MORE
POWERFUL
TOGETHER

MORE
POWERFUL
TOGETHER

CONVERSATIONS WITH CLIMATE ACTIVISTS
AND INDIGENOUS LAND DEFENDERS

JEN GOBBY

FERNWOOD PUBLISHING
HALIFAX & WINNIPEG

Editing: Candida Hadley
Cover design: Jess Koroscil
Printed and bound in Canada

Published by Fernwood Publishing
32 Oceanvista Lane, Black Point, Nova Scotia, B0J 1B0
and 748 Broadway Avenue, Winnipeg, Manitoba, R3G 0X3
www.fernwoodpublishing.ca

100% of the royalties made from the sales of this book are being donated
to Indigenous Climate Action www.indigenousclimateaction.com

Fernwood Publishing Company Limited gratefully acknowledges the financial
support of the Government of Canada, the Canada Council for the Arts, the
Manitoba Department of Culture, Heritage and Tourism under the Manitoba
Publishers Marketing Assistance Program and the Province of Manitoba,
through the Book Publishing Tax Credit, for our publishing program. We are
pleased to work in partnership with the Province of Nova Scotia to develop
and promote our creative industries for the benefit of all Nova Scotians.

Library and Archives Canada Cataloguing in Publication

Title: More powerful together: conversations with climate
activists and Indigenous land defenders
/ Jen Gobby.
Names: Gobby, Jen, 1976- author.
Description: Includes bibliographical references and index.
Identifiers: Canadiana (print) 20200166387 | Canadiana
(ebook) 20200166425 | ISBN 9781773632261
(softcover) | ISBN 9781773632513 (EPUB) | ISBN 9781773632520 (Kindle)
Subjects: LCSH: Environmentalism—Canada. | LCSH:
Environmentalists—Canada. | LCSH: Traditional
ecological knowledge—Canada. | LCSH: Indigenous peoples—
Ecology—Canada. | LCSH: Human ecology—Canada.
Classification: LCC GE195 .G63 2020 | DDC 333.720971—dc23

CONTENTS

Acknowledgements / ix

1. Thinking Together About Changing Everything / 1
   Global Climate and Inequality Crises / 6
   This Research Project / 9
   Working Towards Decolonial Research Practice / 13
   This Book / 15

2. The Climate and Inequality Crises in Canada / 18
   Climate Crisis and Oil and Gas Development in Canada / 18
   Ongoing Impacts of Settler Colonialism in Canada / 20
   Social Movements in Canada / 22

3. Understanding the Crises / 32
   Uneven Impacts of Pipeline Development, Environmental
   Destruction and Climate Disruption / 34
   Structures and Systems that
   Drive Climate Injustice and Inequality / 38
   Worldviews that Justify and Reinforce
   Unjust Systems and Structures / 47
   Why This Analysis Is So Important / 52

4. Envisioning the Alternatives / 54
   Decarbonizing / 55
   Decentralizing and Democratizing / 58
   Decolonizing / 61
   Reconnecting with Land and Each Other / 69
   Possible Tensions / 71
   Note / 72

5. How We Get From Here to There / 73
        The Movements' Theories of Change / 75
        The Context / 76
        How We Understand and What We Value / 80
        How We Take Action / 95
        How We Relate / 111
        Thinking Across the Different Dimensions of Change / 117

6. Taking Stock of Where We Are At
    and What Stands in Our Way / 122
        What's Working and What's Not Working in Our Movements / 122
        The Barriers to Decolonizing and Decarbonizing Canada / 125
        Note / 160

7. Overcoming the Barriers
    and Building More Powerful Movements / 161
        Confronting and Overcoming the External Barriers / 162
        Confronting and Overcoming the Internal Barriers / 165
        Relational Theories of Change and
        Relational Approaches to Movement Building / 177

8. "We Get There Together, or We Don't Get There at All" / 200
        Centring Justice in Our Relations / 200
        Decolonizing Relations / 204
        Climate Change as Catalyst for Decolonizing Relations / 207
        Note / 213

Appendix / 214
        Table of Codes for All Sources of Data / 214

References / 218

Index / 232

To the people, and the non-human ones, on the front lines of climate change and extractivism and to everyone fighting for a kinder world.

Much of daily life tries to facilitate change,
but opportunities to think together about
how change happens are far rarer

— E. Tuck and K.W. Yang,
Youth Resistance Research and Theories of Change

Change can be an end result, measured
in discrete outcomes, and change can be a
relational process of continuous becoming

— J. Ayala, in E. Tuck and K.W. Yang,
Youth Resistance Research and Theories of Change

ACKNOWLEDGEMENTS

This book is made of many collaborations and discussions, the coming together of many minds. First and mostly, I thank the activists and land defenders who sat down with me for interviews, who filled out the surveys and who participated in other ways. Thank you for thinking with me and for bringing all your hard-earned, on-the-ground experience to bear on these questions. But mostly, thank you for doing the risky, vital work of opposing extractivism and fighting hard for a more just and livable world.

To Freda Huson thank you for leading a most powerful site of resistance and resurgence, for welcoming me to the camp and for engaging me on research. To Vanessa Grey for our various collaborations over the years, for your powerful words, your leadership and activism and for teaching me so much about the realities of environmental racism in this country and about the powerful resistance that is ongoing. To Kanahus Manuel for your work of putting the beautiful solutions in the pathways of the pipeline. To Jaydene Lavallie for speaking with such power and integrity, for being willing and able to unsettle a crowd. To Sue Chiblow for some very formative conversations. To Marlene Hale for all the good talks and for all you do.

Gratitude to Bianca Mugyenyi and Jody Chan for supporting me so well through our research collaboration. To Candida Hadley and Fazeela Jiwa and the others at Fernwood for guiding me through this process of writing a book. Your constructive and encouraging feedback and patience with me throughout the process are much appreciated! To Ayendri Riddell, whose help with research for my thesis literature review was very formative in Chapter 5 of the book.

To the people that supervised the research: Peter G. Brown, Ellie Perkins and Kirsten Anker and to those who read and gave feedback on the thesis: peter kulchyski, Aziz Choudry and Chris Dixon. I'd also like to acknowledge the whole Economics for the Anthropocene partnership and SSHRC, which funded the partnership and this research project. Thank you Leah Temper for your mentorship. To Julia Freeman for the many moments of thinking together.

Thanks to folks of Climate Justice Montreal — Dru Oja Jay, Aurore Fauret, Lily Schwarzbaum, Daphne Ben David, Dan Parker, Amy Miller, Cathy Inouye, David Whiteside, Shona Watt, Nicolas Chevalier, Vincent Duhamel, Naomi Goldberg and many others. I've learned so much though our thinking, planning, reflecting, debating and strategizing and from being in the streets together.

A big thanks to Charles Guay-Boutet and Stephen Gobby for help with translating between French and English. And to Jenna MacDonald, Brenda Pollock and Kayla Pollock-McKenna for help with audio transcription. To Jacqueline Lee-Tam for help with formatting. Thank you!

To Cynthia MacDonald, Clare Kenny, Adam Enright, Jeremy Eliosoff, Marika Lhemery, Daniel Svatek, Anna Kusmer, Peter Rudiak-Gould, Michele Molnar, Pachiel Smith, Sophia Rosenberg, Joseph Fall and Brigitte Dorner for many good conversations over the years. To Jenna, Adam, Hayden and Isabella for being wild, funny and beautiful humans.

Thank you to Stephen Gobby for the times you brought me tea, breakfast and then lunch while I wrote hard at my desk. To Chris Gobby for keeping me humble. To Brenda Pollock for the many, many hours of thesis editing, and for your indomitable spirit, for giving me my confidence and for teaching me that change is always possible, that we're all stronger than we think.

Biggest, most heartfelt thanks to Nicolas von Ellenrieder for your support, for bringing such a diversity of life forms into our home, for all the adventures.

CHAPTER 1

THINKING TOGETHER ABOUT CHANGING EVERYTHING

> While the climate justice movement is working hard to address the legacy of white supremacy and colonialism within environmental and conservation movements, it is a work in progress.
> — E. Deranger, *The New Green Deal in Canada*

On the morning of Friday, September 27, 2019, the day of the Global Climate Strike, I woke up smiling. The sun was shining down on Montreal, the streets of the city ready to be taken over by the people. The media was predicting hundreds of thousands of people would attend the march. This is the kind of day I live for — when daily routine is set aside and the most heartfelt and passionate expressions of the human spirit are on full display; when people come together, and the individual acts of showing up combines into a massive, vibrant demonstration of public will.

Placards in hand, my partner and I left our apartment that morning, stepped out into the unseasonably warm fall day and walked towards Mount Royal. In my mind's eye I was picturing streams of people flowing from all directions, from neighbourhoods all over the city, amassing into rivers rushing towards the march. As we turned onto Parc avenue, my heart leapt. We were arriving an hour early and already an endless sea of marchers had converged at the base of the mountain.

Over the next few hours, we were carried along in the singing, dancing, smiling crowds, chanting slogans for climate justice, yelling our love for people and for the planet. Along the way, we ran into new friends and old, exchanging embraces with fellow students and climate organizers. I happily marched along, entertained by the endless stream of protest signs: "Systems Change, Not Climate Change," "People and Planet Over Profit," "Decarbonize and Decolonize," "Wind Power: I'm a Big Fan."

All afternoon I was filled with the feeling — the renewed belief — that we can do this. People are rising. People power is stronger than the entrenched interests of powerful companies. There is hope; look at us! What a force to be reckoned with!

That feeling lingered in me even as the march wound down, as the immense crowd slowly dispersed, as the sun went behind the mountain.

The Montreal march was, by most accounts, a huge success. As part of a week of actions across the world, spanning 185 countries, over six million people marched to demand action to cut emissions and stabilize the climate (Laville and Watts 2019). In Montreal alone, over 500,000 people showed up that day (Shingler 2019). This was an historical moment of global climate action.

But that evening, back at home, when I turned on my laptop and signed in to Facebook, my elation was deflated in a matter of seconds. Posts from Indigenous people who had attended the event reported on violent, racist behaviour that had been directed at them during the march. One tweet stated that the "Montreal climate strike was one of the most racist protest spaces I've ever been in."

Jessica Bolduc, who is Anishinaabe-French from the Batchewana First Nation in Northern Ontario, had travelled to Montreal for the march with 4Rs Youth Movement and Indigenous Climate Action as part of the Indigenous youth delegation. She wrote that soon after the march began,

> non-Indigenous people … swarmed behind and to our right, shouting over and silencing the songs of the drummers … all completely ignoring the safe space that we were trying to hold for the youth and our older relatives. It was at this point that the safety of community began to be challenged. We held hands, grabbed onto each other's bags, called out to each other — strategies to try to stay together.… We were pushed, intentionally separated, provoked and mobbed — all for simply claiming space in this discourse, asking to have Indigenous voices heard and prioritized.

Bolduc reported that settlers yelled at the delegation "It's the peoples march, not the Indigenous Peoples march" and that "others said worse;

Indigenous youth [were] confronted with language steeped in hatred and racism. It was from this point on that we would spend the rest of the march struggling simply to stay safe and stay together."

I sat there that night, staring at my screen, struck by the stark contrast between the joyful day I had just spent, and the profoundly not-joyous experience of racial violence that the Indigenous people at the march had experienced.

Perhaps it was naïve of me in that moment to be surprised by how differently the march was experienced by different people. Like the march was, climate change is experienced very differently by different people. Jessica Bolduc's post explained that

> not all people feel the impacts of climate change the same ... Black, Indigenous and communities of Colour are disproportionately impacted by climate change and yet our stories continue to be forced out of the global narrative, despite our actions being truly at the front lines for Mother Earth. What does this march tell us about the values society is preaching vs. those we need desperately to be practicing? ... Despite coming up on 5 years of the Truth and Reconciliation's final report and Calls to Action ... there are still many privileged Canadians who believe that their needs, their bodies, deserve to come first. Climate change should be a conversation about colonialism, power, privilege, wealth distribution and capitalism, but instead it is flattened into a more digestible conversation about plastic straw bans and "green" campaigns.

Indigenous Peoples, and other marginalized communities, are bearing the brunt of climate impact, and they are leading the fight for climate justice, for keeping fossil fuels in the ground. Yet their voices are continuing to be sidelined in mainstream climate organizing, international climate negotiations and domestic climate policy. And as if all that is not egregious enough, Indigenous people are also facing racist verbal and physical abuse from settler activists at climate marches.

Eriel Deranger, the executive director of Indigenous Climate Action, is a leading advocate in Canada for Indigenous approaches to confronting climate change. She is a Denesuline woman and member of the Athabasca Chipewyan First Nation (ACFN), from Treaty 8 territory in Northern

Alberta. Earlier in 2019, she wrote that "While the climate justice movement is working hard to address the legacy of white supremacy and colonialism within environmental and conservation movements, it is a work in progress" (Deranger 2019: n.p.). Echoing that sentiment, Tayka Raymond, a Quebec-based grassroots advocate and water protector of Ojibwe and Scottish decent, posted on Facebook the day after the march that "despite all the awareness work being done around the country, there is still A LOT of work needing to be done. We have to review our game plan. Cause yesterday was horrible."

The climate movement is growing and becoming more powerful. But there are many dynamics and factors limiting our power. Racism is one among other forms of oppression that continue to play out in movement spaces. These need to be meaningfully and actively addressed, for straight-out ethical reasons and in the interest of human decency. And we must do this work because the kind of internal violence that happened at the Montreal climate march deeply compromises the potential to build powerful, cohesive and effective movements that can generate that much needed "force to be reckoned with."

As people concerned with building a better world, we need to be taking stock of where we are at, where we are strong and what is holding us back. This work is required if we are to be as powerful a force for change as we can be.

This process of taking stock, of deep reflection, of strategizing ways to combine efforts and build diverse, transformative movements that work towards both decarbonization *and* decolonization of our systems, this is the ongoing work to which this book aims to contribute. The overarching message of this book is that strong, just relations are the means and ends of building a better, climate safe world.

This book is based on research I conducted in collaboration with climate activists and Indigenous land defenders as part of my doctoral degree at McGill University. The project was conceived in September 2014, while I was in New York City for another historic moment for global climate activism: the People's Climate March. While there, I also attended the NYC Climate Convergence, which took place over the two days leading up to the march. It featured over one hundred events all around the East Village in community centres, parks, gardens and churches. While listening to the stories and seeing the faces of the people, from all across the globe, who are on the front lines of this crisis, climate change came alive for me in a way it had not before.

That was also the month that Naomi Klein's book *This Changes Everything: Capitalism vs. the Climate* was released. Both the convergence and the book opened my eyes to the fundamental links between the deepening environmental crisis and growing social inequality and injustice worldwide. They, as have others before them, named capitalism and colonialism as root causes of these intersecting crises. Both made clear to me that the solutions to the climate crisis must be deeply informed by the people most directly impacted and that the failure of governments to take action on climate change means that this massive transition that is urgently needed will have to be driven from the bottom up, from grassroots social movements, led by front-line communities.

That week in New York and Naomi Klein's book sparked in me a conviction to do research that is informed by, and of benefit to, front-line communities and others actively fighting for climate justice, but it was not clear then how that could be done. Pursuing a doctoral degree, spending years in the ivory tower immersed in stacks of books and journal articles, at this very urgent moment in human history didn't seem like the best use of my time. Could I not contribute to social change in much more useful ways? Rather than giving up on academia altogether, I sought out unconventional approaches to research, approaches that are action-oriented, that engage closely with communities and movements. I came across long traditions of activist-scholars that do not just sit back and observe and analyze what is going on in the world; rather they take action with communities and movements, co-creating new knowledge along the way.

So in 2014, feeling growing urgency about the climate crisis, deeply inspired by the work going on in climate justice movements around the world and now newly equipped with these unconventional research methodologies, I set out to do research that is not just *about* social change, but that seeks to *actively contribute* to the systems transformations that are so urgently needed to address climate and inequality crises that are mounting globally. There is a lot at stake and there is no time to lose.

GLOBAL CLIMATE AND INEQUALITY CRISES

In November 2017, an open letter entitled Warning to Humanity was published, signed by 160,000 scientists from 184 countries across the Earth. An update to an original warning sent twenty-five years earlier, it states that global biophysical systems have changed dramatically over these last twenty-five years, and almost entirely for the worse. The scientists who issued the letter state that "especially troubling is the current trajectory of potentially catastrophic climate change" (Ripple et al. 2017: 1). This echoes reports from the Intergovernmental Panel on Climate Change (IPCC), which recognize that our globalized industrial activities are increasingly compromising the processes of the planet's life support systems, thus threatening the viability of ecosystems and countless life forms including our own (Field et al. 2014). Climate change is being driven by greenhouse gases (GHGs), such as carbon dioxide, building up in the Earth's atmosphere and trapping heat. GHGs are produced by human activity such as the combustion of fossil fuels (mainly coal, oil and natural gas) as well as deforestation, changes in land use, soil erosion and agriculture (Solomon et al. 2007). The 2018 report from the IPCC stated that limiting global warming to 1.5°C — the temperature increase limit necessary to avert the dangerous destabilization of ecological and social systems — will require "rapid, far-reaching and unprecedented changes in all aspects of society."

While people around the world suffer increasing ecological upheaval, growing social crises of economic, racial and gender inequality are also unfolding and demanding urgent collective response. In one overview of global social inequality, Kate Raworth identified twelve dimensions of social wellbeing including education, peace and justice, political voice, gender equality, health and food. Her work shows that many millions of people around the world are not able to meet their basic needs. She writes, "worldwide, one person in nine does not have enough food to eat. One in four lives on less than $3 a day, and one in eight people cannot find (paid) work. One person in eleven has no source of safe drinking water" (Raworth, 2017: 43). She goes on to describe that almost 40% of people live in countries in which income is distributed highly unequally and more than half of the world's population live in countries in which people have little political voice. A recent Oxfam report found global economic inequality to be growing rapidly:

The year 2017 saw the biggest increase in billionaires in history, one more every two days. This huge increase could have ended global extreme poverty seven times over. Eighty-two percent of all wealth created in the last year went to the top 1%, and nothing went to the bottom 50%. Dangerous, poorly paid work for the many is supporting extreme wealth for the few. Women are in the worst work, and almost all the super-rich are men. (Pimentel, Aymar, Lawson et al. 2000: 2)

Increasingly, masses of people suffer from poverty while a very few powerful people become obscenely rich. The accumulation of wealth of the very rich few is happening at the expense of poor people, women and children and at the expense of ecosystems and non-human life on Earth. Transformation scholar Ashish Kothari writes that "every day, we see new evidence that our current model of development is straining the resilience of the biosphere and producing glaring economic inequalities. Levels of poverty, deprivation, and exploitation remain unacceptable, while conflict over access to natural resources, food, and water grows more frequent" (2014: 2).

Indigenous Peoples are particularly impacted by climate change. Because many Indigenous communities live close to the land and thus rely directly on natural resources and ecosystems, Indigenous Peoples are especially vulnerable to, and disproportionately affected by, climate change. Around the world, they are being forced to leave their lands due to deforestation, sea-level rise, major infrastructure projects and conflict arising from resource scarcity and other climate impacts (Salick and Byg 2007). Impacts of climate change are made worse by the pressure from commercial and extractive interests on their land and resources (Tupaz 2015). Because they are already disproportionately suffering from poverty and other legacies of colonialism, they are disadvantaged in terms of resources to help adapt to climate change and in some cases do not have the ability to reject unwanted extractive projects on their territories. Yet despite this poverty and disadvantage, Indigenous communities bearing the brunt of extractivism and climate change are leading the climate justice and environmental justice movements. The UN's *Global Assessment Report on Biodiversity and Ecosystem Services*, released in 2019, finds that, while biodiversity is declining in all areas across the globe, it is declining much less rapidly in those lands still managed by Indigenous Peoples (IPBES 2019). In countless places around the world, Indigenous Peoples are actively blocking the expansion of extractive industries (Gedicks 1994, 2001; Temper and Bliss 2015).

These converging climate and inequality crises speak to deeply troubled *human-Earth* and *human-human* relationships. Both these sets of relationships are in urgent need of healing and transformation. The interconnection between environmental and equality crises is not just functional (i.e., poor people reliant on land hardest hit by climate change) but are symptoms of a deeper pattern of dysfunctional relationship based on domination. Some scientists, policy makers and activists discuss the environmental crises as separate, or of a different nature, from social crises. Though some may prefer, for simplicity's sake, to create policies and solutions addressing *social* crises and *ecological* crises separately, Raworth reminds us that "that simply won't work: their interconnectedness demands that they be understood as part of a complex socio-ecological system and hence be addressed within a greater whole" (Raworth 2017: 47; see also Folke, Jansson et al. 2011).

In the spirit of seeing and responding to the depth, breadth and interconnection of the social and ecological crises unfolding currently, climate justice activists and organizers around the globe are calling for *systems change* (Klein 2014). Scientists too are acknowledging that in order to address the crises being faced, there needs to be a profound transformation in the economic, political and thought systems that are driving the crises (Moore et al. 2014; Beddoe et al. 2009; IPCC 2018). Some scientists too are recognizing that a transformation towards sustainability will require radical systemic shifts in deeply held values and beliefs, patterns of social behaviour and governance (Westley et al. 2011). Indeed "the roots of these crises lie in structural problems within the economy, society, and humanity's relationship with nature. All of this calls for a fundamental rethinking of the human project in the twenty-first century" (Kothari 2014: 2).

The need for massive systemic transformation is clear. Small adjustments in our economic and social systems are not enough. Adapting to the changes already occurring, that is not enough. We require a "fundamental restructuring of the way modern societies operate" (Scheidel et al. 2017: 11). We need transformative change. By transformation I mean intentional change that confronts not just the symptoms but the root causes of social injustice and environmental unsustainability, including unequal power relations, and rather than merely improving an existing system, alters the overall composition and behaviour of the system in ways that drive desirable change across temporal and spatial scales, towards increased social wellbeing, equality and ecological sustainability.

Governments across the world have been failing to lead the transformations necessary for addressing the climate and inequality crises. As such we need to be seeking out other avenues for social change.

Given that many people in decision-making positions of power benefit from the systems remaining as they are, and given that individual people do not, alone, constitute the kind of force required, many scholars argue that *social movements* — ordinary people coming together, engaging in collective action to push for change — are crucial for bringing about transformative change (Carroll and Sarker 2016; Solnit 2016; Scheidel et al. 2017; Kothari et al. 2014; Temper and Del Bene 2016; Choudry 2015).

Social movements are one of the "social forms through which collectives give voice to their grievances and concerns about the rights, welfare, and wellbeing of themselves and others" (Snow, Soule and Kriesi 2008: 3). Though there are other ways by which social change is driven — such as through legislation and court proceedings, through educational systems and through electoral outcomes etc. — social movements provide regular people a means by which to combine forces to influence change without needing to hold certain specialized or elite roles in society (Glasberg and Shannon 2010). Movements drive social change from the bottom up by empowering regular folks and oppressed people to effectively challenge and resist the decisions and actions of those with more power and advantage in a society (Glasberg and Shannon 2010).

THIS RESEARCH PROJECT

It is in social movements that I place my hope for transforming our systems towards climate justice. For the past five years, I have been working closely with people in the Indigenous land defence, environmental/climate justice and anti-pipeline movements in Canada. Together we've been discussing what we can do to increase our power to bring about transformation in Canada towards both decolonization and decarbonization. We have been thinking hard about how large-scale systems change happens and how social movements can work together to bring this change about.

Since the fall of 2014, I have spent time at Indigenous anti-pipeline blockades, washing dishes, hauling wood and learning decolonization practices and theory. I've worked with grassroots organizations to organize protests and marches, helped plan training events and panel discussions and fundraised legal fees for activists criminalized for direct action. I have also conducted a series of interviews, surveys and think tank sessions to work together to analyze the crises, envision the future we want, theorize about how change happens, reflect on what is working and what is not, and strategize together about how to strengthen the movements' power to transform Canada. This has been a process of theorizing from the ground up.

I developed this approach in response to the critiques of conventional forms of social movement research which can be done in ways that are extractive, disconnected from and of little use to movements (Choudry 2015). These critiques are not unique to research with social movements. Social science, especially Euro-Western research, has been extensively critiqued as "extractive, insofar as universities and governments send their 'experts' to a community, extract information from 'subjects,' and take away the data to write their papers, reports and theses with no reciprocity or feedback to the community" (Santos 2008: 321). Indeed, this has been the endemic approach in the social sciences more generally, and particularly in anthropology and the study of Indigenous Peoples (Smith 1999).

The work of Chris Dixon, Aziz Choudry, Harsha Walia, Eric Shragge, Sandy Grande, Dip Kapoor, Alex Khasnabish, Anne Harley, Jonathan Langdon and others offer new and promising approaches to research involving social movements. These more engaged forms of research tend to centre around several principles: reducing the disconnect between scholars and activists, valuing the intellectual work of movements, doing research that is relevant to movements, and doing research that helps bring about social change.

Rather than *learning about social movements,* I have, from the start, approached my research as being about *learning with movements.* I've been working to convene conversations that can contribute to our shared understandings of how we can effectively address climate crisis and mounting social inequality, to *think together* how we can bring about transformation towards more just and ecologically viable systems.

Early on in the project I engaged in several research collaborations that helped me refine my research questions and approaches. One collaboration was with the people at Unist'ot'en camp in north-central BC, who have been actively blocking multiple oil and gas pipelines by re-inhabiting their traditional territory, which is on the pipeline route between the Alberta oil sands and the BC coast. In 2016, I worked with them to research how social marketing can be used as a tool for social change. This project was prompted by their own research interests and culminated in the preparation and delivery of a day-long workshop at the annual Unist'ot'en Action Camp in 2016, training activists and community members in using social marketing tools for social change.

A second research collaboration was with Vanessa Gray, an Anishinaabe kwe land defender from Aamjiwnaang First Nation, located in Canada's Chemical Valley. Vanessa and her sibling Beze have been raising awareness about the rampant environmental racism and the devastating heath impacts on her community caused by the oil and gas refineries around her reserve near Sarnia, Ontario. In 2015, Vanessa was facing criminal charges for shutting off Enbridge's much contested Line 9 pipeline. Facing the possibility of many years in prison for this act of protest that she considered "community self-defence," Vanessa and I convened and facilitated a think tank of scholars and other experts in Canadian and Indigenous law to brainstorm about Vanessa's defence. The transcription from this session was sent to her lawyer, who used it in the court case.

A third research collaboration was with the team from The Leap Manifesto. This manifesto sets out a vision for a justice-based energy transition in Canada centred on "Caring for the Earth and One Another." In 2017, the team that launched the manifesto formed a new organization, called The Leap, to work towards implementing the manifesto's vision. I collaborated with the team by helping them conduct and analyze over a hundred phone interviews with representatives of the organizations that had signed on to the manifesto. In these phone calls we asked for feedback and input on how The Leap could be most useful to the movements in Canada.

Bolstered with important learnings from these collaborations and from my ongoing involvement with these movements, during the summer and fall of 2017, I conducted forty in-depth interviews with people active in Indigenous land defence, anti-pipeline and environmental/climate justice movements in Canada. This sample of forty people represents an incredible wealth of experience in working to make change in Canada. The range of people, from youth to elders, included twenty women, twenty men, seven people of colour, eight Indigenous people and twenty-five white settlers. It included twenty-six anglophones and five francophones, mostly people residing in Quebec and British Columbia, but with a few from other provinces, including Saskatchewan, Ontario and Nova Scotia. It included twenty-one activists in grassroots organizations, twelve people who worked in NGOs, five community organizers and eight who were involved in other ways (e.g., First Nations governance, education, policy). Most interviews involved myself and one interviewee, though I did conduct a few group interviews, which I refer to as think tank discussions, in order to think together with several people at a time about specific questions.

I also conducted an in-depth online survey, which was completed by a total of thirty-six people: thirteen women, sixteen men (the rest didn't specify), three people of colour, three Indigenous people and nineteen white settlers (again, the rest didn't specify).

Through the interviews and surveys, I asked activists and land defenders many questions about how they understand the climate and inequality crises, how they think large-scale social change happens, what they see as the most significant barriers to the change they want to see, and what they think can be done to build more powerful, transformative movements in Canada. Through a process of coding-based data analysis, guided by grounded theory, I've been able to bring these into dialogue with each other. This book presents the rich insights and ideas that emerged from this process of *thinking together*.

Though it was not my intention, a majority of the people I interviewed and surveyed were white settlers. To try to ensure Indigenous voices remain central to this work, despite the failure to engage as many Indigenous people as I would have liked, I raise up and disproportionately report on the views and theories of the Indigenous people that I spoke with. The voices of Indigenous people and people of colour have been given more weight in the data analysis and presentation. In an effort to further bolster the contribution of Indigenous voices to my research, I also attended public events where land defenders and water protectors were speaking. I took notes and incorporated the insights and ideas presented there into my data analysis.

Quotes from various sources of data are represented in the chapters of this book in the following ways:

Quotes from interviews — (Int#),
Quotes from surveys — (S#)
Quotes from think tank sessions — (TT#)
Quotes from public event — (E#).

A table of codes is presented in the Appendix, providing basic information about each interview, survey, think tank and event interlocutor.

WORKING TOWARDS DECOLONIAL RESEARCH PRACTICE

In her influential book *Decolonizing Methodologies*, Māori scholar Linda Tuhiwai Smith makes clear that research is a site of ongoing colonial relations (1999). Academic research is an institution that is "embedded in a global system of imperialism and power" and with it has come "new waves of exploration, discovery, exploitation and appropriation" (Smith 1999: 24). This is so to such an extent that "research," is "probably one of the dirtiest words in the indigenous world's vocabulary" (Smith 1999: 1). "We need an understanding of the complex ways in which the pursuit of knowledge is deeply embedded in the multiple layers of imperial and colonial practices" (Smith 1999: 2). And we need to work hard at undoing these.

Settler researchers, such as myself, need to be vigilantly alert to the ways their research may be replicating colonial dynamics.

I am a settler living on stolen Indigenous land. My family arrived on Turtle Island, from various countries in eastern and western Europe, in the late 1800s and early 1900s. They were working-class people seeking employment, homes of their own and better lives for their kids. These better lives that my great-grandparents sought and found in Canada were available and accessible to them because of the European colonization of North America — the lands and resources taken from Indigenous Peoples without their consent and the systematic destruction of their cultures and lifeways in order to facilitate this land and resource dispossession. My ancestors directly benefited from the colonial process of land dispossession and the oppression of Indigenous Peoples here on Turtle Island. As Mi'kmaw warrior and decolonial thinker Sakej Ward said to a room of settlers at an event I attended in Vancouver in 2017: "As settlers, your ancestors were the architects of my people's apocalypse."

What this means to me is that the position I hold in Canadian society — as an able-bodied, cis-gendered, white woman born to middle-class parents with access to higher education and financial ease — was afforded to me based on colonial relations and the ongoing dispossession of Indigenous Peoples from their lands. My material wellbeing is based on, and my worldview has been shaped by, these ongoing relations of colonial domination. I continue to benefit from the ongoing injustice in Canada. This understanding demands that I think hard about how self-interest may be clouding and distorting my understandings and visions for change, and about how this has shaped my research project.

In responding to this growing understanding, I commit my research and activist work to helping bring about radical transformation in Canada and to unlearning the racist, dualistic, hierarchical and oppressive world-view that I was born and raised in. I commit this work and my future work to help dismantle the structures of capitalism and colonialism. I have been seeking to learn as much as I can about the systems of domination that undergird the current status quo in Canada, which continues to drive ecological devastation and social injustice. I have been seeking to respectfully learn from and raise up Indigenous voices and worldviews, which offer radically more just and sustainable ways of knowing, living and working for change.

Realizing early on in this research project that settler-led research involving Indigenous Peoples and communities can be highly problematic, I spent a lot of time reading about decolonizing research methods. In reflecting on the learnings from these readings, I developed a set of principles to help guide me through the whole research process.

1. Engage in critical self-reflexivity (Fortier 2015), continually working to "critically reflect on and understand the underlying assumptions, motivations and values which inform my research practices" (Smith 1999: 20). To ask myself: who is benefiting from this research and who is not?
2. Acknowledge, learn about and promote an understanding of

Canada's colonial history and present and to ensure that my framings of current political struggles and efforts for change in Canada are situated "within the structures of settler colonialism, white supremacy, heteropatriarchy, and the capitalist world system" (Fortier 2015: 19).

3. Endeavour to practise decolonization "not only in my research but as a life praxis" (Fortier 2015: 19).

4. Develop and practise a research approach that is radically participatory (Smith 1999) and aimed at social transformation.

5. Support and enhance an Indigenous agenda for transformation (Smith 1999) in my research and in my activism.

6. Commit to developing reciprocal relationships with the people with whom I work, such that the collaborations and alliances are of benefit to them at every stage (Riddell et al. 2017).

7. Ground my theoretical work in multiple ontological realities and worldviews and to work towards raising up and learning about relational worldviews drawn from Indigenous ontologies (Fortier 2015; Kovach 2010).

8. Rather than uncritically apply social movement theories to Indigenous change agency, seek to emphasize insights and theories from diverse Indigenous perspectives (Coburn and Atleo 2016).

9. Use my dissertation and position as scholar and researcher to create space for Indigenous voices, theories and agency in the academy (Kovach 2010) and in social movements in Canada.

10. Take any financial gain from this work and redirect it towards Indigenous front-line communities.

THIS BOOK

This book tells a story about distinct but overlapping movements in Canada, a powerful convergence of Indigenous and non-Indigenous people, impacted communities, grassroots groups and non-governmental organizations (NGOs). These have come together in the common cause of opposing the criss-crossing network of proposed and existing oil and gas pipelines in Canada. While grappling with very real inter- and intra-movement tensions and differences in worldviews, strategies and long-term goals, the environmental/climate justice, anti-pipeline and

Indigenous land defence movements are directly challenging the status quo of the Canadian extractive economy.

As I will argue, these movements are contesting the story Canada tells itself about being a peaceful, nature-loving, human-rights-abiding nation. These movements are helping expose the contradictions and injustices at the heart of Canada — that its economy is based on the destruction of natural systems, theft of Indigenous land and violation of Indigenous rights, that Canada is a country guided predominantly by the logics and relations of capitalist accumulation and settler colonialism.

Though the Liberal government purports to care about forging better relationships with First Nations, it continues to pressure them to extinguish their rights at land claims negotiations tables (Manuel 2017). While Prime Minister Trudeau continues with his simplistic rhetoric about climate action that balances the "environment" and the "economy," these movements are offering a different story. It's a story that doesn't pit the economy against the environment but conceives of the economy, and the wellbeing of people, as fundamentally dependent on clean water, clean air and a stable climate.

Meanwhile, collaborations with social justice groups and Indigenous communities are expanding mainstream environmental movements' narrow understanding of "environment," as they learn about solidarity across diverse movements, rendering the movements less "siloed." These movements are working to coordinate efforts across vast geographies and diverse ideologies and coming to see themselves as part of a movement ecosystem — a larger whole in which different groups play differentiated and interdependent roles, contributing in ways that are necessary but insufficient on their own. Conceiving of "movements as ecosystems" and learning to see diversity as a strength holds promise for better collaborating and coordinating movement efforts.

Indigenous Peoples engaged in these struggles are defending their lands and rights and reinvigorating traditional practices and livelihoods. They are directly and indirectly teaching non-Indigenous activists about reciprocal relationships: relationships of responsibility to land and to each other. These teachings are ultimately the promise of stronger, more effective social movements. They offer new ways of relating that can help overcome the relational and ideological tensions and divisions currently weakening and fracturing the movements. However, to realize this promise of a "movement of movements" powerful enough to transform Canada, there is much work to be done to undo the power imbalances — the ongoing racism, classism, sexism and other forms of "power-over" that still exist within and across movements.

This book presents the diverse voices in these movements. While struggling with divergent worldviews, sometimes-competing interests and deeply wounded relationships, activists, organizers and land defenders are working together and apart to forge paths forward — paths that work simultaneously towards decarbonizing and decolonizing Canada.

I am more hopeful about the state of the world now than I was when I began this project. Spending these five years talking and working closely with so many people who care so deeply and work so hard to fight against injustice and build a just and thriving world has provided me a much-needed antidote to the despair and anxiety that this moment in history can generate.

CHAPTER 2

THE CLIMATE AND INEQUALITY CRISES IN CANADA

CLIMATE CRISIS AND OIL AND GAS DEVELOPMENT IN CANADA

Like many places around the globe, Canada has been facing more and more occurrences of climate change–induced extreme weather, such as wildfires, floods and storms (Environment and Climate Change Canada 2019). A report released in April 2019 by Environment and Climate Change Canada, shows Canada warming at twice the global rate and confirms that the majority of warming is the result of burning fossil fuels. To have any chance of warding off the worst of the impending climate impacts, much of the remaining fossil fuel reserves must stay in the ground, and other forms of energy and revenue must be developed (McGlade and Ekins 2015).

At the opening of the 21st Conference of the Parties (COP21) meeting of the United Nations Framework Convention on Climate Change (UNFCCC) in 2015 in Paris, the newly elected Canadian prime minister, Justin Trudeau, promised real action on climate change, claiming "it's the right thing to do, for our environment, economy, and as part of the global community" (Morin 2015: n.p.). Despite these seeming commitments to climate change mitigation, the Trudeau Liberals continue to expand Canada's oil and gas industry to the detriment of ecosystems, local communities, long-term economic sustainability and a stable climate.

Canada is the fifth largest producer globally of both petroleum and gas (Natural Resources Canada 2018). The 2016 report about Canadian GHG (greenhouse gas) emissions from Ivey Business School at University of Western Ontario states that

> Canada emits about 1.6 percent of the world's GHG emissions. Despite this relatively low share, Canada is among the top 10 global emitters on an absolute basis and stands firmly in the top 3 for emissions per capita. By way of comparison, Canada's population makes up about 0.5 percent of the world total so that our emissions' share is about 3 times our population share. (Boothe and Boudreault 2016: 4)

The centre of Canada's oil extraction is in the Alberta tar sands, which holds 170.2 billion barrels and is the third largest known oil reserve in the world after Saudi Arabia and Venezuela (Nimana, Canter and Kumar 2015). NASA scientist James Hansen has calculated that the tar sands contain twice the amount of CO_2 than has been emitted by global oil use in human history. He said that if we were to burn all the oil in Alberta at once, the atmospheric concentration of CO_2 would go from the present level of 400 ppm to 540 ppm, and this has led him to conclude that continuing exploitation of the tar sands is "game over" for the climate. The tar sands are thus a key front in the fight against climate change (Hansen 2012).

Resistance to oil and gas pipelines has been a primary manifestation and catalyst for the growing environmental/climate justice movement in Canada. To get Canada's land-locked fossil fuel resources to refineries and to domestic and international markets, and to continue to expand the industries, transport infrastructure is needed. "Pipelines are the vital arteries of the industry, bringing bitumen to refineries and ultimately to market, and they already stretch over thousands of kilometers across North America" (Black, D'Arcy and Weis 2014: 4).

The ongoing effort to propose, approve and build new oil and gas pipelines is currently a critical point of tension in Canada and has sparked unprecedented resistance to Canada's oil and gas industry (Lukacs in Black, D'Arcy and Weis 2014). As extractivism and climate change exacerbate existing social injustice and inequality in Canada, communities and social movements have been mobilizing to resist new fossil fuel infrastructure and to push for more just and ecologically viable energy and economic systems. These movements are being led by Indigenous Peoples on the front lines of both the climate and the inequality crises. Like the uneven and unjust distribution of climate impacts, the impacts of fossil fuel extraction and transportation are felt by some people in Canada more than others, reflecting more general patterns of environmental injustice (Martinez-Alier et al. 2016). Whether at the points of extraction, transport, processing or combustion, Indigenous communities are bearing an unfair brunt of Canada's ongoing dependence on the oil and gas industry.

Indeed, the expansion of the oil and gas industry in Canada is directly related to Canada's colonial history and to the very real neo-colonial forces still at play in this country. This includes but is not limited to struggles over land, water and resources. Resource extraction in Canada has been, from the start and continuing today, closely linked with colonization and the dispossession of Indigenous Peoples from their lands.

Despite recent attention to reconciliation and increasing international pressure to respect Indigenous rights, the Canadian government continues to infringe on Indigenous rights through the development of oil and gas pipelines, expansion of the tar sands, mining and other extraction projects. Canada's economic base is dependent on the land stolen from Indigenous Nations, lands that are still contested. This places Canada and Canadians at odds with Indigenous Peoples, who have prior and competing claims to land (Barker and Lowman 2015). Thus, Canada's ongoing extractive economic development is not only driving the climate crisis, it is dependent on the ongoing theft of Indigenous land and violation of Indigenous Peoples' rights. The late Arthur Manuel, influential thinker and political leader from the Secwepemc Nation, put it clearly: "The forces of cultural genocide that you launched against us were not because you are wantonly cruel people ... it was because only by destroying us could you have uncontested ownership of the land" (2017: 88). Canada's wealth has been created on the backs of Indigenous Peoples and through the extraction and destruction of lands that are the basis of Indigenous cultures and economies.

ONGOING IMPACTS OF SETTLER COLONIALISM IN CANADA

The Truth and Reconciliation Commission (TRC) Report, released in 2015, starkly exposes the huge suffering that has come directly from historical and ongoing colonial relations between the Canadian state and Indigenous Peoples, naming the historical treatment of First Nations by the Canadian state as "cultural genocide" (TRC 2015: 1). The 1996 Royal Commission on Aboriginal People explicitly lays out Canada's imposition of a colonial relationship on Indigenous Peoples, including

> residential schools, forcible relocation, the imposed Band Council system, institution of a pass system, germ warfare, outlawing of ceremonies such as the potlatch and traditional activities such as fishing, failed treaty processes, and other forced assimilation policies. Currently, it takes the form of the imposition of foreign governance systems legislated through the Indian Act and state-sanctioned appropriation of Indigenous lands and resources. (Walia 2012: 241; see also Dussault and Erasmus 1996)

Indigenous Peoples continue to lose their land base while facing infringement of their rights from resource extraction, mining companies, property developers and the pressure of urbanization. This "massive land dispossession and resultant dependency is not only a humiliation and an instant impoverishment, it has devastated [Indigenous] social, political, economic, cultural and spiritual life. We continue to pay for it every day with grinding poverty, broken social relations, and too often in life-ending despair" (Manuel 2017: 70). A disproportional number of cases of missing and murdered Indigenous women, discrimination by social services and police brutality underscore the reality that colonialism is ongoing (Barker and Lowman 2015).

Indigenous Peoples in Canada are currently facing the ongoing impacts of a colonial past, as well as impacts from ongoing colonialism as a persistent structure. These manifest in stark systemic social, economic and health inequalities between Indigenous Peoples and settler Canadians (see Manuel 2017: 78; TRC 2015: 146–147). These inequalities stem from the violation of Indigenous rights to land and self-determination. In its 2018 *World Report*, Human Rights Watch states that the Canadian government "has yet to pay adequate attention to systemic poverty, housing, water, sanitation, healthcare, and education problems in Indigenous communities." In 2017, the United Nations Committee on the Elimination of Racial Discrimination urged the Canadian government to address what it found were persistent violations of Indigenous rights (Human Rights Watch 2018: n.p.).

These stark racial inequalities in Canada are being driven by ongoing colonial relations. Arthur Manuel wrote: "Our dependency was not some accident of history. It is at the heart of the colonial system. Our poverty is not an accident, the result of our incompetence or bad luck; it is intentional and systematic.... Our poverty is not a by-product of our domination but an essential part of it" (2017: 68). As Leanne Betasamosake Simpson puts it, "the 'social ills' in our communities ... are the symptoms, not the disease. 'Fixing' the 'social ills' serves only to reinforce settler colonialism, because it doesn't stop the system that causes the harm in the first place" (2017: 42). As Kanien'kehá ka Elder Ellen Gabriel has commented, "what we need is systemic change" (quoted in Serebrin 2018: n.p.).

The federal government has been paying lip service to climate action and to reconciliation with First Nations; meanwhile they continue to approve pipelines and new tar sands mines, forcing unwanted projects on Indigenous territories without Indigenous consent, violating Indigenous rights and breaching Canada's commitments to reducing GHG emissions. As a counterforce to this Liberal hypocrisy, social movements and front-line communities have been organizing and mobilizing, pushing for real transformation of Canada's economic, political and energy systems; targeting the underlying drivers of both climate change and racial inequality in this country.

SOCIAL MOVEMENTS IN CANADA

Resisting proposed pipeline after proposed pipeline over the last decade has brought together diverse social movements in Canada, working in courtrooms, in the media, in the streets and on the land. Although specific social movements are dynamic and hard to define and delineate, I see three distinct but overlapping movements as making up the bulk of the anti-pipeline resistance. They are the Indigenous land defence movement, the mainstream environmental movement and the environmental/climate justice movement.

Indigenous Land Defence Movements

Indigenous resistance to oil and gas pipelines is one manifestation of a much longer and much broader struggle. Indigenous resistance to colonial violation of Indigenous lands, rights and lives has been ongoing since European contact over five hundred years ago (Hill 2010; Simpson

2017). Indigenous struggles against colonization have been ongoing in many regions of the world. Indigenous communities globally struggle to resist the capitalist mode of production and the logics of domination that maintain the structure of settler colonialism (Wolfe 2006), while also defending relations and forms of social organization based on mutuality and reciprocity (Amadahy 2010; Simpson 2011; Coulthard 2014).

That Indigenous Peoples are still here after centuries of Canadian federal "Indian policy," with its explicit goals to eliminate and assimilate Indigenous Peoples, is testament to this ongoing resistance (Coburn 2015; Simpson and Ladner 2010; Manuel 2017; Simpson 2017). This resistance has taken, and continues to take, multiple overlapping forms, including legal actions defending constitutional (inherent and treaty) and international rights in provincial and federal courts. This legal approach has led to important court rulings that affirm the rights of Indigenous Peoples to their lands. These key rulings include Calder (1973), Van Der Peet (1996) and Tsilhqot'in (2014).

While some Indigenous Peoples and communities have been fighting colonialism though the court system in Canada, others have been resisting through the direct action of blockades and land occupations, creating what Anishinaabe scholar of Indigenous Law John Borrows refers to as vitally important "flash point" events (2007). There is a long history of this kind of direct action resistance by Indigenous Peoples in this country, including at Oka, Caledonia, Ipperwash, Gustafsen Lake, Burnt Church and more recently Elsipogtog and Unist'ot'en. These flash point events tend to arise when 1) Indigenous rights have been violated, 2) years of political and legal means of addressing the violation have been ineffective and 3) despite the ongoing dispute over land rights, governments authorize unwanted development on Indigenous land (Russell 2010). Currently there are multiple sites in Canada where Indigenous communities are actively blocking the development of gas terminals, mines, dams, pipelines and oil and gas extraction on their lands. These types of resistance efforts work on many fronts of socio-ecological transformation: "Beyond the disruption of the flows of capitalism and the denial of the movement of resources out of the territory, the blockade can create a space for the control and practice of Indigenous economic and political authority in the face of the cultural and economic dislocation forced upon them" (Temper and Bliss. 2015: 21).

Very often these two strategies of legal action in the courts and direct action on the land have been combined (e.g., the Gitxsan, Lubicon Cree and Eeyou). Different strategies are effective in different contexts, and in many key cases (e.g., Northern Gateway) combining both court action and direct action has led to important wins. Dene scholar Glen Coulthard wrote that "if history has taught us anything, it is this: if you want those within power to respond swiftly for Indigenous Peoples' political efforts, start by placing Native bodies … between settlers and their money" (2013: n.p.).

Indigenous resistance was also mounted in the form of the Idle No More movement during the winter of 2011, triggered by legislation of the Harper government — an omnibus bill — which included bills to weaken environmental protection laws, including those protecting all of Canada's navigable waterways, many of which pass through Indigenous territory. The Omnibus bill also included ten bills that would affect Indigenous sovereignty (K.N.N. Collective 2014). This movement erupted across the country in the form of flash-mob circle dances and drumming and other beautiful and disruptive expressions of Indigenous agency and cultures in public spaces, such as shopping malls and blockades of rail lines (K.N.N. Collective 2014). The Idle No More movement was and is part of a larger movement of *resurgence* that is at the heart of Indigenous change agency currently in this country. While resistance over the last five centuries has been critical to defending Indigenous lands, rights and lives, in pushing back against the forces of colonial capitalism (Alfred 2009), "at their most powerful … Indigenous movements move beyond resistance to resurgence; that is the joyful affirmations of individual and collective indigenous self-determination" (Coburn 2015: 25). There is a move currently in Indigenous movements and communities to turn away from approaches that seek to gain recognition from non-Indigenous people and colonial governments, and a turning inwards instead, towards healing, strengthening and reinvigorating traditional cultures, practices and governance structures (Coulthard 2007; Simpson 2017).

Many powerful expressions of Indigenous agency, such as the Unist'ot'en camp in BC, are currently pursuing transformation through both resistance *and* resurgence. For the past ten years, these people have reoccupied their traditional territories, which are on the pathways of multiple oil and gas pipeline routes. This most certainly is a site of resistance, having seen multiple confrontations with police and industry, but it has also provided space to practise and assert sovereignty and enact their responsibility to their lands (Temper and Bliss 2015). Guided by their natural law and traditional governance system, they have built traditional structures and a healing centre, and they teach traditional practices of hunting, trapping and gathering to Indigenous youth (Unist'ot'en Camp: 2017).

Many strands of anti-authoritarian social movements in Canada have come to see the Indigenous fight for decolonization as deeply connected to other liberational, transformative goals, and indeed foundational to them (Fortier 2017). While the environmental/climate justice movements tend to align with this understanding, the mainstream environmental movement has been slower to centre Indigenous voices and struggles in their practices and conceptions of environmentalism (Fortier 2017: 117).

Given the shared focus of protecting land, there have been numerous partnerships between mainstream environmentalists and Indigenous Peoples against resource extraction, development and pollution (Fortier 2017). Though these collaborations have at times succeeded strategically in stopping or slowing unwanted development projects, they have been "fraught with colonialist logics and instrumentalism" (Fortier 2017: 118). The transformative potential, as well as the conflicts and tensions present in these relationships between Indigenous and environmental movements, are a central theme of this book and are explored in greater depth in the following chapters.

The Mainstream Environmental Movement

The environmental movement in Canada emerged and evolved along a similar trajectory as did environmental movements in the US and Europe. It began in the late 1800s and early 1900s as a predominantly white movement for the conservation of pristine nature and the setting aside of "wilderness" (Indigenous lands) as national parks (Guha 2014). In the 1960s, with the publication of *Silent Spring* by Rachel Carson, environmentalism gained traction around issues of chemical pollution and impacts to human health and to other species, and became more of a popular movement (Guha 2014). In Canada in the 1970s, 80s and 90s, the environmental movement gained strength and numbers as it mobilized around direct actions to oppose clear-cut logging and other pressing issues. "This predominantly white environmentalist movement broke into the mainstream through tree sits, flotillas, and other forms of direct action that brought groups like Greenpeace, Rainforest Action Network ... and others into popular consciousness" (Fortier 2017: 118–119). While environmental causes gained more popular support, the movement was slowly becoming institutionalized with the increase in non-governmental organizations (NGOs), as I will discuss in Chapter 6.

Ramos and Rodgers argue that the environmental movement in Canada has followed a similar pattern to other social movements that emerged at this time. This involved the gradual professionalization and institution-alization of social movements, moving them from what had been "risky, contentious, and outside-of-the state in the 1960s" to be more "predict-able and accommodating, and partially incorporated into the state" by the 1990s (2015: 4).

Indeed, in his book *Environmentalism of the Rich*, Peter Dauvergne argues that environmental movements in the Western world turned not only to institutionalization, but to corporatization — increased collabora-tion and cooperation with large corporations. He understands this trend to have significantly reduced the transformative impacts of environmental movements (2016). He claims that this decreasing effectiveness of the environmental movement stems from a loss of a sense of "outrage" at the deep injustices inherent in the destruction of the natural world. This critical "outrage" that had been at the heart of environmental struggles of earlier decades is still at the heart of what Martinez-Alier and others refer to as Environmentalism of the Poor and currently at the heart of environmental justice and climate justice movements around the world (Guha 2014).

Clapp and Dauvergne analyze the divergent strands of global environmental movements, which they find are divided by "radically dif-ferent visions of the best way forward: ones rooted in radically different explanations of the causes and consequences of global environmental change" (2011: 1). They identify four distinct strands, which include: 1) *Market liberals*, who call for reforms to facilitate a smooth functioning of markets. They want eco-efficiency, voluntary corporate responsibil-ity and more technological cooperation; 2) *Institutionalists*, who call for reforms to facilitate global cooperation and stronger institutions. They call for new and better environmental regimes, changes to international organizations and efforts to enhance state capacity to manage environ-mental change; 3) *Bio-environmentalists*, who call for reforms to protect nature from humanity. They call for lower rates of population growth and consumption as well as a new economy based on an ethic of sustainability, one that operates at a steady state, designed to preserve the globe's natural heritage; and lastly 4) *Social greens,* who call for reforms to reduce inequality and foster environmental justice. "People must rise up and dismantle global economic institutions to reverse globalization. The new global political economy must empower communities and localize trade and production. And it should respect the rights of women, Indigenous communities, and the poor" (Clapp and Dauvergne 2011: 1).

Where the mainstream environmental movement in Canada is made up of some messy combination of market liberals, institutionalists and bio-environmentalists, the environmental justice and climate justice movements are much more aligned with Dauvergne and Clapp's social greens categorization. Some people in the mainstream environmental movement "continue to see environmental endeavor detached from questions of social justice … some proponents of environmental agenda remain not only disinterested in challenging racialized oppression, but in fact view racial hierarchies and racist practices as necessary to the pursuit of an 'environmental vision'" (Gosine and Teelucksigngh 2008: 5). The environmental justice and climate justice movements, in contrast, are generally more committed to social justice and undoing all forms of domination, thus making for somewhat easier alliances with Indigenous movements than the mainstream environmental movement has.

The Environmental Justice and Climate Justice Movements

The environmental/climate justice movement in Canada emerged more from the anti-authoritarian social justice movement than from the mainstream environmental movement (Fortier 2017). The environmental justice movement is understood to have been born in the United States in the early 1980s with roots in the civil rights movement, defending people of colour against environmental and health damage. The concept of environmental justice arose because minority communities were disproportionately impacted by environmental burdens (Scheidel et al. 2017; Bullard 2002, 1993). Environmental justice movements tend to focus on "the structural and political dimension of environmental problems that cannot be solved apart from social and economic justice" (Temper and Del Bene 2016: 2). Canadian activist and journalist Harsha Walia describes the environmental justice movement in Canada:

As part of the international movement under the banner of "system change, not climate change," a growing number of environmentalists are rejecting green capitalism. Green-washing attempts such as the Canadian Boreal Forest Agreement and the Ontario Far North Act were challenged by anti-capitalist environmentalists, as well as by Indigenous communities who saw such efforts as continuing to marginalize front-line voices. An inspiring example of anti-colonial environmental justice organizing has been resistance to the Alberta Tar Sands and Enbridge Pipeline in BC. (2011: n.p.)

Climate justice activism in Canada has emerged in the last decade within the context of a new bottom-up global movement (Bond 2012) that has mobilized to contest the unequal impacts of climate change, both geographically and socially (Featherstone 2012). This movement is growing as more communities around the world are being impacted by changes in the climate.

The term "climate justice" was coined by activists protesting the failed negotiations at the Copenhagen UNFCCC COP meeting in 2009 (Foran and Widick 2013). Climate justice emerged in reaction to the failure "from above," as "failure is the only way to summarize sixteen years of talk by United Nations negotiators from national states influenced by fossil-fuel-dependent capital, neoliberal multilateral agencies, and the big Environmental NGOs" (Bond 2012).

Since Copenhagen the global climate justice movement has grown, bringing together an emerging alignment of previously separate social justice and environmental activist movements. It is being led by those on the front lines of the impacts of a changing climate and those on the front lines of the destructive extractivism that is fueling the problem. These people on the front lines are primarily poor and Indigenous.

Characteristic of this movement is that it aims to not just tackle climate change, but "challenge the unequal social and environmental relations which carbon emissions are embedded in and locate it within the broader crisis of contemporary capitalism" (Chatterton, Featherstone and Routledge 2013: 7). It squarely rejects capitalist solutions to climate change (e.g., carbon markets) and exposes the "uneven and persistent patterns of eco-imperialism" (Featherstone 2013).

Climate justice principles were articulated in the Klima Forum's declaration during Copenhagen and included leaving fossil fuels in the ground; reasserting peoples' and community control over production; re-localizing food production; massively reducing over-consumption, particularly in the Global North; respecting Indigenous and forest people's rights; and recognizing the ecological and climate debt owed to the peoples in the Global South by the societies of the Global North necessitating the making of reparations. These principles are now accepted by a broad range of climate justice campaigning networks (Chatterton, Featherstone and Routledge 2013).

Climate justice–focused activist groups and organizations have been emerging over the last decade in Canada, such as Climate Justice Montreal, Climate Justice Edmonton, The Leap, Indigenous Climate Action and others. Climate justice conferences, such as Powershift, have occurred several times since 2009, bringing diverse groups and activists across Canada to train and plan together.

Convergence of These Diverse Movements to Oppose Pipelines

These three distinct but overlapping movements — the mainstream environmental, Indigenous land defence and environmental/climate justice — have come together in other forms at other times, but never more so than during the past decade of opposing pipelines, tar sands and extractivism. A "large number of industrial projects have actually been delayed or completely halted as a result of community resistance engaging in diverse tactics" (Walia 2011: n.p.).

Pipeline expansion is currently a shared primary target of these movements. "There are many possible points of intervention but struggles around pipelines appear to have distinct significance as a point of weakness for the tar sands industry" (Black, D'Arcy and Weis 2014: 3). Pipelines are viewed as a strategic vulnerability for the tar sands industry, for two major reasons. One is that the industry fears bottlenecks, which can "constrain expansion, and hence both increased pipeline capacity and access to a wider set of refineries are deemed to be essential to continuing growth and investments" (Black, D'Arcy and Weis 2014: 16). While bottlenecks remain in place, opposition to pipelines can slow investment in the industry as investors are wary of delays. Secondly, pipelines provoke resistance by threatening serious ecological and health risks to more and more regions. These multiple and widespread risks have served to "galvanize front line mobilizations against pipelines and refineries, and these have grown into a major part of the struggles against the tar sands" (Black, D'Arcy and Weis 2014: 17).

When I began this research in 2014, there were several large-scale pipelines proposed for development in order to expand markets for Alberta bitumen and BC natural gas, including TransCanada's Energy East, Trans Mountain's Kinder Morgan and Chevron's Pacific Trail, among others. In October 2017, TransCanada announced the cancelling of the Energy East pipeline, and social movements who had been working hard to oppose this project celebrated the victory (Tucker 2017). These convergences continue to protest the building of the Trans Mountain (Kinder Morgan) pipeline, which, if built, will nearly triple the capacity of the current pipeline system to 890,000 barrels a day and significantly increase tanker traffic off the Pacific coast (Crawford and Mooney 2018).

The fierce opposition to the Trans Mountain pipeline, like the opposition to the other proposals that have come before, is being led by Indigenous communities. Opposition to pipelines by Indigenous Peoples and their non-Indigenous allies in Canada is posing a real challenge to the state and to the extractive, fossil fuel-based economy. Indigenous Peoples in Canada have been called the "last line of defence" and "the only real threat to energy projects such as oil and gas pipelines" (Curtis 2015: n.p.). The *Montreal Gazette* stated that though "they don't have the backing of major political parties, corporations or any major funding source.... First Nations are becoming the de-facto face of Canada's anti-pipeline movement" (Curtis 2015: n.p.).

The alliances between these diverse movements is a powerful force for transformation in Canada, a force dependent on the leadership of Indigenous Peoples and also on the support and the awakening of settlers. Arthur Manuel expressed it in these words: "I still see hope, a faint light on the horizon. This is the gradual dawning of awareness among ordinary Canadians that things are not right and things have to change, that there may be important projects in protecting land and fixing Canada to make it a land of justice for all" (2017: 56).

The crises of climate change and of racial inequality and Indigenous poverty, all rooted in ongoing colonial relations in Canada, demand a fundamental rethinking and restructuring of the economic and social relations at the heart of Canada. The path forward for healing these unjust relations lies in the practice of settler Canadians following the leadership of Indigenous Peoples who are actively protecting their lands and waters (Klein 2014; Davis 2010). The alliances and collaborations that have been forged in anti-pipeline fights hold much promise for cultivating the kind of people power required to transform Canada. That said, the transformative power of these movements is currently being hampered in various ways.

Canadian journalist Naomi Klein has pointed out that there is a long legacy in Canada of movements working in silos on "separate issues" and failing to see the crucial overlap in their visions. She contends that moving past this siloed approach and creating a "movement of movements" is necessary for creating a strong enough force to shift the trajectory of the Canadian energy and economic systems (2014). Others have also argued that, in Canada, social movements' efforts have been fragmented, often working at cross purposes and unwilling to collaborate, which renders them unable to build a "counter-hegemonic" political force (Findlay 2002). Tensions over conflicting end goals and theories of change, as well as over preferred tactics, are driving the fragmentation. But ongoing racism, sexism, classism and other forms of domination playing out within and across movements is also blunting the transformative power of these movements.

How do we unblunt this force of social movements? How do we work together better, combine forces and pose a real treat to the status quo of extractivism and settler colonialism in Canada? The rest of this book grapples with these and other questions, drawing on the many conversations I have been having with people in these movements.

CHAPTER 3

UNDERSTANDING THE CRISES

We are at a moment. We either change the narrative, change the story, bring in the people who have been marginalized, or we go ahead with business as usual. — E. Deranger, *The New Green Deal in Canada*

To stand a chance of being able to build a socially fair and ecologically viable society, we need to identify and take aim at the root causes of the climate and racial inequality crises we face. Climate justice activists, especially those of the Global South, have been leading the call for attention to the root causes of climate change (Chatterton, Featherstone and Routledge 2013), and scholars have been arguing too that transforming systems requires addressing not just the symptoms, but the deeper causes of social and environmental challenges (Temper et al. 2018; Abson et al. 2017; Ehrenfeld 2004; Pepermans and Maeseele 2016). Indeed, the fact that societies have made very little progress towards sustainability is due in no small part to the continued focus on quick fixes, rather than on the drivers of current trajectories (Ehrenfeld 2004, Abson et al. 2017).

Mainstream discourses about climate change and racial inequality in Canada generally fail to name the systems and structures driving the crises, and this allows for solutions and initiatives which leave the underlying drivers of the crises unaltered, or even reinforce them, foreclosing on the potential for real, transformative change.

For example, the Pan-Canadian Framework on Clean Growth and Climate Change, which encapsulates Canada's current approach to addressing the climate crisis, centres on pricing carbon and technological innovation (Government of Canada 2016). It does not acknowledge the deeper issue of the Canadian economy's ongoing dependence on fossil fuels and ignores the vested corporate interests that seek to perpetuate this dependence. It ignores that Canadians are not all evenly responsible for creating carbon emissions, and it ignores that some people in Canada are being impacted by climate change much more than others. It fails to acknowledge the systems and structures that hold the carbon polluting energy system in place, the forces which are driving fossil fuel dependence and carbon pollution. This shallow analysis of the crisis informs shallow, inadequate climate policy.

Within this depthless framing of climate change the Liberal government has been able to rationalize building and even purchasing new pipelines to help get bitumen from the Alberta tar sands to the coasts and then to overseas markets. Their shallow discourse allows Prime Minister Trudeau to claim that the building of a new pipeline is somehow not in conflict with Canada's climate goals, that revenue from the Trans Mountain pipeline will be part of funding the transition to clean energy (Government of Canada 2019). Only from very shallow understandings of the climate crisis can the status quo of extractivism and pipeline development in Canada be rationalized and justified.

And along similar lines, only through egregiously superficial framings of racial inequality in Canada have mainstream conversations about reconciliation been carried out without centring the very real and ongoing drivers of inequality. This framing allows the continuation of policies and projects that violate the rights of Indigenous Peoples and continue to dispossess them of their lands, waters and ways of life. Maintaining the destructive status quo requires that we do not look too deeply at the underlying systems and structures driving climate and social injustice. But that is precisely what this chapter aims to do.

In my interviews with activists and land defenders across Canada I asked them how they understand the social and ecological crises that their work seeks to address and what they see as the root causes driving the crises. Their answers reached deep to expose the structural connections between extractivism, the violation of Indigenous rights, climate change, uneven impacts, inequality and other issues. Many discussed these as symptoms of systems such as capitalism and colonialism, which in turn are influenced by and influence worldviews that justify domination and a fundamental disconnection from land and from each other. Amid the superficial, wholly inadequate mainstream discourses about climate change and racial inequality, activists and land defenders engaged in social movements across the country are providing much needed counter-narratives about what is wrong and what kind of futures are possible.

UNEVEN IMPACTS OF PIPELINE DEVELOPMENT, ENVIRONMENTAL DESTRUCTION AND CLIMATE DISRUPTION

Although most of the people I spoke with have been actively involved with stopping oil and gas pipelines, no one I talked to framed pipeline development as the crux of the problem. Rather, people see them as driven by, and poignant symbols of, unjust and unsustainable political, economic and belief systems — systems that are driving both climate change and inequality. Pipelines "connect local communities all across Canada with the larger issues of tar sands extraction, climate change, and the violation of Indigenous rights" (Int#17). Where global climate change can feel abstract and far away to people who are not yet impacted, "pipelines are something that people can connect to … something to hold on to … otherwise climate change is too big" (Int#15). As new pipelines threaten to cut through towns, cities, forests and waterways to get landlocked oil and gas to the coasts, more and more communities have become engaged with big concerns and big questions — about spills, carbon emissions, health impacts, jobs and justice. Whose health, wellbeing and livelihoods are being put in danger? And for whose benefit? Who gets to decide whether these projects are rejected or built? Controversies about pipeline development have been teaching Canadians, in many cases first hand, what many marginalized peoples and people in the Global South have long known: that the benefits and the costs of polluting industrial development are not evenly distributed across society. Some people, mainly those with power and wealth, are benefiting while others, those already marginalized by poverty, racism and other forms of systemic inequality, are disproportionally bearing the negative impacts. These patterns are playing out in oil and gas pipeline development and they are shaping the ways that global climate impacts are being felt and responded to.

A climate justice activist from Quebec said that, "when it comes to climate change, we know who's responsible for the worst of emissions historically and also who is profiting from [the crisis]." Later in the interview she made clear that "climate change is about power and who has the power in society" (Int#39).

It is not just activists alone who have been pointing this out. Scholars too are identifying the ways that environmental and climate crises are exacerbating existing social strains and reflecting existing inequalities on local, national and global scales. The increasingly frequent impacts of anthropogenic climate change are hitting poor, racialized and Indigenous communities first and hardest. Nations and communities most impacted by climate change are often those least responsible for the problem and those who have the fewest resources to cope with it (Parks and Roberts 2006). Citing flooding from Hurricane Mitch in Honduras, rising sea levels swamping entire Pacific Island atoll nations and devastation from flooding among squatter settlements in Mozambique, Parks and Roberts explain that existing social and economic inequalities are rendering communities such as these "brutally vulnerable to forces outside their control" (2006: 1). The understanding about the interrelations between the climate crisis and social inequality crisis has been deepened by climate justice activists and scholars across the world (Bond 2012).

Like the uneven and unjust distribution of climate impacts, the impacts of the extraction, transport and processing of fossil fuels are felt by some people more than others, reflecting more general patterns of environmental injustice (Martinez-Alier et al. 2016). One interviewee explained:

> The development of fossil fuel projects [happens in] communities that are already more marginalized because of the way that society is set up. Think about the tar sands. Who's living on the land? Whose land is there? [Industry and government think] 'it's undeveloped, and we're just going to go and develop the tar sands over those people's land'. It's the same with refineries that are causing climate change and pollution of land and water. (Int#13)

Environmental racism, one form of environmental injustice, refers to the disproportionate impact of environmental pollution and other hazards on people of colour (Taylor 2014; Waldron 2018). In a discussion about the Line 9 pipeline in Ontario, one person I spoke with told me the siting of that pipeline route is a clear example of environmental racism: "It's how violence is enacted on communities and land. The pipeline goes through Jane and Finch, which is a highly racialized neighbourhood, and then goes through Indigenous territories" (Int#32).

Another person, reflecting on the siting of pipelines in Canada, argued that "it's ... environmental racism. But there is classism also. Because you have poor people living in these areas where [unwanted development] is happening" (Int#7 Kanien'kehá:ka). "People of lower economic means are usually the first to be affected by environmental pollution" (Int#23).

Intertwined with the ways the impacts of climate change and extractivism are unevenly being borne along racial and class lines, women are also disproportionality impacted. In a webinar hosted by Indigenous Climate Action, Eriel Tchekwie Deranger (2018a), the executive director of ICA and member of the Athabasca Chipewyan First Nation, made clear that "climate justice is gender justice" and that "violence against land is violence against women." Women are "disproportionately impacted by climate and the drivers of climate change," in many ways including the increase in sexual violence that accompanies man camps (Deranger 2018a). Man camps are temporary housing for transient workers. These camps accompany many pipeline construction projects, and the 2019 Final Report from the National Inquiry into Missing and Murdered Indigenous Women and Girls states that there is substantial evidence of a "correlation between resource extraction and violence against Indigenous women, girls, and 2SLGBTQQIA people" (Walia 2019: n.p.).

Here we see the links between climate change, colonialism and the oppression of women. Kanahus Manuel, of the Secwepemc Women Warriors and leader of the Tiny House Warriors movement, argues that the solutions to climate change need to be shaped and led by women. She states clearly that "we need to confront patriarchy and other things that drive climate change" (2018).

Of all the many unjust and unequal relations that people I interviewed described, the most common was the ways Indigenous Peoples are most directly and pervasively impacted by climate change and extractivism in Canada. As one interviewee put it, "Indigenous Peoples are the first to be subject to environmental injustice, all in the name of economic progress" (Int#23). Mascarenhas too observes that "whether by conscious design or institutional neglect," First Nations communities face the worst environmental devastation in Canada (2007: 570).

Indigenous Peoples are disproportionately suffering the impacts of the tar sands expansion (Stewart 2015: n.p.). Indigenous communities downstream from the tar sands in Alberta are suffering from devastating levels of water and soil pollution and the associated health effects. These communities are also being impacted as tar sands development destroys the habitats of animals and plants that are a vital part of these local cultures and livelihoods (Droitsch and Simieritsch 2010).

Other Indigenous communities, rather than being impacted by extraction, are being impacted by the processing of fossil fuels at refineries and petrochemical plants. The Anishinaabe people in Aamjiwnaang First Nation near Sarnia, Ontario, a centre of petrochemical processing in Canada, are suffering serious health impacts due to water and air pollution (Fung, Luginaah and Gorey 2007; Mackenzie, Lockridge and Keith 2005). The Inuit in the north of Canada are being impacted by the effects of fossil fuel combustion driving planetary warming and the quickly changing weather conditions. This is having deep impacts on Inuit livelihoods and wellbeing (Ford et al. 2008). Meanwhile many First Nations (such as the Secwepemc, Wet'suwet'en and Coast Salish Nations in BC) are facing the impacts and risks of oil and gas pipelines currently proposed to go through their territories. Whether at the points of extraction, transport, processing or combustion, Indigenous communities are bearing an unfair brunt of Canada's ongoing dependence on the oil and gas industry.

What these movement voices, corroborated by scholarship, are making clear is that environmental degradation, pollution and other impacts from extractive development affect first and foremost the people already marginalized by the current systems, by way of class, race, gender and other systems of domination (Martinez-Alier et al. 2016; Gosine and Teelucksingh 2008). But these dynamics are not just about who is being negatively impacted, we also need to pay attention to who is benefiting and who is making the decisions that allow these injustices. The inequalities inherent in dirty energy extraction and production don't just negatively impact marginalized communities, but directly benefit rich, white ones: "For every single industrial town that exists, there must be a Westmount.… For every single marginalized community, there is a core community that is benefiting from that marginalization" (TT#2). "The people that are upholding the actions of fossil fuel companies … are upholding racial injustice and social injustice (Int#23).

Where mainstream discussion places the blame for climate change on some faceless, generalized *human activity* and abstract *carbon pollution* (Government of Canada), these movements' analyses help us see that not all people are equally responsible, nor do all people have equal access to decision-making power about what projects get built and what fossil fuels are burnt. These more nuanced and in-depth analyses serve to compensate for and push back against the shallow understandings about climate change and inequality in Canada.

STRUCTURES AND SYSTEMS THAT DRIVE CLIMATE INJUSTICE AND INEQUALITY

As described, the conversations I had with activists and land defenders exposed the uneven, unjust ways that climate change and extractivism are impacting different groups. But their analyses dig down deeper, bringing to light the ways that these uneven impacts are driven by underlying structures and systems that lock in unjust and unsustainable trajectories. Though some people may see Canada as a generally peaceful, nature loving nation, with a slight inequality issue and a minor problem of carbon pollution, many of the people I spoke with see Canada, at its very core, as premised on the extraction of natural resources and the theft of Indigenous land, as an ongoing settler colonial state. Colonialism came up again and again in the conversations I had with activists across the country. Both Indigenous and non-Indigenous people are naming colonialism as an ongoing system in Canada and a root cause of both the climate crisis and crisis of inequality.

"We're still living in the midst of colonialism" (Int#34 Anishinaabe/ Ojibway). "It's not just that there is inequality [in Canada], we are operating in a violent system of disparity and systemic violence and injustice" (Int#36). "Canadian culture is not built around having an equal relationship with Indigenous people. It's about colonization and domination" (Int#9 Kanien'kehá:ka). "Colonization and disregard for Indigenous rights is what has allowed for all the fossil fuel extraction projects in Canada … the silencing of voices, for generations. That is pretty foundational" (Int#26).

"Though some Canadians may not see this, it is because these unequal, unjust systems are so ingrained and foundational to Canadian culture and economy that it can remain invisible" (Int#34 Anishinaabe/Ojibway). "It's what we call institutionalized racism. Racism on Indigenous Peoples is so ingrained in legislation and policy and rules and regulations and attitudes that it's hard to see it clearly. Canadians can't see it" (Int#9 Kanien'kehá:ka).

Colonialism is the exertion of control of territory or resources outside the official boundaries of a state or empire. Nation states establish colonies beyond their borders with various motivations — for trade, for military purposes, for the general extension of central power (Barker and Lowman 2015). Colonialism has been enacted around the world in different forms and can be defined in different ways, but one characteristic they all share is uneven power relations between settlers and Indigenous Peoples. These "relations of power are shaped by hierarchies of race, culture, gender, and class, and lead to the political, social, cultural, and material subordination of the less powerful groups through domination and exploitation" (Waldron 2018: 38).

Settler colonialism is one particular form of colonialism, and it is the way by which the European take-over of Turtle Island has played out over the last five hundred years. Settler colonialism "functions through the replacement of Indigenous populations with an invasive settler society that, over time, develops a distinctive identity and sovereignty" (Barker and Lowman n.d.). With settler colonialism, the colony is not just a place to extract resources to send back home; the colony becomes home (Waldron 2018). Making home for colonizers requires the elimination of Indigenous Peoples and their relationships with the land (Wolfe 2006; Shoemaker 2015; Veracini 2011). Within settler colonialism, it is land which is "most valuable, contested, required" (Tuck and Yang 2012: 5).

Many people spoke to me of how Indigenous Peoples in Canada have been pushed off their lands continually over Canadian history, so that governments and industry can access, extract and exploit resources. "What we have seen over centuries is the forced displacement of people from the lands they inhabit ... for the wholesale destruction of those lands" (Int#30).

Dene scholar Glen Coulthard makes clear that the primary purpose of settler colonialism is access to land, for settlement and for capital accumulation (2014). Nishnaabeg scholar Leanne Betasamosake Simpson writes that "the Canadian state has always been primarily interested in acquiring the ... rights to [Indigenous] land for settlement and for the extraction of resources" (2017: 42). "Over the past 200 years, without our permissions and without our consent, we have been systematically removed and dispossessed from our territory" (Simpson 2017: 4).

The lands and waters that Canadian settlers now claim as their own were not freely handed over by Indigenous Peoples. These territories were never ceded — neither by treaty nor through war. In the cases where treaties were signed, the land was often seized through violation of treaty agreements (McFarlane and Schabus 2017). In various ways, Canada's claim to state control over these lands and waters rests on racist and legally weak foundations (Reid 2010). The basis of Canadian jurisdiction over lands generally rests on two assumptions. The first assumption is that the Doctrine of Discovery permitted the assertion of sovereignty by the colonists. The second assumption is that by signing treaties Indigenous Peoples ceded title to their lands.

"Racism is at the foundation of Canada's claim to sovereignty, of having power over us. A Canadian state shouldn't exist. But because of racism, because of the Doctrine of Discovery they claim the right to exist. [Canada] exists because of racism" (Int#38 Mi'kmaw). When Europeans began to settle Turtle Island, the Doctrine of Discovery was how they "claimed rights of sovereignty, property, and trade in regions they allegedly discovered" (Reid 2010: 336). The Doctrine is rooted in two fifteenth-century papal bulls: one gave Christians the right to take non-Christians as perpetual slaves, and the other justified the colonization of the Americas with the idea that since the non-Christians around the world were not using the land as Europeans deemed proper, Europeans had the right to claim ownership of the lands (Vowel 2016). This papal bull was a starting point in the "historic efforts by Christian monarchies and states of Europe in the fifteenth and later centuries to assume and exert conquest rights and dominance over non-Christian Indigenous Peoples in order to take over and profit from their lands and territories" (Frichner 2010: 8).

As the British Crown asserted control over Indigenous lands, it negotiated Treaties with First Nations or the land was simply seized and occupied. There are several ways that negotiation of Treaties, "while seemingly honourable and legal, was often marked by fraud and coercion" (TRC2015: 1). Firstly, Treaties were understood by Indigenous signatories as agreements to share the land, where this was clearly not what transpired. Secondly, often the treaty negotiations were not conducted with the lawful hereditary chiefs and excluded women, who in many Nations had final authority. And thirdly, Treaties have been breached many times by the Crown and/or Canadian government, notably by the residential school system and through resource extraction (Vowel 2016; McFarlane and Schabus 2017).

The United Nations Declaration on the Rights of Indigenous Peoples affirms "that all doctrines ... based on, or advocating, superiority of peoples or individuals on the basis of national origin or racial, religious, ethnic or cultural differences are racist, scientifically false, legally invalid, morally condemnable and socially unjust" (United Nations 2007: 3). Even though Canada has signed this declaration, no meaningful actions have been taken to relinquish the control over the territories claimed through this racist doctrine. An Anishinaabe kwe water defender and scholar I spoke with reflected on Canada's treaty process:

> Back then, we hadn't realized yet that what the Crown, and eventually the Canadian Government, wanted to do was resource extraction. It was kind of a forced Treaty. The Treaty was signed under duress. And so, today, has anything changed? Has the Canadian Government consulted with us? Time and time again ... they end up in their own court system and they are proven wrong ... [reprimanded for] not properly consulting with us, but yet they just continue. (Int#12 Anishinaabe)

> The government and industry have never given up a single inch of Indigenous soil back to us. They've never given us our freedoms back. (Int#38 Mi'kmaw)

Several people explained to me that the theft of land, the violation of Treaties and settler colonialism in general have been driving both the ecological crisis and the systemic inequality and poverty crises in this country — but further to that, to add insult to injury, Indigenous Peoples are often blamed for the suffering they face: "We are rebuilding from an apocalypse.... [Yet] somehow it's our fault. Poverty is our fault. Social dysfunction is our fault. If anything, white society constructs itself as the hero, coming in to save us from ourselves" (Int#38 Mi'kmaw).

Settler colonialism and extractivism in Canada depend on notions of settler superiority and on the dehumanization of Indigenous Peoples and communities. "They condescend to us ... make us think we're stupid, that we don't know the science about the extractive projects ... they say it's for the economy. It's part of the system, to break [us] down ... to open the land to exploitation and occupation" (Int#7 Kanien'kehá:ka).

These conversations have helped me see that both the inequality and climate crises are deeply rooted in ongoing colonial relations in Canada. Settler colonialism, from the moment Europeans stepped foot on the shores of Turtle Island, was about establishing racial domination so that colonial control over land and resources could be established, so that settlers could acquire wealth through the extraction and exploitation of natural resources. This was the case in the days of the fur trade (Dawson 2016), and it is true now, with ongoing deforestation, mining and the extraction of unconventional oil and gas. Canada's wealth depends on theft of Indigenous lands and the violation of Indigenous rights. As the climate crisis deepens and we become ever more urgently in need of alternative ways of life and livelihood, the economic and political systems in Canada continue to exert racial dominance over Indigenous Peoples, the very peoples who, as evidenced by their presence on these lands since time immemorial, offer beautiful alternatives and solutions to the climate crisis. "What we're seeing is the taking of land from people who have a completely different relationship to that land than us settlers. And destroying it. Destroying their way of life. Destroying their traditions. Destroying the things that have kept them alive for millennia" (Int#30).

Colonial violence is not a thing of the past. One settler activist I interviewed expressed the view that "during the colonial days [it took] a much more brutal and overt form, a very violent form. These days it takes place in a more bureaucratic sense and happens through laws and permanent approvals" (Int#30). Though the face of colonialism has changed over time, and indeed injunctions and project approvals are a key means by which colonialism in Canada is currently enacted, overt colonial violence is still very much still alive in Canada. This week, as I was writing this chapter, an article was published in the *Guardian* newspaper regarding notes from a strategy session of the Royal Canadian Mounted Police (RCMP), Canada's national police force, which showed that Canadian police had been prepared to shoot Indigenous land defenders (Dhillon and Parish 2019: n.p.). Wet'suwet'en people and their allies at Gidimt'en checkpoint near Houston, British Columbia, were blockading construction of a natural gas pipeline through their traditional territories. While preparing to remove the land defenders and dismantle the barricade to enforce the injunction filed by Coastal Gaslink Pipeline in January 2019, RCMP officers were instructed by commanders to "use as much violence toward the gate as you want." Commanders argued that "lethal overwatch" was required. This term refers to the deployment of snipers. The Wet'suwet'en people have, for the last decade, been re-inhabiting their traditional territories to protect the lands and waters and people from proposed pipeline after proposed pipeline. They have cultivated permaculture gardens, installed solar panels and built a healing lodge. They have welcomed people from all over Canada and the world to visit and learn about defending lands and waters. Their motto is Heal the People, Heal the Land. The RCMP had been instructed to shoot. Colonial violence is not a thing of the past. It is ongoing. And it is being directed at the very people who are devoting their lives to the fight for climate justice and social equality.

How has such blatant injustice been able to be perpetuated in a country like Canada, by a government that self-identifies as a climate leader and prides itself on its relations with Indigenous Peoples? Many of the people I spoke to described capitalism as a main driving force that not only incentivizes but actually requires the ongoing colonial relations and power asymmetries described above. Capitalism, too, is a root cause of both climate change and inequality.

"We're never going to have climate justice or any sort of sustainable energy system under capitalism — it just doesn't make sense. Capitalism is a system that necessitates infinite growth" (Int#20 Michif-Cree). Capitalism can be defined as "the economic, political, and social system that is based on property, business, and industry being privately owned, and is directed towards making the greatest possible profits for private people and organizations" (Cambridge Dictionary: n.p.). Capitalism has certain inherent characteristics that are deeply problematic for both people and the planet. In his book about capitalism as a driver of the current extinction crisis, Ashley Dawson (2016) explains that capitalism, which must continuously expand in order to survive, tends to degrade the conditions of its own production, including the natural world and its resources. With the existential need to grow, profit making becomes the driver, the goal, the predominant incentive for human social endeavours (Whyte 2017; Kohn and Reddy 2017). This drive then overpowers other possible social goals, such as human wellbeing, social equality and a livable planet.

Endless economic growth requires the accumulation of economic surplus. This economic surplus is rooted in exploitation of people's labour and of raw materials. Given the dynamics of competition between firms, this exploitation must occur on an ever-larger scale. Capitalist production is dependent on a constant supply of raw materials to sustain operations on an ever-greater scale (Clark and York 2005). Given that capitalism requires increasing use of energy to continually increase production, the use of fossil fuels — as an abundant form of cheap energy to drive the machines of production — has become locked in. "Capital's constant demand for energy *necessitates* the continual plundering of the Earth for new reserves of fossil fuel" (Clark and York 2005: 409, emphasis mine). The climate crisis demands a swift transition away from the dependence on fossil fuels, but under capitalism's drive for profit and growth, this transition becomes antithetical. "It goes back to over-consumption. It's a big vicious circle we are living in. The government is promoting it. They're corporate driven and they're promoting it and they're not coming up with good long-term solutions" (Int#12 Anishinaabe).

A Kanien'kehá:ka activist I spoke with likened capitalist greed for money and oil with rape culture and drug addiction. He told me a story of being at a meeting with oil executives trying to convince his community to allow an oil pipeline through their reserve:

> I got up and said, "When you talk to Indigenous communities you remind me of a bunch of horny teenage boys that'll say any-thing to get laid." … You say "oh ya, we got the best technology for extraction that'll make for no waste, no pollution, no mess." … When I said this, people had a laugh, but people stopped and thought. These companies are like hard core addicts — they'll do anything to get their fix. (Int#7 Kanien'kehá:ka)

Naomi Klein's book *This Changes Everything: Capitalism vs. the Climate* documents how the rise of neoliberalism — a global movement since the 1990s to super-charge free-market capitalism through deregulation, privatization, austerity and removal of trade barriers — constituted a case of very bad timing. As people and nations became aware of the mounting climate crisis and began to understand that it was being caused by human activity and the burning of fossil fuels, the very means of addressing the crisis — through government regulation, through constraining corporate greed, through massive public spending in clean energy — were becoming politically unthinkable under growing neoliberal, free market ideology (Klein 2014). It is for these reasons that capitalism is driving the climate crisis and hindering efforts to address the crisis. To tackle the climate crisis, our economic systems need to be transformed away from growth-driven capitalism (Clark and York 2005; Klein 2014).

And capitalism is not only disastrous for the environment; it also requires and drives deep social inequality among humans. It brings wealth to a few through the exploitation of many (Marx 1976). Like its endless need for more raw materials, capitalism relies on the exploitation of human labour. Those who own the means of production make profit from workers' labour, driving class inequality (Harvey 2014). Feminist economists bring important insight about how capitalism rests on the backs of women, whose unpaid labour in the reproduction of life and labour is exploited, but unacknowledged, in the process of capital accumulation. Just as capitalism depends on the labour of the working class, the working class is in turn completely dependent on the unpaid reproductive work of women (see Perkins 2009; Waring 1988).

The problems with capitalism do not end there. Capitalism drives not just the exploration of nature, workers and women, it also depends on racial discrimination. Malcom X articulated this, calling capitalism a "rotten system" of exploitation, and stating "You can't have capitalism without racism" (quoted in Taylor 2016: 197). Racism justifies hierarchies of labour and employment, which distribute the benefits of the systems unequally across people in society (Waldron, 2018). Racial capitalism describes the commodification of racialized people for the purposes of acquiring social and economic value and benefits. Intersectional Marxist feminist Keeanga-Yamahtta Taylor argues that capitalism not only justifies and drives inequality, it then uses racism to divide and rule, blunting the class consciousness of everyone, and thus quelling the fire of resistance (2016).

As we see, capitalism requires the exploitation of the Earth and it drives the exploitation of workers, women and racialized people. It is also deeply implicated in colonialism. Its drive for endless growth and expansion has also manifested in land theft and colonization in the pursuit of new markets and new lands to exploit. Under capitalism, imperialism in some form or another is inevitable (Kohn and Reddy 2017):

> There's an ongoing process of empire, the Leviathan that continues, that requires constant growth of resources, expansion of territories and constant growth. It's part and parcel of capitalism. Imperialism and capitalism are two sides of the same coin. It has different faces; the face of misogyny, it includes the face of racism. All of those things are true, but empire, imperialism and capitalism are flip sides of one another. (Int#11)

Borrowing from Marx's concept of primitive accumulation Dene scholar Glenn Coulthard develops the concept of *accumulation by dispossession* to help draw the connection between capitalism and colonialism, describing how capitalism necessitated dispossession of Indigenous Peoples from their land in the quest to expand to new territories (Coulthard 2014). In Canada, "the primitive accumulation of capital through the colonial theft of land is foundational to both current capitalist wealth and to state jurisdiction … colonialism is by its very nature capitalist because it dispossesses Indigenous people of their land and resources and subjugates their communities" (Waldron 2018: 44). Kyle Whyte, Potawatomi scholar states it simply: "Colonialism often paved the way for the expansion of capitalism" (2017).

Settler colonialism in an ongoing encounter of domination of white settlers over Indigenous Peoples with the main incentive being the opportunities and wealth acquired through the acquisition of land. Inherent to capitalism is the "assimilation, depopulation, removal, and erasure of Indigenous Peoples; and the dispossession, expropriation, and territorial occupation of Indigenous resources, land, property, homes … all toward the end goal of profit" (Waldron 2018: 41).

Inextricably tied together, colonialism and capitalism have laid the groundwork for "industrialization and militarization — or carbon-intensive economics — which produce the drivers of anthropogenic climate change" (Whyte 2017: 154). These are the root causes driving both the climate crisis and the inequality crisis in Canada and beyond. It is vitally important that people actively working to address these crises can see this. "Seeing capitalism and colonialism as structural forces generating exploitation and ecocide" is of critical importance as we need to be able to acknowledge that colonial capitalism will not and cannot solve the crises it is causing (Dawson 2016: 63). "We have to decolonize things: the capitalistic, extractive, destructive, money-making activities in the dominant society. All that has to change. That would work hand in hand with solving the issues of climate change" (Int#9 Kanien'kehá:ka).

It becomes clear how deeply the roots of these crises have burrowed and how deeply the analyses happening in these movements must go. Being able to see the systems and structures holding injustice and polluting energy systems in place is critical for being able choose effective targets and strategies — to identify the levers of transformative change, to know what is at stake, what needs to be done and what is in our way.

WORLDVIEWS THAT JUSTIFY AND REINFORCE UNJUST SYSTEMS AND STRUCTURES

Digging deep to excavate and bring to light the inner workings of the economic and political systems that currently run societies is vital work happening in social movements. But some of the people I spoke with are also uprooting the inner workings of people's hearts and minds — exploring the ways that people understand the world, the assumptions we make about what is and what should be. How has the stronghold that colonial capitalism has over our social organization and relations shaped how we understand the world, what and who we value, and what we think is possible. What kind of worldview can justify the actions of settler climate protesters in Montreal, as they harassed and pushed Indigenous youth during the march, yelling "this is not your land"? Through what kind of lens on the world can building new oil and gas pipelines in a time of mounting climate chaos seem reasonable? What kind of worldview can justify, in the heart and mind of that RCMP commander, telling his officers to "use as much violence as you want" against Indigenous Peoples protecting their lands and waters? "We have to look at the mindsets of people" (Int#7 Kanien'kehá:ka):

> [It's] not just the government and the physical, financial and economic conditions … can we create transformation of the self along the way? That's critical because we may change the government, we may change the industry, but if we don't change ourselves, we're going to still have that insatiable need and greed

that will drive us to find new ways of exploitation. So, we have to change ourselves. And until we do that, none of these strategies work. (Int#38 Mi'kmaw)

Our mindsets — or worldviews — tend to be made up of "unstated assumptions ... our deepest set of beliefs about how the world works" (Meadows 1997: 11). Worldviews are our perceptions of how the world works and what is possible, including how we understand humanity's place in the natural world, the kind of goals and outcomes we consider socially desirable, as well as what we deem fair or unfair (Meadows 1997; Beddoe et al. 2009). Our worldviews tend to be unstated, deeply felt but unquestioned (Beddoe et al. 2009). They remain unstated because there is no need to state them; they are the things that we assume everyone knows (Meadows 1997). Worldviews are important to attend to because they play a very significant role in "how institutions and technologies are designed to function" (Beddoe et al. 2009: 2484).

One of the fundamental problems with current dominant worldviews is the objectification of the natural world. As one land defender I spoke with explained: "These companies, the mindsets where they are coming from.... They've trained the public to think about the natural world as a resource.... Everything that exists becomes a commodity. Things to be bought and sold" (Int#7 Kanien'kehá:ka):

The carbon problem is a by-product of industrialism. Industrialization is one of the pillars of power of Western society ... and is the manifestation of Western relationships with nature. In Western society, especially the ones that are dominated by Christian worldview ... nature is a spiritual wasteland. The trees, the animals, the mountains, the rivers don't have spirit. Only humans have spirit. So, it's easy to objectify nature ... as nothing more than material. This becomes very supportive of capitalism. Because capitalism is all about objectifying something, exploiting it, and turning it into a commodity and then profit.... The faster you can turn something into a commodity, the faster you can sell it, the more money you'll make. Christianity and capitalism work together that way. The relationship is one of dominance, control, destruction, death. For profit. (Int#38 Mi'kmaw)

The tendency of the Western worldview to devalue non-human forms of life allows and justifies the exploitation of the natural world. And the idea, also strongly held by the Western worldview, that some human lives are more valuable than other human lives has allowed for and justified many forms of oppression and social injustice. This worldview fosters domination — of people over nature and of people over other people. "It has always been connected ... that capitalism ... patriarchy ... it is designed to subjugate not only the natural world but also people" (Int#14):

> This idea of colonization, this idea that we can be above other peoples because of where we come from, you see that again and again, the notion of dominionism. In the Bible .... God made the Earth and gave Man dominion over the Earth. It's all here for you to exploit. It's very specific. Man has dominion. And women have been struggling so long, collectively, for rights, because in that biblical notion, women are a burden. This is something [Indigenous Peoples] fight against all the time. Because our society was opposite of that — women were the title holders. Women decide what happens on the land." (Int#7 Kanien'kehá:ka)

Social ecologist Murray Bookchin wrote that the idea that humans must dominate nature stems directly from the domination of humans over other humans and that "this centuries-long tendency finds its most exacerbating development in modern capitalism. Owing to its inherently competitive nature, bourgeois society not only pits humans against each other, it also pits the mass of humanity against the natural world" (Bookchin 2004: 24–25). Capitalism generates a social system in which "people want to be on top of other people" (Int#24).

Social psychologist Irina Feygina also argues that exploitation of the natural world and social injustice stem from the same ideological root, which she describes as the "hierarchical arrangement of power which places some groups and the environment in a position devoid of power or rights" (2013: 363).

This hierarchical arrangement of power is undergirded by the Western worldview's tendency to reduce the world into rigid compartments, dividing rich complexity into simple binaries of this/that, me/you, us/them, good/bad, etc. It's not just that the world is reduced to oversimplified *binaries*, but that we create *dualisms*, whereby one half of a binary is superior to the other. Our simple categories are organized hierarchically — men over women, humans over nature, white people over people of colour, rich people over poor, colonizer over colonized (Plumwood 2002; Escobar 2018). Worldviews organized by such dualistic conceptions undergird systems of domination such as racism, sexism, colonialism and the destruction of nature by humans (Plumwood 2002; Collins and Bilge 2016). Dualisms are not merely arbitrary groupings of ideas; they are at the service of domination and accumulation (Plumwood 2002: 42), including settler colonialism. Coulthard sees settler colonialism as power "structured into a relatively secure or sedimented set of *hierarchical social relations* that continue to facilitate the dispossession of Indigenous people of their lands and self-determining authority" (2014: 6–7, emphasis mine). Dualisms justify the mistreatment of the "other"; they are the building blocks of worldviews that are allowing and reproducing the social and ecological crises we face (Moore 2014; Head 2016). The "binaries of Eurocentrism, racism and sexism, Nature/Society [are] directly implicated in the modern world's colossal violence, inequality, and oppression" (Moore 2016: 2).

Dualism oversimplifies the world into people above/people below, into people above/nature below; it is the "ontology of disconnection and oppression" (Escobar 2018: 65). "The distance that allows us to exploit the Earth is the same distance that allows us to exploit other people" (Int#10). This way of understanding the world separates and disconnects us from each other and from the natural world, severing us from the collective knowledges and transformative relations and collaborations that are so urgently called for at this moment in history.

If we are to unlearn these ideologies of domination and learn different ways of seeing the world, it is helpful to understand that the Western worldview, though it seems so entrenched, is not a given. It did not emerge out of nowhere. It did not take hold because it was righter, or somehow superior. It came from particular places and times and cultures, for the benefit of certain people, and was spread to others around the world, often through the use of force.

As the Christian church and doctrine, as discussed earlier in the chapter, provided justification for European colonization of Indigenous land, it also provided conceptual undergirding for the domination of humans over the natural world. The Bible gave humans "dominion over the fish of the sea and over the birds of the heavens and over the livestock and over all the Earth and over every creeping thing that creeps on the Earth." Ecofeminist philosopher and historian Carolyn Merchant documents how human domination over the Earth was then further extended and strengthened during the Enlightenment and scientific revolution. Francis Bacon, renowned father of the scientific method, wrote that "nature takes orders from man and works under his authority" (quoted in Merchant 2006: 282).

The reductionist worldview that developed in Europe during the Enlightenment dissected the world into parts, fostering the idea that the world is a machine, and nature is the raw material to run the machine (Merchant 2006), with women, nature and non-European "others" to be dominated. This reductionist worldview allowed for the flourishing of dualistic concepts and hierarchical social organization, which in turn facilitated colonial capitalism. Meanwhile Enlightenment thinkers, such as Descartes, Locke and, later, Kant, were establishing the notion that abstract reason is the superior form of knowledge generation, rendering other ways of knowing inferior or invalid, establishing epistemological dominance, further facilitating and justifying violent colonial expansion (Kerr 2014).

These legacies of Eurocentric ideologies of dominance still preside and are propping up the social and environmental injustices currently playing out in Canada. It is only through a deep belief that some lives are less valuable, and the conviction that domination of some people over others is natural, that an RCMP commander can advocate for shooting Indigenous land defenders on their own territories. It is only through the persistent belief that nature and humans are separate and that humans are above and in control of nature that Prime Minister Trudeau can claim that the Trans Mountain pipeline is in the national interest and that the project is part of his work to balance the economy and the environment.

Problematic worldviews serve to prop up ongoing capitalist colonialism and the uneven benefits and burdens they generate. But luckily worldviews are not fixed. And importantly, though the Western worldview of dominance and disconnection is dominant and prevails, it is not the only worldview present in the world. I live and work and write this book on the unceded lands of people with radically different ways of understanding the world, of governing human relations and of relating to the land. These people, the Kanien'kehá:ka, are very much still present and offering other ways of knowing and being and doing.

All across this country and the world, there are Indigenous Peoples living worldviews that have relationship and reciprocity, not domination, at their foundations (Bear 2000). By these understandings, humans are not separate from and above nature. And as such there is no "environmental" issue compartmentalized off from social issues, there is no climate movement separate from the struggle for social justice, anti-capitalism and decolonizing. All life is connected, all forms of oppression are linked.

Melina Laboucan-Massimo, member of the Lubicon Cree First Nation and leader in community solar energy projects, says:

> We are fighting resource extraction, we are inheriting violence against the land, but we're fighting for justice for our women. Our families are constantly fighting on many spheres, it's not justice [for the] climate, it's justice for the women, for the four-legged ones, the two-winged ones, that are all integral to our being on Mother Earth. (2018)

WHY THIS ANALYSIS IS SO IMPORTANT

Where mainstream discourse in Canada about climate change and inequality focuses on the surface layer of the problems — the symptoms of the crises — people in these movements are digging down much more deeply, uncovering the root causes. These conversations explain climate change and inequality as both being driven by colonial capitalism, which is undergirded by Western worldviews that promote domination of people over nature and of people over other people. These systems have bred systemic disconnection from land and from each other, cutting us off from the knowledge and relations we need to get ourselves out of this mess.

This deep-reaching, collaborative analysis of the root causes of climate change and inequality, generated in social movements and front-line communities, offers Canada much-needed counter-narratives. These are not the stories we hear in the media, government policy briefs or corporate publicity. They offer a fundamentally different story of what is wrong in Canada and what needs to be done about it. These conversations provide an important challenge to the shallow discourse about climate change and inequality in Canada, which centres around carbon emissions, renewable energy, tearful apologies and reconciliation schemes. These things are valid and important but do not go nearly far enough.

Understanding the ways that institutional racism, settler colonialism and land dispossession are related to extractivism, climate change and social inequality is critical for being able to understand what is driving the crises, as well as being able to devise effective ways of intervening. That said, these understandings, which have been and are being developed and refined in movements and scholarships, are wholly missing from the mainstream discourses about inequality and climate change and pipelines in Canada. They are even missing from some of the strands of climate activism in this country.

It is only through an exceedingly shallow understanding of what is causing climate change that people could show up to that climate march in Montreal on September 27, 2019, and bring to their climate activism an anti-Indigenous racism. Those people, the perpetrators of racist, colonial violence, displayed an understanding of the climate crisis that grossly fails to see the links between climate change, capitalism and colonialism. It fails to see that "Climate justice is social justice. Social justice is environmental justice" (Int#23). It fails to understand that it is only though fostering the links between anti-racist, decolonial and other social justice struggles that the climate movement will stand a chance of building a better world.

What this discussion offers is the understanding that the systemic mistreatment of Indigenous Peoples, the climate crisis, and the abuse of land and waters in the name of unsustainable resource extraction are inextricably linked. They are deeply linked through their shared root cause of colonial-capitalism and the "pathological drive for accumulation that fuels [it]" (Coulthard 2010: 82). To truly address these pressing crises in Canada, they need to be addressed simultaneously and in ways that targets the root causes driving both. We need to actively work towards *both decarbonizing and decolonizing* Canada. These two pathways and goals are entwined and inextricable.

And importantly — these understandings of the root causes, the systems of domination and the worldviews that underlie them, open up the possibilities for much more transformative solutions and alternatives. Solar panels, carbon pricing and reconciliation apologies will not transform colonial capitalism. We need to be able to envision radically different futures.

It is the movements' visions of the future that we turn to next.

CHAPTER 4

ENVISIONING THE ALTERNATIVES

I want a ton of things — the destruction of capitalism, the destruction of patriarchy, the destruction of colonialism, return of lands to the Indigenous folks. Equality. What else? Not to have to work so much. A place where my kid can feel safe.... I want all of that. — Int#30

The climate and inequality crises in Canada will not be solved by smoothing out the rough edges of capitalism and colonialism. These systems need to be unrooted, dismantled, transformed. As climate justice activists argue, we need systems change. We need to get past "the kind of solutions that would allow capitalism to continue" (Int#8). Unfortunately, the solutions presently on the table in Canada do not seek to transform capitalist relations nor relinquish colonial control. If anything, they are designed to maintain these systems. Part of that is due to the vested interests of the people designing the solutions and making the decisions. And part of it may be due to people's inability to envision viable alternatives. Colonialism and capitalism are so ingrained in Canadian culture that it can be hard to see beyond them, to see that they are not inevitable.

But activists and land defenders in the climate justice, anti-pipeline and Indigenous land defence movements are dreaming up radically different futures. The worlds they describe evoke visions of equality and justice, of healing relationships, of decentralized, autonomous communities powered by clean energy. They talk about decolonizing relations between settlers and Indigenous Peoples. They envision self-determination and the rebuilding of diverse Indigenous Nations, a fundamental redistribution of power and land. And they talked about re-establishing mutually beneficial relations with the land and with each other.

In interviews, I asked people what their end goal is, how they envision the worlds they are working hard to bring about. Their answers, their beautiful visions, are presented below along the following four themes: decarbonizing, decentralizing and democratizing, decolonizing and reconnecting with land and with each other. In order to corroborate these visions as viable, I intersperse the activists' and land defenders' words with references to relevant scholarship and examples of existing initiatives in Canada and across the world that reflect these visions. It may not be obvious that there are concrete, achievable yet radical solutions to racial inequality and the climate crises. These may seem to be intractable problems, especially when we become attuned to how deeply the roots of the crises go. But there is a lot of inspiring work being done, around the world and in Canada, to identify and develop alternative governance structures, economic systems, policies, technologies, energy, housing and food systems, all aiming towards justice and ecological sustainability, and working towards the future worlds envisioned by the people I spoke with.

All the beautiful visions I heard hinge on human survival. One person told me that his "end goal is a society that works for the benefit of all beings. That's my aspiration. But mostly I'm focused on humans; human survival being the main priority" (Int#16). Another's end goal is "to ensure that the people who come after us have what they'll need to survive" (Int#6). It's not simply any kind of human survival these folks are interested in. People spoke about a future of equality between humans, "a world where people can just live like they want to live, regardless of sexuality, gender, race … where people are able to move where they want, no borders … living like they want — not just living to survive" (Int#24).

DECARBONIZING

Addressing the climate crisis requires decarbonization, the transformation away from fossil fuel–based energy and economic systems towards ones based on clean renewable sources of energy. Several people's visions of the future emphasize a rapid energy transition away from fossil fuels and Canada's responsibility to play a leadership role in this:

As a country that has benefited so thoroughly from the current order, at least in terms of its industrial development, I think it's incumbent upon Canada, in particular, to not only reduce its emissions, but to be investing billions of dollars, hundreds of billions, into developing the technology that can move us past this and give it away to the rest of the world, at highly subsidized prices. Whether it's transportation infrastructure, power generation, investing in geothermal energy or renewables of various kinds, we should be just pouring all of our collective resources into that in order to make that transition happen globally at a very rapid pace. (Int#16)

Canada is a major producer of greenhouse gas emissions, due both to its high consumption rates and it being a major producer of carbon polluting fossil fuels. To have any chance of warding off worsening climate impacts, fossil fuel reserves must remain in the ground, and other energy and economic systems must be developed. The Trudeau government claims that building pipelines will fund the transition to a clean energy economy and hopes that carbon taxes will inspire the changes needed. The IPCC states that the way to decarbonize most quickly and effectively is to transition away from carbon-intensive fossil fuels completely (2018). Despite research showing that this complete energy transition is possible (Jacobson et al. 2017) and affordable (CCPA 2015), it is not happening in Canada at anywhere near the necessary scale and speed it needs to.

A just transition away from carbon polluting fuels means creating jobs in climate-friendly industries. It means creating good jobs so people do not have to choose between decent work and a healthy environment. A community organizer in northern BC who works closely with First Nations on alternative energy projects expressed her vision for her community's future: "Industry can come in here and they can say whatever they want, [but] our vision is that we want jobs and we want a solid economy and we want fish and clean air and rich, alive, functioning cultures that are respected. We don't think these things are mutually exclusive" (Int#37).

Currently, a strong coalition has formed in Canada to design and promote a Green New Deal (GND), inspired by the Green New Deal in the US. It is a detailed plan for eliminating poverty while creating millions of jobs and tackling climate change. The GND calls for massive public investment to fund clean energy, transit and climate adaptation work: "But the vision is bigger than that: it's about transforming our entire economy to be safer and fairer and give everyone a better life" (The Leap 2019: n.p.). The GND is premised on a rapid transition from a fossil fuel–based energy system to one based on renewable energy. This can be done in ways that would generate millions of jobs by 2025 in building trades, such as renewable energy, green building construction, building retrofits and transportation infrastructure (Bridge and Gilbert 2017).

That said, renewable energy sources are not the panacea we may want to believe they are. Indeed, in some cases they have negative environmental impacts that can be as bad as some conventional energy sources (Abbasi and Abbasi 2000). Alternative energy sources, despite contributing less to climate change, are problematic in various ways and are limited in the extent to which they can solve the crises. Renewable energy's

> dependence on a massive amount of material resources (steel, concrete, rare earth metals) often leads to the dispossession and forced labour of vulnerable people, such as the Congolese who produce cobalt in terrible conditions. And it can also be difficult to increase the production of certain metals to meet growing demand. (Gauthier 2018: n.p.)

This doesn't mean that a massive and rapid energy transition is not possible; it means that there are "no purely technical solutions to the problems we face. To be successful, the energy transition must also be based on a change in needs and habits.… We need to rethink consumerism and growth" (Gauthier 2018: n.p.). The solution is not to replace one extractive industry by another, but rather to address the mode of consumption leading us to such dependency.

We need to massively reduce rates of per capita energy consumption in Canada. According to the 2018 report *Canada's Energy Outlook*, on a per capita basis Canadians consume energy at more than five times the world average (Hughes 2018). In 2016, Canada consumed 2.5% of the world's energy, and consumption rates have been increasing over the past five years (Hughes 2018). As over-consumers, reducing energy consumption in industry, housing and transport is an obvious and relatively easy way to begin making significant progress in the energy transition. This will help "maximize the effectiveness of investments in renewable energy and will minimize overall expenditures on new energy supply and the inevitable economic costs and environmental impacts of developing it" (Hughes 2018: 24).

But targeting consumption is not enough; production rates of oil and gas also need to be rapidly decreased. An important step to tackling production rates is to eliminate fossil fuel subsidies. According to Environmental Defence: "Every year, the federal government and some provinces pay billions in hand-outs to Canada's coal, oil and gas companies, undermining climate action in Canada. Fossil fuel subsidies to producers total $3.3 billion annually, which amounts to paying polluters $19/tonne to pollute" (2016: 3). The cost of these annual subsidies is equivalent to the cost of installing solar panels on 13,200 schools across Canada or retraining 330,000 workers (Environmental Defence 2016).

However, a massive reduction in consumption and production, and the elimination of subsidies is not likely within a capitalist economic system that is addicted to growth. Luckily, there are many who are working on this problem as well. Degrowth is both a global movement and a field of research that deeply questions capitalism's pursuit of endless growth (Kalllis and March 2015). It is concerned with "a downscaling of production and consumption that increases human wellbeing and enhances ecological conditions and equity on the planet" (Research and Degrowth 2020: n.p.). Research by Paulson (2017) shows that are many examples worldwide of diverse communities exemplifying these values in localized practices of prioritizing wellbeing, equity and sustainability instead of growth and expansion. There are exciting degrowth initiatives in Canada, especially in Quebec's cooperative movement (Abraham 2018).

DECENTRALIZING AND DEMOCRATIZING

A Toronto-based social justice activist told me that she envisions a world where "people have more control over the decisions that affect their lives." She told me: "I want decisions to be informed by people who are most affected by the decisions" (Int#28). Decarbonizing energy systems is required but does not go far enough towards addressing the social inequalities and systems of domination that are driving climate change. Energy systems need to be decentralized and democratized as well. A Montreal-based divestment activist shared his vision for this:

There's this opportunity that if we fix the climate crises, we have the opportunity to solve the energy crises forever.... The disparities in income and access to energy and access to clean water and to basic education, these opportunities can be facilitated with a decentralized form of energy. If people have access to energy, decentralized forms of energy, they have autonomy in a lot of other respects. It can help with access to clean water, it can help with access to food. It can help with access to income generation ... all these things are interconnected. (Int#23)

This vision reflects the movement for "energy democracy," which works towards "asserting social control over energy generation, distribution, and waste disposal; advocates often envision publicly and/or locally-owned energy systems, created to provide safe, sustainable, and affordable power" (Griffin and Vukelich n.d.). Energy democracy advocates seek to transform power relations, addressing dispossession and environmental injustice, while working to replace monopolized fossil fuel energy systems with renewable and democratic ones (Burke and Stephens 2017). Energy democracy is being forged in many places around the world, including Nigeria, South Africa, Germany and Canada (Griffin and Vukelich n.d.).

Energy democracy reflects a larger trend of building solidarity economies, an alternative to capitalism and state-dominated economic systems whereby "ordinary people play an active role in shaping all of the dimensions of human life: economic, social, cultural, political, and environmental" (RIPESS 2015: 2). Degrowth, energy democracy and solidarity economies all call for producing less, sharing more and making genuinely democratic decisions about how to live together (Abraham 2018). Schweickart (2009) shares a similar contention that radical democratization of the economy — specifically democratization of work places and democratic control over investment — is critical for transforming society away from capitalism.

To some people I spoke with, democratizing and decarbonizing energy systems does not go far enough. Some have visions that involve a fundamental restructuring and even dismantling of the Canadian nation state. A Montreal-based journalist told me: "My long-term goal is to build a society that is stateless, non-capitalist, and is based on principles of decolonization, mutual aid, direct democracy and solidarity" (Int#5).

Another anarchist activist pointed to the connection between decolonization, autonomy from the state and defending the land:

> There's a slogan that says a lot: 'For a life unmediated by the state, we must defend the land.' The more contaminated everything is, the more depleted the soil, the more water filtration is necessary, the more you require the forms of technology that require resources that we may not be able to produce.... In terms of decolonization, we need to get back to basics and meet our own needs in the territories we inhabit. I don't see decolonization as returning to the past ... that's impossible. But as a way forward.... The goal is the creation of autonomous zones where people are able to meet their own needs without the fossil fuel economy and the state. (Int#8)

As communities build autonomy, social power and ecologically sustainable systems through cooperation and solidarity, they can link through regional, national and international networks. For example, the Symbiosis network is working towards building a confederation of community organizations across North America. These communities are "fighting for a better world by creating institutions of participatory democracy and the solidarity economy through community organizing, neighborhood by neighborhood, city by city" (Symbiosis 2019: n.p.). This, and other similar networks, inspired by social ecologist Murray Bookchin's libertarian municipalism, work to democratize city governments through popular assemblies, connecting them along confederal lines (Bookchin 1991). Symbiosis' vision is to bring radical change by organizing at the community level, meeting basic human needs and building "popular power outside the governing institutions of the present system, to challenge and displace those institutions through truly democratic ones of our own ... [to] eventually supplant the institutions of capitalism to become the governing structures of a liberated society" (Symbiosis 2019: n.p.).

This vision of autonomy links to dreams of flourishing decentralized communities that a Vancouver-based social justice organizer of colour shared with me: "I dream of decentralized, self-determining communities.... It's better for health care, better for decision making.... Most things would be better if things were smaller and we didn't have these monolithic political, economic systems that we all need to contend with" (Int#32).

She offers this vision as a radical alternative to the systems of oppression that her activism works to oppose and transform:

> Hetero-patriarchal colonial capitalism is so predatorial. It just doesn't allow anything else to exist. This idea of having this mosaic of beautiful ecosystems of self-determining communities is very decolonizing in my imagination. I truly believe that there's a world out there that is so much better. There are communities out there that can be determined through place and collective tradition and culture. Decentralizing that power would be incredibly powerful … not all small communities need to run the same way. Different communities will create different decision-making processes. Energy needs can be defined by your community and your land. Everything is defined by where you are…. There are a lot of traditional systems that can be reinvigorated. (Int#32)

DECOLONIZING

> For Indigenous nations to live, capitalism must die. And for capitalism to die, we must actively participate in Indigenous alternatives to it — G.S. Coulthard, *Red Skins, White Masks*

All these aforementioned visions of autonomous communities powered by decentralized, democratized renewable energy systems are important and powerful, but they are not the answer if they are built by settlers on stolen Indigenous land. Really addressing climate change and inequality in Canada requires a transformation of the economic systems and social relations driving the crises. It is not enough to just wrest power from the state and distribute this to settler communities. The fundamental injustice at the heart of Canada — settler colonialism — must be transformed through the return of self-determination and land to Indigenous Peoples. Reconciliation — tinkering with Indian policy and making tearful apologies — will not solve inequality, nor will it contribute to addressing climate change.

A Dene writer and organizer told me that her end goal

> is to better the life of Indigenous Peoples so that there's no feeling

of imposition and being stuck ... that kind of suffering my father went through in residential school and that I feel the after-effects of in my life. I need to care for and nurture Indigenous culture and people. Hopefully Canada will be on this side of the story too. (Int#25 Dene)

When I asked her more about her vision for decolonizing Canada, she emphasized the need for more settlers to be better educated about Indigenous Peoples, evoking a future in which settlers are "less ignorant." To her, decolonizing means "that Indigenous Peoples will have power and that there will be strong matriarchs heading their communities once again" (Int#25 Dene).

For a Mi'kmaw warrior and thinker I spoke with, decolonization is about reinstating Indigenous self-determination and the rebuilding of Indigenous Nations:

When I say Indigenous Nationhood — that will be the displacement of Western nation state sovereignty over Indigenous lands and it will be the rebuilding of Indigenous Nations.... My vision of decolonization really is about let's wipe away the effects of colonialism. Let's wipe away the cultural dominance. Let's wipe away the political power. Let's push this stuff all to the side and rebuild Indigenous Nations. (Int#38 Mi'kmaw)

To him, Indigenous self-determination means "dismantling the political, economic, social structures that support colonialism." And it means rebuilding Nations: "The rebuilding of Indigenous Nations ... involves the political, social, economic ... rebuilding social institutions. We are rebuilding from an apocalypse. We are rebuilding everything. We're rebuilding the social institutions, we're rebuilding culture and language. We're rebuilding the customs, the ceremonies, the spiritualism, the economy" (Int#38).

Decolonizing Canada may seem impossible to some people, but there are many concrete steps that can be taken by settlers and the Canadian state to meaningfully work towards this. These include, but are not limited to, repudiating racist legal doctrines; respecting international, constitutional and inherent Indigenous rights; heeding the recommendations of the RCAP, TRC and other government-commission reports; and fairly redistributing land.

A first step is to "repudiate the concepts behind the colonial Doctrine of Discovery and recognize that every Indigenous Nation in Canada has underlying title to their entire territory" (Manuel 2017: n.p.). The federal and provincial governments must begin to make their policies, projects and legal directions consistent with the rights of Indigenous Peoples, which are set out in section 35(1) in Canada's Constitution (Manuel 2017).

A Prairie-based journalist and activist raised the issue of "Respect, respect for treaties. Canada has been ignoring these for 150 years. It's had awful environmental consequences and other consequences" (Int#26). A Kanien'kehá:ka Elder made clear that this process is long term, but has concrete steps that can be taken now: "I don't know if we'll ever fully decolonize. Canada has to decide to let go. And we will see [if they are willing to do that]. I think that the UN Declaration [on the Rights of Indigenous Peoples] is a good way to start that" (Int#9 Kanien'kehá:ka).

A concrete step towards decolonization is respecting the international right to Indigenous self-determination as set out in Article 3 of UN Declaration on the Rights of Indigenous Peoples[1] and Article 1 of the International Covenant on Civil and Political Rights and International Covenant on Economic, Social and Cultural Rights: "The Supreme Court of Canada must understand the international context of our Aboriginal and Treaty Rights as the grounds to decolonize Canada" (Manuel 2017: n.p.). Indigenous Peoples' right to self-determination

> is spelled out in UNDRIP, in regard to land rights, governance and Indigenous prior informed consent (PIC). The latter principle is also increasingly enshrined in multilateral environmental agreements that recognize Indigenous PIC and therefore Indigenous decision-making power regarding access to their lands and resources.... It is clear that including Indigenous peoples as decision makers and respecting their knowledge, which is the most long-term knowledge regarding the respective territories, will ensure more economically, culturally and environmentally sustainable development. (McFarlane and Schabus 2017: 65)

Further concrete steps towards decolonization would be to heed the recommendations of the many reports commissioned by the federal government over the last thirty years. These include implementing the recommendations of the Royal Commission on Aboriginal Peoples (1996), the Truth and Reconciliation Commission (2015) and the National Inquiry into Missing and Murdered Indigenous Women and Girls (2019). Canada has commissioned these extensive and expensive reports and then failed to implement the many important recommendations that came out of them. Heeding these recommendations is a concrete step towards decolonizing Canada. Writing about the RCAP process, Kanien'kehaka scholar Taiaiake Alfred explains that

> so much work went into that document, from all across the country and taking into account the perspectives and voices of all regions, generations and segments of our Indigenous peoples.... What they told the Commission in a unified voice was that it's all about the land. In a rare show of integrity and respect on the part of government, the commissioners listened and the voices of our ancestors echoed in the multiple volumes of the Commission's lengthy and comprehensive report when they stated clearly and emphatically that what is needed to achieve the full decolonization of Canada is a massive transfer of land back to the Indigenous peoples. (quoted in McFarlane and Schabus 2017: 11)

Fair redistribution of land is the core of decolonizing Canada. Phrases such as "decolonizing the academy," "decolonizing your mind," "decolonizing movements" are becoming more common. Indeed, colonization is a multi-dimensional, wide-reaching process that emanates through most if not all aspects of society (Fortier 2017), and decolonization, in turn, must do the same. That being said, Tuck and Yang make the important argument in their influential paper "Decolonization Is Not a Metaphor" that one must not lose sight of the core meaning of decolonization, which is material (about land) and by definition unsettling to the status quo. They write that "though the details are not fixed or agreed upon, in our view, decolonization in the settler colonial context must involve the repatriation of land" (2012: 7). Arthur Manuel also makes clear that settling the land issue is foundational to the process of decolonizing relationships between Indigenous Peoples and settlers in Canada (2018). Alfred states: "A notion of reconciliation that rearranges political orders, reforms legalities and promotes economics is still colonial unless and until it centres our relationship to the land" (quoted in McFarlane and Schabus 2017: 13). As colonization has, by definition, sought to sever this relationship, decolonization by necessity must involve the full reconnection between Indigenous Peoples and their lands. As Eriel Deranger, the executive director of Indigenous Climate Action, states: "Decolonization is in its simplest terms a return of and connection to the land" (2018: n.p.).

There are Indigenous thinkers who have been doing important work of proposing how land repatriation can roll out: "Canada is the second-largest country in the world … the size, population, constitutional and legal framework could accommodate fundamental change in expanding the land base of Indigenous Peoples from 0.2 per cent to a size that could accommodate our right to self-determination" (Manuel 2017: n.p.). Enough land needs to be relinquished by the Canadian state such that each Indigenous Nation has enough of a land base to protect their language, culture, laws and economy (Manuel 2017).

This land issue is often considered a non-starter by many settlers who fear being pushed off the land they live on. And though some Indigenous Peoples would indeed like settlers to go back to where they came from, many leading Indigenous thinkers on decolonization make clear that there is enough land to be shared, but it needs to be shared fairly. Arthur Manuel said to settlers: "If you recognize our collective right to our lands and territories and decision making over it, we will recognize your human right to stay here in our territories" (quoted in McFarlane and Schabus 2017: 67).

Colonization has violated Indigenous rights to self-determination, and so another key principle of decolonization is reinstating Indigenous self-government. In his book *Peace, Power and Righteousness: An Indigenous Manifesto*, Taiaiake Alfred characterized the process of decolonization as "the mechanics of removing ourselves from state control and the legal and political struggle to gain recognition of an Indigenous governing authority" (1999: 2–3).

This focus on land and governance points to decolonization as a radical restructuring of social organization and relationships in Canada, including the relationship between people and non-human nature. Harsha Walia states that "striving toward decolonization requires us to challenge a dehumanizing social organization that perpetuates our isolation from each other and normalizes a lack of responsibility to one another and the Earth" (2012: 252).

Decolonization does not just focus on the removal or destruction of the colonial systems, but the creation of new systems — ones not based on domination:

> Decolonization is more than a struggle against power and control; it is also the imagining and generating of alternative institutions and relations. Decolonization is a dual form of resistance that is responsive to dismantling current systems of colonial empire and systemic hierarchies, while also prefiguring societies based on equity, mutual aid, and self-determination. (Walia, quoted in Fortier 2017: 283)

There is no one-size-fits-all approach to building alternatives to colonialism. Different Nations are forging different paths and visions. As one person explained:

> Indigenous people have their own governance, have their own decision-making process and leadership selection process. That's all part of self-determination, to determine our own political structures, and our own relationship with Canada. Canada can't try to have one formula that fits everybody because we are all different. The Mohawks are different from the Mi'kmaq, the Haida are different from the Cree. We are not all the same. We all have something in common and that's the land and the relationship with Canada. We've all been oppressed and dispossessed. That's what we have in common, but how we want to go from here, we might have different points of view. And Canada can't say, "well now all you Mi'kmaqs, you Mohawks, Crees and Haida all need to do the same." That just won't work. We all have to develop our own way, at our own pace. You have to phase out colonization by exercising the right to self-determination … piece by piece. (Int#9 Kanien'kehá:ka)

Decolonizing Canada, Indigenous self-determination and nation-building have significant implications for the Canadian state and its sovereignty. These goals as well as the Indigenous title and jurisdiction undergirding them, constitute a fundamental threat to the systems of power in this country. And disrupting and transforming the systems of power in this country is what is needed to address the mounting social inequalities and the climate crises. It is the promise of a justice-based transformation that will benefit Indigenous Peoples and settlers alike.

A 2019 report entitled *Land Back,* put out by Yellowhead Institute, presents many rich examples of what communities are doing to get land back. The authors write that in light of the fact that the whole planet is "at risk from the type of economic philosophy and practices perpetuated by colonialism and settler colonialism" and the structural conditions that act as barriers to real transformations of our relationships to the land, water and each other, the efforts of Indigenous Peoples to get land back represents a "movement towards hope" (2019: 64–65).

Land repatriation and other dimensions of decolonization require huge transformations of economic and political systems (Yellowhead Institute 2019). They will be deeply disruptive to the current political and economic order. But that's the point. A transition that doesn't force us to dig up the foundations of our current society — which is built on extraction, accumulation, oppression and theft — won't be a just transition.

"Respecting Treaties and Indigenous self-determination goes hand in hand with a very rapid transition, all the way from fossil fuel extraction towards other forms of social order, community living, energy use" (Int#26). Decolonization is inseparable from decarbonizing our economic systems. As one person told me, "the rebuilding of Indigenous Nations becomes the answer to how we deal with climate change. It isn't just another issue of political justice off to the side, away from the issue of climate change and pipelines. It's one and the same. [Decolonization] is a bigger solution to these problems" (Int#38 Mi'kmaw).

One of the many reasons that Indigenous self-determination is central to addressing climate change is that Indigenous Peoples hold important knowledge and practices for living outside the clutches of capitalism. As Simpson argues, "Indigenous people have extremely rich anti-capitalist practices in our histories and current realities … and more experience in anti-capitalism and how that system works than any group of people on the planet. We have thousands and thousands of years of experience building and living in societies outside of global capitalism" (2017: 72–73).

> If non-Indigenous readers are capable of listening … they will discover that while we are envisioning a new relationship between [Indigenous Peoples] and the land, we are at the same time

offering a decolonized alternative to the Settler society by invit-
ing them to share our vision of respect and peaceful coexistence.
The non-Indigenous will be shown a new path and offered the
chance to join in a renewed relationship between the peoples and
places of this land, which we occupy together. (Alfred, quoted
in Fortier 2017: 1)

Equipped with thousands of years of accumulated knowledge gained
through actively participating in "the many ecosystems that inhabit their
lands and territories … [and helping] enhance the resilience of these
ecosystems," Indigenous Peoples hold important wisdom, insight and
skill for surviving and addressing the crises we all face (United Nations
2008). Meanwhile, instead of drawing on this knowledge, Canada continues to violate Indigenous lands and rights, compounding poverty and
suffering. Effectively addressing climate change cannot happen while we
continue to organize economies on colonial social relations of domination.
Decolonizing and decarbonizing are inextricable. Or as the Idle No More
slogan puts it, "Indigenous Sovereignty is Climate Action."

In Naomi Klein's preface to Arthur Manuel and Grand Chief
Derrickson's book *Reconciliation Manifesto*, which was also her speech
at Manuel's funeral in January 2017, she stated:

What is good for Indigenous people, what will ultimately fight
poverty and heal trauma, is the return of the land … what is
good for Indigenous people, is good for the land, is good for the
water, and ultimately is our only hope for fighting catastrophic
climate change and ecological collapse. Our only hope. The connection between respect for Indigenous rights and the safety
of all humanity is the greatest lesson. (quoted in Manuel and
Derrickson 2017: 10)

The work of decolonization is different for Indigenous Peoples and for
settlers. For settlers interested in transforming Canada to a place that is
radically more just in our relationships with each other and with the land,
this means working in active solidarity with

Indigenous people fighting against the colonization of Indigenous
lands and peoples, and fighting against the assimilation of

Indigenous world-views and ways of life. I believe we must also be able to see ourselves, as non-natives, as active and integral participants in a decolonization movement for political liberation, social transformation, renewed cultural kinships, and the development of an economic system that serves rather than threatens our collective life on this planet. (Walia 2012: 241)

RECONNECTING WITH LAND AND EACH OTHER

Woven through all these powerful visions is respect, love and reconnection with land and with each other. A young Montreal-based Jewish woman spoke to me about love as central to the world she wants:

> The essence of what I believe in is love. Cornel West said it best when he said "Justice is love in public." It is about how we interact with each other … creating spaces where people feel they're most able to be themselves. At the bottom of it is love. The Earth needs to be loved also, and the Earth needs to be healthy in order for us to have love. (Int#10)

A filmmaker and climate justice organizer also from Montreal gave similar reasons for why she does the work she does:

> It's like Alice Walker's famous quote, "Activism is the rent I pay for living on this planet." That's the thing. We get our core sense of self through compassion and caring, empathy and collective work for the transformation for all. It goes back to the Indigenous worldview — how people understand. If people are taught that they are all stewards of the land, then it becomes a natural way to respond to the crisis. If we're taught from an early age that your job is to be kind and support people, we try to figure out ways to do good with whatever passions and gifts we have. (Int#11)

People spoke to me about how capitalism and colonialism have separated us from one another and from the land and that to create a more just and viable world, we need to reconnect with each other and with land. A community organizer in northern BC said, "connection to land helps foster better decision making" (Int#37). A Mi'kmaw warrior and thinker explained to me why he focuses much of his life on working with youth, on the land: "By getting the youth back on the land they're going to rediscover what it means to be Indigenous. 'Cause that's what it is. Giving them the tools to go back out on to the land and to start to have the experiences that are driven by the interaction with nature" (Int#38 Mi'kmaw).

> Decolonization doesn't have to be complicated — it is the return to and connection with the land. Return it to the rightful owners and we all return to it. Develop that connection, then the solutions come more naturally. The people who can adapt to the changes are land-based people. Ceremony and connection are part of decolonization. If you want to stop the projects, decolonize your mind. Listen to what the wind says to you, what the land says to you. And put your bodies on the land. We have to reaffirm our connection to the land and stop the machines. (Deranger 2018: n.d.)

The visions of more just and ecologically viable futures that these activists shared go far beyond renewable energies, carbon markets, reconciliation schemes and apologies. They conjure up a future of flourishing networks of decentralized self-determining communities, powered by renewable energy and learning from the land. This is a future where a hard process of decolonizing relations will have rendered us all much more capable of living and making decisions together — decisions that benefit all beings. This future depends on a fundamental restructuring of our systems and a massive redistribution of wealth, power and land. This means some people — those most benefiting from our current system — will have to relinquish some things (namely land, power and wealth). But I would say that is a reasonable ask in exchange for a livable planet on which everyone's basic needs are met.

For some of the people I spoke to these visions of the future are not new, they are based in longstanding Indigenous worldviews and theories that understand the fundamental link between people and lands and waters. For others, it is through beginning to feel and fear the impacts of the fossil fuel economy and/or through engagement with Indigenous Peoples and other radical struggles that they are deepening their understandings of the problems and beginning to envision beautifully different futures.

POSSIBLE TENSIONS

I have presented these analyses of the crises and visions of the future in such a way that they are assembled together like pieces of a puzzle, each interview quote contributing something to the bigger picture. I believe that there are ways that all these visions of the future are compatible and could co-exist. But this is not necessarily the case. Different analyses and visions may be in conflict — *if* they do not take each other into account. For example, the anarchist vision of decentralized autonomous communities would work against transformative goals if they build their autonomous zones on stolen Indigenous land. Or if settler communities develop community-based solar power projects that are only affordable to wealthy residents, this would be counter to the work of undoing class-based oppressions. It is important to think deeply about what and who any given end goal or vision of the future benefits and who it does not. We need to be asking ourselves whose visions matter and who gets to decide what the future will be like.

We don't all have to hold precisely the same end goal or pathway in mind, but if we want to combine forces to transform things at the systems level, we need to be paying attention to make sure our end goals and our paths to get there do not impede the end goals and paths of others. And we need to make sure that the people most impacted by the crises are determining the solutions.

The Indigenous youth delegation that came from across Canada to attend the climate march this past September had come bearing a large beautiful hand-painted banner that took six of them to carry together through the streets. It expressed their end goal:

#LANDBACK

From post-march debrief sessions I was part of, I learned that some of the racist verbal violence these young Indigenous folks had faced that day had been in response to that "land back" message. The settler Quebecois protesters yelling at the Indigenous youth "this is not your land!" were in essence saying that the climate future they imagine, the justice they are fighting for is for themselves, for the preservation of a system that benefits them, for ongoing white privilege. Indeed, a common message chanted again and again that day by a sea of white youth was *"Whose future? OUR future!!"* — a variation of the popular chant *"Whose streets?*

OUR Streets!!" The question of whose future we are fighting for is a critically important one.

People in the current climate movement do not all share the same end goals. That in itself is not a problem. The problem is that some of the end goals espoused in the climate movement reproduce the same logics and ideologies that are driving the climate crisis — the idea that some lives are more valuable than others. Indeed, as Paul Farmer so cogently put it, "the idea that some lives matter less is the root of all that is wrong with the world." It's not that we all have to share the exact same goal, but we do need to share a commitment to undoing the systems, structures and ideologies that are driving the climate and inequality crises. That's the only way we're going to win. As Robert Jones Jr. put it: "We can disagree and still love each other, unless your disagreement is rooted in my oppression and denial of my humanity and right to exist" (quoted in Powell 2016: n.p.).

The movement is growing at an amazing rate, and that is wonderful. But the analysis needs to catch up. I hope that these chapters help illuminate why the fight for the climate will not win, that it cannot build a better world, unless it is addressing the drivers of the crisis — capitalism, racism, colonialism, white supremacy, hetero-patriarchy. This kind of deep systems change, this work of both decarbonization and decolonization, involves huge shifts that may seem politically infeasible. Certainly, there is great resistance to these changes, in the form of vested interests by those in power and many ordinary folk who are benefiting from the unjust and unsustainable status quo. It is the work of social movements to build counter-power and to change what is politically possible. We turn now to this pressing question: how can we change what is politically feasible? How do social movements bring about large-scale systems change?

Note

1   It's important to note that there is a fundamental weakness in the UNDRIP, which Hayden King and others point out, which provides a loophole for states and deeply compromises the transformative and decolonial potential of UNDRIP. Article 46 states: Nothing in this Declaration may be interpreted as implying for any State, people, group or person any right to engage in any activity or to perform any act contrary to the Charter of the United Nations or construed as authorizing or encouraging any action which would dismember or impair, totally or in part, the territorial integrity or political unity of sovereign and independent States. See <https://www.opencanada.org/features/undrips-fundamental-flaw/>.

CHAPTER 5

HOW WE GET FROM HERE TO THERE

How does change really happen?… These are pedagogical questions, meaning they are meant to be asked in community, in conversation with lived life. The answers are important, yes, but more important is the opportunity to think and feel through these questions collectively. — E. Tuck and K.W. Yang, *Youth Resistance Research and Theories of Change*

The mounting social and ecological crises we face call for massive transformations to social, economic and political systems. *But how does such large-scale intentional systems change come about? How can social movements push this change towards more just and sustainable futures for humanity and non-human life on Earth?* These are the questions at the heart of my research; this is what I have been trying to understand though my conversations with others.

Well thought-out theories of social change that can inform effective action are crucial at this moment in time. Yet scholarship and research that focus explicitly on social change remain limited, and activists generally do not have the time to step back from urgent work on the ground to reflect on their own theories of change. Our understandings of change often remain in the shady realm of unstated assumptions, rather than being pulled out into the light of day for rigorous debate, scrutiny and reflection (Tuck and Yang 2013). But when our assumptions remain unspoken, they can render our strategies for change less effective and hinder collaboration between different people, groups and movements that hold conflicting, unspoken ideas.

Duncan Green, author of *How Change Happens,* said this about conflicting theories of change:

> Relationships between ... activists are often fraught. People bring their own worldviews to the questions of change. Do we prefer conflict ("speaking truth to power") or cooperation ("winning friends and influencing people")? Do we see progress everywhere, and seek to accelerate its path, or do we see (in our darker, more honest moments) a quixotic struggle against power and injustice that is ultimately doomed to defeat? Do we believe lasting and legitimate change is primarily driven by the accumulation of power at the grassroots/individual level, through organization and challenging norms and beliefs? Or by reforms at the levels of laws, policy, institutions, companies and elites? Or by identifying and supporting "enlightened" leaders? Do we think the aim of development is to include poor people in the benefits of modernity (money economy, technology, mobility) or to defend other cultures and traditions and build alternatives to modernity? Do we want to make the current system function better, or do we seek something that tackles the deeper structures of power? (2016: 3)

Change is a complicated, unpredictable process and the systems we seek to change are themselves remarkably complex. There is a lot at stake. Understandably, people have wildly different ideas about how change happens, and theories of change are hotly contested. Explicit study of the process of intentional social transformation and deep reflections about our own theories and assumptions of change are needed in order to generate more effective strategies and to forge wider, stronger collaborations towards systemic change.

We spend much of our lives trying to affect change, but our opportunities to think together about how change happens are rare (Tuck and Yang 2013). And so, in my conversations with activists and land defenders, I asked them: *How do you think large-scale systems change happens? What is your theory of change?* In the following pages, I assemble the many different answers I got to these questions, bringing them into dialogue with each other and with other theories of change I gathered through a review of diverse bodies of scholarly literature, including social movements studies, socio-ecological systems transformation, Indigenous resistance and resurgence, historical materialism and intersectional feminism.

The wide variety of perspectives on the process of change that are presented below reflects the complexity of the problems and the complexity involved in the kind of change necessary. So much needs to change, and so many things are required to make such changes transpire. I have approached this with the contention that systems change is so complex that none of us can fully understand it, none of us can see the whole picture, but that each person's viewpoint contributes insight, a piece of the puzzle. By bringing them together we gain access to a wider and richer understanding of the process of transformation.

THE MOVEMENTS' THEORIES OF CHANGE

In a wide sweep, these conversations provide insight that systems transformation happens through a convergence of the context, how we understand and what we value, how we take action and how we relate. Each of these four themes is broken down further into sub-themes. I have conceptualized these in Figure 5-1.

Figure 5-1 How Systems Change Happens

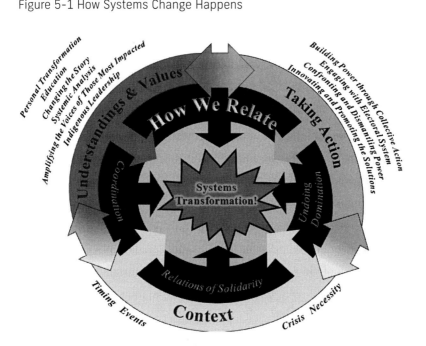

THE CONTEXT

When I asked folks how they think large-scale change happens, many pointed out that so much depends on context. It's the relationship between what we do and the context in which we do it that shapes change. Context can determine which tactics work and when. It determines whether your action gets traction (Int#19). "There is no one size fits all ... you have to examine the context, the location, the political climate you're in" (Int#20 Michif Cree). This requires activists to be fluid and "constantly attentive to context" (Int#34 Anishinaabe/Ojibway). By being attentive to context, we can adapt our strategies and targets as conditions change. One person explained this attentiveness to context as "revolutionary acupuncture ... you put the needle at the right spot at the right moment" (Int#19). Being attentive to context can help us be more effective agents of change.

The systems we seek to change are already and always changing. Human struggles for change happen within the context of complex socio-ecological systems that are continuously changing in ways that are unpredictable, shaping and being shaped by many diverse factors and forces, including but not limited to human agency (Green 2016). Indigenous philosophy sees the "world as in motion, that all things are constantly undergoing processes of transformation, deformation, and restoration ... the essence of life and being is movement" (Alfred 2005: 9).

The activists that I spoke with discussed how at certain points in time change is more possible than at others, describing this in various ways: political opportunities, tipping points, key moments and political sweet spots. Social-ecological systems scholars similarly describe how ecosystems move through cycles of growth, collapse, reorganization, renewal and re-establishment and that cycles of social change can follow similar patterns (Berkes et al. 2008). Intentional transformation of a social system may be more possible at certain phases than others (Olsson, Galaz and Boonstra 2014), namely the collapse and reorganizations phases; it is at these stages that new structures and dynamics are most likely to emerge (Holling and Gunderson 2002; Folke et al. 2010; Westley et al. 2011). Activists can assess which cyclical phase the system they are trying to change is currently in and then use this to help inform strategy (Green 2016).

Social movements scholars such as Tarrow (2011) refer to opportunity structures: moments when the state is more receptive or vulnerable to movements' collective action. Activists need to be "mindful of these changes as they come into view" (Carroll and Sarker 2016: 16). For example, election outcomes and changes in political power can create differing constraints and opportunities for change, and these call for different strategies for "wedging open and undermining the power structures.... With the more liberal government, you have to work around slippery rhetoric. While with conservative power, you have to deal with the hammer of law of enforcement and fear" (Int#29).

Different times in history call for and enable different forms of collective change agency, reshaping "the terrain on which movements move" (Carroll and Sarker 2016: 25). The question becomes: *What approaches to change work at which points in time?* One activist told me that change is more likely to happen when our actions and messages resonate with the cultural zeitgeist of the moment in a certain place. According to him, we need to ask: "What's currently possible, politically, here and now? And is our activism reflecting that?" (Int#6).

As we take action in the world, and our work has impact, we change the context in which we act, shaping the opportunity structures that open to us (Tarrow 2011). "Movements move in a dialectical relationship with *opportunity structures*, and success or failure in one conjuncture leads on to a new conjuncture that can open up new opportunities and threats" (Carroll and Sarker 2016: 16).

And to make matters even more dynamic and complex, when movements' hard work is successful and does catalyze a transformation, the way that that transformation process plays out is in itself dynamic. Transformation scholars have developed frameworks for describing the stages that social-ecological systems transformations tend to go through (see Olsson, Galaz and Boonstra 2014; Moore et al. 2014). Early stages often involve disruptions; later stages involve routinization and stabilizing the new direction. The important point here is that different stages of change call for different kinds of strategies and different kinds of actors. In other words, they require different approaches to activism (Olsson, Galaz and Boonstra 2014; Moore et al.2014). It's important to ask which people or groups are best equipped and positioned to do the work necessary at each phase of systems transformation. For example, direct-action groups may be best positioned and skilled to take the lead during the disruptive phases, whereas perhaps NGO policy analysts may best provide leadership during institutionalization phases.

Another main takeaway here is that transformations are generally catalyzed by triggers, such as disruptive events or crises that open up opportunities for change (Moore et al. 2014). These can be brought on intentionally or unintentionally by social forces, such as civil unrest, election cycles, direct action or blockades of major infrastructure. Or crises in the system can be brought about through ecological forces, such as abrupt changes in resource availability or disruptive weather events (Moore et al. 2014). Crises can come about on their own, or they can be triggered by human agency.

Activists I spoke to discussed the significant impact that events have on change processes: "Unfortunately, it can take drastic things to happen so people will start changing" (Int#7 Kanien'kehá ka). These drastic things happen in the form of events that trigger change (S#34). "There's always a little spark that starts it. [Many] revolutions in history started with a riot and a bread line…. There were people organizing beforehand, but then all of a sudden there's a flashpoint and then everybody comes out" (Int#5).

Marx also saw "that revolution is most likely when economic crises converge with growing class consciousness" (Buechler 2016: 18). The many contradictions inherent within capitalism serve as grievances and opportunities for collective action (Harvey 2014). Movements looking to transform systems away from capitalism are well advised to understand the various contradictions inherent in capitalism that create instability and crises, and develop strategies that can take advantage of the crises as they emerge (Harvey 2014).

During times of disruption or crisis, certainty and predictability crumble, control is weak and confused. At these times, space is also created for reorganization and innovation (Berkes et al. 2008). Change becomes more possible when the powers that be are weak or experiencing crises of legitimation, when events disrupt people's taken-for-granted understanding of social reality (Snow et al. 1986; Buechler 2016) or when social controls are weakened enough that people become available and able to participate in collective action (Piven and Cloward 1979).

"When authority is weak because its legitimation is undermined, the social space for social movements increases and they are more likely to emerge and flourish" (Buechler 2016: 37). Additionally, change can become more possible at these critical junctures because to the people making decisions, "the status quo suddenly appears to be less worth defending" (Green 2016: 17). It is these phases in which activists have the best chance of influencing events (Berkes et al. 2008). At these key moments activists' "long-term work … can suddenly come to fruition" (Green 2016: 18).

Sometimes, at these critical moments, crises can create conditions in which transformative change becomes necessary. Several people I spoke with suggested that people don't change unless they have to, that systems don't change unless they are forced to. For example, "most people are never going to be vegan, unless we run out of meat" (Int#14). Reflecting on the collective effort that was mobilized during the Second World War, another activist told me "it wasn't voluntary.… That was decided at a high political level, because it was a national emergency. The [government] said, 'this is the new deal.' It wasn't a choice. So, everyone did it" (Int#2). Certain kinds of events create conditions that necessitate changes in how we understand, in how we live and in how society is organized.

"We need some kind of other story to take us over, and sometimes that happens through crisis and catastrophe" (Int#34 Anishinaabe/Ojibway). Crisis can change people's perceived self-interest and what they will stand up for and stand up to. "A lot of people engage in conflict because there is no choice. They know that their future depends on engaging in conflict" (Int#38 Mi'kmaw).

But for these crisis moments to trigger transformative change *in desirable directions*, we need to be paying close attention, be prepared with alternatives and be ready to seize the opportunities that open up. As one person said to me:

> There are windows of opportunity that are presented, often in times of crises, often manufactured by massive systemic forces we have no control over. The people who are able to have a massive impact in those moments are the ones who are expecting them and are organized and able to take those opportunities. (Int#28)

Progressive organization are not always nimble enough to take advantage of such opportunities (Green 2016).

According to several people I spoke with, echoing Naomi Klein's arguments in *The Shock Doctrine: The Rise of Disaster Capitalism* (2007), the political right has proven better than the left at creating and seizing crises. They do so through a politics of fear that produces hostility towards others. One activist made clear that though the answer is not to organize like the right does, "we need to understand that over the last few decades they've done an incredible job of seizing those crises and taking over all the institutions. [They are] better than us at movement building and at actually governing" (Int#28).

The key lesson from this discussion about context is that timing really matters in determining what interventions will work and when. Activists and organizers need to be attentive to timing, opportunities and stages of change and chose our moments and strategies accordingly. Matching strategy to context is key to driving transformative change:

> If we approach strategy from a rigid template, as in — this is how you do it in every single place, every single time, follow step one through ten and you'll win. No. It ignores the social conditions. It ignores the cultural conditions. It ignores the resource condition of what you have available to you and it ignores the political will. Every place. Case by case. The scenario has to be strategically analyzed to determine its vulnerabilities, to determine its opportunities. And that's why we say "be like water" because you can't come in with this rigid template of strategy. (Int#38 Mi'kmaw)

Given how much needs to change on such a pressing timeline, learning to understand the contexts in which we act and to strategically seize moments of opportunity can help speed up and leverage our work. Context is important, but there are many more forces and factors that determine change.

HOW WE UNDERSTAND AND WHAT WE VALUE

In this dimension of change lies culture, worldviews and values. Many activists' and land defenders' theories of change emphasize this realm of hearts and minds. As one Indigenous land defender from Ecuador told an audience at the 2016 World Social Forum in Montreal when I asked him what was holding back the changes that are needed: "The barriers are inside of us. The most important thing is to change our mentality" (E#2). As another person put it, we need to "shift the conversation, shift the frame, the imagination" (Int#26). It is the stories we tell ourselves and each other about what is important. It's the narratives that help us make sense of unfolding events. It is how we work to shift the thought patterns and values systems that prop up the structures and institutions that drive the social and ecological crises. It's how we nurture values, understandings and worldviews from which a more just and sustainable future can grow. It's the values and emotions and belief systems that spark our willingness to take action to defend what we love, inspiring and driving the long, hard work of resisting injustice and environmental destruction.

The academic literature on social change also emphasizes that, along with the material world, the less tangible world of worldviews, understandings, values, ideas, identity, stories and emotions matters greatly in the process of social change, playing a key role in who participates in social change efforts and why (Kznaric 2007; also see Weber 1905). Karl Mannheim and Pierre Bourdieu explored the ways that worldviews guide human actions, shaping and constraining social action, playing an important role in social change (Kznaric, 2007). This focus shifts the way we understand change, allowing us to see that it isn't just a matter of who has resources and the formal power to force change, instead "placing social action in a deeper framework of meaning" (Kznaric 2007: 12–13).

Power — who has it and how it is wielded — is central to how change happens, and why it doesn't. Much of our conversations in movements, and much scholarship on social change, focuses, for understandable reason, on the formal, overt and direct forms of power, such as the power exerted by the state when they send in the RCMP to enforce injunctions and remove Indigenous land defenders from their territories to make way for pipeline construction. Understanding and transforming this kind of power is absolutely crucial for driving transformative change. But we also need to understand and address the ways that power functions and is wielded in more indirect ways. Habermas, the German philosopher and sociologist, offered important insight about the way power shapes processes and outcomes not only in the public sphere but also in the private sphere of everyday life (Carroll and Sarker 2016; Habermas 1987). Transformation scholars Temper, Walter, Rodriquez et al. describe these less visible forms of power:

Power also works in an "invisible" way through discursive

practices, narratives, worldviews, knowledge, behaviours and thoughts that are assimilated by society as true without public questioning. This invisible, capillary, subtle form of power often takes the shape in practice of cultural violence, through the imposition of value and belief systems that exclude or violate the physical, moral or cultural integrity of certain social groups by underestimating their own value and belief systems. Here, people may see certain forms of domination over them as "natural" or immutable, and, therefore, remain unquestioned. (Temper et al. 2018: 8; see also Lukes 1974; Gaventa 1980; Foucault 1971; Galtung 1990)

Power is used directly through force to bring about change, or more indirectly through propaganda or education systems to change people's preferences, opinions or worldviews (Krznaric 2007). The Italian Marxist Antonio Gramsci developed the concept of hegemonic power to describe the domination of society by the ruling class through the manipulation of culture — through shaping common understandings, values and beliefs. These softer forms of power serve to render the status quo as "natural and inevitable instead of as social constructs meant to benefit the ruling class" (Carroll and Sarker 2016: 41; see also Gramsci 1971 2000).

Gramsci explained that modern capitalist democracies' "formal freedoms and electoral rights exist alongside the class inequalities of the bourgeois state; therefore, relations of domination need to be sustained with the consent of the dominated" (Carroll and Ratner 1994: 5). As far as the interests of capital come to be culturally "common sense," hegemonic control comes to do what direct coercion never could: "it mystifies power relations and public issues; it encourages a sense of fatalism and passivity toward political action" (Carroll and Sarker, 2016: 41). Hegemonic power prevents people from being able to clearly see, let alone act upon, their interests. By functioning through our own internalized values and worldviews, hegemonic power constrains the potential and likelihood that large numbers of people will push for transformative change.

Overcoming this significant barrier to social change requires deliberate, counter-hegemonic strategies and ideas. Counter-hegemony is the work of critiquing and dismantling hegemonic power. It is the confrontation with or opposition to existing status quo and its legitimacy. Building on

Gramsci's work, MacKay writes that, "as power in hegemonic states is based on perceived legitimacy, then a counter-hegemonic movement of movements must work to delegitimize the rule of elites, while simultaneously building the legitimacy and transformative capacity of the movement" (Mackay 2017: 205). One of the key insights that emerges from the concept of hegemony is that we require an immense scale of counter-force to oppose and dismantle hegemonic power. We need efforts on the scale of social movements to deconstruct hegemonic power and to build counter-hegemony.

Demonstrations, protests and other collective actions can generate emotional energy that can be transformative to people and fuel social mobilization processes (Buechler 2016). The collective rituals and heightened emotional states generated when we take to the street together can amplify and transform into a force for change. They also "help nurture beliefs about and visions for alternatives to the status quo ... increas[ing] the success of movements through helping sustain the commitment and motivation of members" (Buechler 2016: 51; see also Durkheim 1965). Worldviews themselves change through new experiences, empathetic relationship with other social groups and long-term changes in educational systems (Krznaric 2007). Movements create spaces and events that can transform people, deepening their commitment to activism and land defence, strengthening the possibilities for transformative change in the world.

Personal Transformation

One young settler activist told me the story of the five months he spent at Unist'ot'en camp in 2012 and how deeply transformative it was for him:

> That was an incredible experience for me. Everything that I did there was very meaningful for me. I'm someone who has a deep, deep need for meaning. I knew that everything I was doing there mattered. I chopped wood, that's direct action. I hauled water, that's direct action. Everything that I was doing was contributing — not just preventing something bad from happening but also contributing towards the creation of something really beautiful, a nurturing vision of a different society. Since that point, I've been really committed to doing this for life. (Int#8)

According to several of the people I spoke with, personal transformation — how hearts and minds change — is an important dimension of social transformation. It is the work of unlearning the internalized hierarchy that hinders our capacity for just relationships. It is the work of unlearning the idea that there is no alternative to the status quo, that we are not powerful enough to change the world. We wake up to the crises and wake up to our own power and agency. Transformation on the personal level can help drive social change. As we develop different values, different understandings of the world, we begin dreaming of profoundly more just futures and we become better equipped to act. When people no longer accept hegemonic stories as common sense they become more willing to stand up, speak out and take action against injustice. All this can help build counter-hegemonic force. That said, narratives around personal healing and individual change can encourage people to focus inwardly and stop there, but several people I spoke to made the important point that personal transformation must lead to collective action or it does not contribute to systems change.

Several people pointed out that for personal change to be transformative it needs to address power and privilege. We discussed how personal transformation looks different for Indigenous Peoples and for settlers. Healing and personal transformation for Indigenous Peoples is the "turning inwards" to community, land and culture, a resurgence and rebuilding of Nations and collective identity and strength; it is relearning and revitalizing existing culture and ways of life (see the works of Coulthard, Alfred, Simpson). Whereas personal transformation for settlers is more about unlearning and relinquishing. Personal transformation for settlers means a profound humbling, an acceptance that we are not the heroes and do not have all the answers. It involves a relinquishing of the privilege and uneven power we hold. Settlers are being asked to "overcome the system of oppression that we have perpetrated" and to forge a culture "beyond rape and pillage" (Int#4). When settlers can humble ourselves, unlearn superiority and accept that we do not have the answers, we become more "ready to hear other solutions, other answers. And maybe that's where transformation starts to take place" (Int#38 Mi'kmaw).

Activists and land defenders also spoke to me about the role education plays in social change. "The general public has very limited knowledge on what colonialism actually is, what the Treaties actually are, and even about what climate change is" (Int#12 Anishinaabe). A lack of education among the general Canadian population about what is wrong and what is at stake helps maintain the unjust and unsustainable status quo and impedes systems change in this country. People spoke about education in various ways: educating youth in school systems, pedagogical and curriculum change, popular education to mobilize more people and educating within our movements. The contention here is that "the more people know about things the more likely things are to change" (Int#29).

Popular movements help educate the wider public. But for movements to be able to bring about change more effectively we need internal education as well:

> We need to do more trainings, more education, we need a sense of history of the movements … about how to fight, what happened before us, what can go wrong, what can go right, how to build a strategy, a more collective strategy. That's a lot of work, that's long work, that's tiring work. But it has to be done. (Int#19)

As much as some people argued for the need for more public education, others argued that there are very important limits to this approach. One person told me: "I don't have a whole lot of optimism around the idea of educating the general Canadian public. There are just too many barriers there, things that people don't want to hear" (Int#38 Mi'kmaw). As another person put it: "We're facing cowards who don't understand that they've grown up colonized, that they've grown up racist" (E#21). Education on its own does not lead to transformative action. It is important but insufficient on its own. Many people spoke about the importance of *changing the story*, the narratives we tell ourselves and each other.

Changing the Story

Alongside the previsioning and dissemination of information through education are the storylines that link bits of information together through compelling narratives that evoke emotion and inspire action. Some social movement scholars emphasize the importance of *collective action frames*, which movements formulate to express their grievances, the need for change and reasons for action (Davis 2002). The ways that movements frame problems and solutions and how they justify the need for change is crucial to their ability to make change. Snow and Benford (1992) define "collective action frames as emergent action-oriented sets of meanings and beliefs that inspire and legitimate social movement campaigns and activities" (paraphrased in Carrol and Sarker 2016: 15). Through collective action framings, movements identify injustices, attribute responsibility for the injustices and express visions of alternatives (Snow and Benford 1992; Tarrow 2011).

Socio-ecological systems transformation scholars Moore, Tjornbo, Enfors et al. (2014) identify *sense-making* as an important stage in bringing about transformative change. It is through sense-making that people "construct meaningful explanations for situations" they want to change (Gioia 1986: 81). Related to this process of framing and sense-making is the work of *envisioning*, which helps foster the idea that a different order of things is possible and helps flesh out what the alternative order of things may be like (Moore et al. 2014).

Stories are central to this. We live by stories. Stories turn information into meaning. Movement stories can foster "a powerful collective identity" that compels action and brings in new participants to the movements (Davis 2002: 24). As Reinsborough and Canning put it: "Every social change effort is inherently a conflict between the status quo and the change agents to control the framing on an issue. This is the battle of the story" (2010: 17). They go on to say that

> many of our current social and ecological problems have their roots in the silent consensus of assumptions that shape the dominant culture (e.g., humans can dominate and outsmart nature, women are worth less than men, racism and war are part of human nature, economies must grow). To make real and lasting change, these stories must change. (5)

Identifying and challenging underlying assumptions is vitally important to social change efforts.

This realm of change is about both creating and sharing stories that can undergird a just and sustainable human presence on these lands we call Canada. But it is also about disrupting the problematic stories that hold injustice in place. People spoke to me about the need to develop compelling stories of radical change that make it clear that it is a real possibility. We need new stories that disrupt the old narratives such as "jobs versus the environment." We need stories that re-embed humans as part of nature, stories that compel us to believe that humans are capable of so much more beauty, empathy and cooperation.

The activists I spoke with reflected on the fact that so often in the work of culture change, we are talking to people who already agree with us. We need to reach beyond the usual suspects and not just preach to the choir. This means talking to people that don't already agree with us. It means meeting them where they are and finding common ground. Many people emphasized that person-to-person contact is a powerful way to change hearts and minds. "There's no greater force than minds coming together to understand and respect how we're going to share this Earth. Dialogue is best" (S#37).

Many people made the important point that it matters deeply who is telling the stories. A Dene woman told me: "Being able to tell stories and to say things truthfully in a good way.... That's a bit of an obstacle. Who gets to talk? What does it mean to have a voice and to share that voice? That's a big thing" (Int#25 Dene). The person doing the telling shapes the story. Stories told from the front lines are very different from those told through mainstream media or big NGO media campaigns. And "it matters who are the heroes, who are the villains in the stories we tell" (Int#38 Mi'kmaw).

Many of the Indigenous people I spoke to emphasized storytelling as central to their cultures and their approaches to change. "Indigenous people have long enough collective memories to recall a time when our worlds were organized on different principles and could be again" (Coburn and Atleo 2016: 193). Stories are a way to centre Indigeneity in bringing about change. Simpson writes: "If we want to create a different future, we need to live a different present, so that the present can fully marinate, influence, and create different futurities. If we want to live a different present, we have to center Indigeneity and allow it to change us" (2017: 20). "Storytelling then becomes a lens through which we can envision our way out of cognitive imperialism" (Simpson 2011: 33).

Kelly Aguirre, mestiza scholar of Nahua and Ñuù savi descent, writes about the "difficult process of relearning our own stories, internalizing them, as well as challenging and dislodging those that have been imposed on us" (quoted in Coburn 2015: 33). Understanding and interpreting Indigenous stories may be a "principled way of beginning to reimagine healthy relationships among Indigenous Peoples — and perhaps if they are willing to listen, with non-Indigenous people as well" (Hayden King, quoted in Coburn 2015: 37).

Story work, crucial to movements building counter-hegemony, is different for Indigenous Peoples and settlers. Where Indigenous Peoples are reclaiming and retelling stories deeply rooted in their cultures and traditions, and are doing so to strengthen the resurgence of their unique and rich life ways and practices, settlers need to create new narratives, not appropriated from Indigenous cultures, but rather created anew, without replicating the values and understandings that help prop up the unjust systems of the status quo. We need to be developing narratives that undo colonial power. Narratives that undo colonial power require a solid and clear-eyed understanding of the complex systems we seek to transform.

Systemic Analysis

The activists and land defenders I talked to also emphasized that systems change requires that we understand the complex systems and structures that underly the social and ecological crises we seek to address; that *systemic analysis* is crucial for transformative change. As we can turn complex systems analysis into compelling and accessible narratives, we build counter-hegemonic power. This is not easy because the roots of the crises lie in systems and structures that are hard to see. We need to uncover and lay them bare, developing shared political analyses that allow us to agree on targets that can bring about transformative change. To change a system, we need to understand how that system works. This is no easy task.

As one person said, "part of my theory of change is that it is very difficult to see what the structures are because we are so deep in them" (Int#29). But it is vital to be able to, to ensure that we're choosing effective targets for our change efforts. We must ask: "Do we have our eye on the proper problem? The real thing that's concerning us?" (Int#28). In comparison to other times in the history of social movements, "our political consciousness is a little less deep now" (Int#32).

To develop "more than a superficial understanding" of what's wrong (S#37), we need a really deep "systemic analysis of colonialism and capitalism, to really build revolutionary mindsets that don't sacrifice anything" (E#15). Do we want to "just replicate what the system looks like now? Just replace the people in power? Or can we move on to a more meaningful dialogue and start talking about how to change the system that created this?" (Int#38 Mi'kmaw). Indeed, much promise for social transformation lies in these "analyses and connections [that] are only starting to be made" (Int#11). Cox and Nilsen contend that if activists can "engage in a critical interrogation of the structures that engender the problems they seek to address," they then stand a chance of developing counter-hegemonic power for transformation (2014: 82).

To systems thinkers, the world is understood as a system of systems. A system is a grouping of things (or elements) — people, organisms, cells, communities — interconnected in such a way that patterns of behaviour are produced through time (Meadows 2008) and whereby something is achieved (Green 2016).

Systems thinkers emphasize that understanding of systems comes from the examination of how the different elements of a system relate to each other and operate together, and not from the examination of the components in isolation. These relationships determine how a system responds (Meadows 2008).

An example could be a very simplified ecological system consisting of two subsystems; a prey population and a predator population. These two subsystems can be studied in isolation, analyzing the variation in populations depending on food or space availability, but the behaviour of the predator-prey system is defined by the interaction of these two subsystems. In the absence of external forces, the interaction can either lead to the collapse of the system or to one of two stable behaviours; a steady state of fixed populations or a cyclic behaviour in which an increase in the prey population leads to an increase in the predator population, which in turn results in a decrease in the number of prey followed by a decrease in predators, which starts the cycle again.

The systems' behaviour, or what is achieved, is not necessarily what was intended by any single actor or element in the system. In fact, one of the most frustrating aspects of systems is that the purpose of individual elements or subsystems may add up to an overall behaviour that brings about the systems' own downfall (Meadows 2008).

For example, the purpose of an economic system should be to bring material wellbeing to a society. Subsystems would be the monetary system, trade unions and the ecosystem, which provides raw materials. Individual elements could be coins, persons and goods. In this context, capitalism is

a system ripe with dire unintended behaviours, such as the marginalization of parts of the society the system is supposed to serve, the depletion
of non-renewable resources and the disastrous disruption of the Earth's
climate. In looking at the relationship between the system's structure and
its behaviour, we begin to understand how a system works, what makes
it produce undesired results, what locks certain behaviours in place and
how to shift them to better behaviour patterns. It gives us the ability to
identify root causes of problems and see new opportunities (Meadows
2008). It can help us steward the systems we are part of in ways that are
more beneficial for all.

Critical social scientists emphasize that an important part of understanding a system is understanding the way power functions, enabling
some people and some institutions to influence outcomes more than
others: "In order to generate social change, we first need to understand
how power is distributed and can be re-distributed between and within
social groups" (Green 2016: xii). "Power analysis helps identify who
holds what kind of power related to a social or environmental issue, and
what might influence them to change" (Green 2016: 38). This includes an
understanding of the kinds of power we, as individuals and activist groups,
hold and where we are most likely to exert influence. Power analysis
should also help us understand how both our allies and our opponents
perceive the change (Green 2016: 38). As interests are closely related to
power, effective change agency requires that activists conduct analyses
of convergent and divergent interests of all the actors involved (Carroll
and Sarker 2016: 16). We need to ask: Who will benefit from the change
we seek? Who will be harmed?

Intersectional feminist scholarship has contributed greatly to analyzing
how different forms of domination and different forms of power interact
to shape people's lives and societal dynamics. Collins and Bilge argue
that to create powerful strategies, "power relations are to be analysed
both via their intersections, for example of racism and sexism, as well as
across domains of power" (Collins and Bilge 2016: 27). Understanding the
systems and structures that drive the crises requires understanding the
power relations of class, gender, race and nations, and how these power
relations shape institutions and organizations (Collins and Bilge 2016: 9).
This kind of analysis of systems and power can inform more powerful and
complex strategies that can transform the political and economic status

quo (Smith 2016). For example, really understanding the economic and political systems that drive extractivism in Canada — analyzing which people in the country are benefiting the most and which are benefiting the least from it, who is making the decisions and who is excluded from decision making and why, how decisions are made, and what underlying forces prop all this up — can help us design more deeply transformative strategies.

Systems scholar Donella Meadows developed a helpful framework for seeing that there are many places to intervene in a system and that some are more impactful than others. There are many areas to target when trying to make social change: policies, laws, emissions levels, people's worldviews, institutions. Understanding these as different kinds of leverage points, with different kinds of potential impacts, can help inform more effective strategy.

Systemic analysis also helps people connect the dots between struggles that are often understood and waged separately — environment, labour, Indigenous rights, women's rights and others. Developing this systemic analysis can help us get past some of the ideological infighting that plagues the left. It deepens our understanding of what's wrong and strengthens our ability to make radical change by forging connections across struggles. Taking an intersectional approach to analyzing systems and power helps us consider the interaction between the capitalist system and other root causes of oppression — colonialism, white supremacy and cis-heteropatriarchy, for example. Collins and Bilge explain that though people often, when referring to intersectionality, refer to race, sex and class as the three primary forms of oppressions, many other important forms of oppression exist and need to be considered, as they are "enmeshed in the process of social justice and injustice" (2016: 38). These other forms of oppression include age, disability, gender identity, sexual preference, mental health, geographical (dis)location, rurality, colonialism/imperialism, Indigeneity, ethnicity, citizenship and the environment (Collins and Blige 2016). Though many scholars of intersectionality focus on the systems of oppression between people, there is some scholarship that explicitly brings the ecological and climate crises into intersectional analysis (see for example Kaijser and Kronsell 2014).

There is tendency for movements to take a piecemeal approach, addressing one crisis at a time, rendering us ineffective in bringing about the social change we seek. "There is a crying need for some more cata-lytic conception to ground and animate political action" (Harvey 2014: 266–267). Developing and sharing, through compelling narratives, deep and clear understandings of the systems and power dynamics that drive the current crises can help movements develop the coalitions and strate-gies required to build counter-hegemonic power.

Amplifying the Voices of Those Most Impacted

Many activists and land defenders I interviewed made the point that the people who can most clearly see the systems and what is wrong with them are those most impacted by them. The call to centre, raise up and amplify the voices of those marginalized and most impacted is essential to bringing about systems transformation. It is both a moral imperative and a strategic one because when those impacted have a say, better deci-sions get made. Indigenous Peoples, racialized people, women, LGBTQ2S peoples — those most harmed by and least benefiting from the current system — have critical perspectives about what is wrong and what needs to be done. Hearing and heeding these voices are keys to decolonizing and decarbonizing Canada. A major challenge and point of tension with this pathway for change is that "narratives are usually hijacked and dominated by the more powerful media sources" (Int#21) and the voices that need to be heard are silenced or tokenized.

S. Smith argues, and this is a key point for theories of change, that the most important lesson to be learned is that mass movements for liberation "must be based not on the needs of the least oppressed, but rather on the needs of those who are the most oppressed" (2017: n.p.).

Indigenous Leadership

Most of the theories of change shared with me by activists and land defenders raised up the conviction that Indigenous leadership is the a most important ingredient for transforming Canada. I heard this again and again in my research, expressed in many different ways: "Militant organizing by Indigenous Peoples is the most promising force we have for real change" (S#3). "These are constructive movements. They are resist-ing pipelines but they offer an alternative to how we can live together in peace and how to be wiser with our lifestyles" (Int#17). "Indigenous Nations, and the ones specifically fighting pipelines are the ones with the solutions, not just the band-aids" (Int#12 Anishinaabe). "The fact that so many environmental initiatives are now being led by Indigenous activists. That gives me hope" (S#23).

To put dignity and justice into our relationships in this country and to build powerful movements, it is crucial that settlers, especially those who continue to benefit most from the status quo (wealthy, white, cis, straight men, for example), step back from positions and attitudes of leadership and instead listen to, take leadership from and actively support Indigenous Peoples and others marginalized by the unjust systems. This is central to many people's theories of change.

Many factors prompt the need for centring and elevating Indigenous leadership in these movements: Indigenous communities are most, and first, impacted by the social and environmental crises and as such their struggles have the urgency of struggles for survival; Indigenous Peoples hold special rights in relation to their territories; their agency inherently targets the systems driving the crises; they have been fighting this fight for hundreds of years; their worldviews, identities, livelihoods and laws, characterized by connection to land and water, inspire a powerful willingness to defend them; and their worldviews do not separate human from non-human nature. They are best positioned to envision beneficial futures for both. Also, it's their land.

All these factors stand in contrast to settler agency. Though people I talked to raised the important point that Indigenous change agency should not be essentialized or overgeneralized, there is clear consensus that Indigenous communities are powerful leaders. Settlers seeking radical change can best help make change by actively supporting Indigenous communities on the front lines of these struggles. Though settlers need to follow direction from Indigenous Peoples, this doesn't mean settlers should leave the fight up to Indigenous Peoples. Importantly, while playing an active but supportive role can mean strategic use of colonial privilege, mostly it means relinquishing this privilege and giving up the plunders of colonialism that have accrued to settlers.

Building movements that are genuinely led by Indigenous Peoples, settler allies need to understand Indigenous land defence from within Indigenous theories of change. It is important to engage with Indigenous theories and approaches to change from the perspective of Indigenous Peoples themselves, working to understand Indigenous perspectives and traditions on their own terms rather than through Western categories and frameworks (Ladner 2008).

Current Indigenous scholarship focuses on the dual work of *resistance* and *resurgence*. Indigenous resistance has been ongoing since contact and is documented in works such as Gord Hill's *500 years of Resistance* (2010). In a recent short film about the Secwepemc resistance to the Kinder Morgan pipeline, Indigenous land defenders opposing Kinder Morgan evoke the intergenerational fight against the Canadian state when they say that "we were raised for this fight" (Guy and Suess 2017: n.p.). Resistance has been necessary for the survival of Indigenous Nations under settler colonialism.

The key insight of the work of Indigenous scholars such as Alfred, Simpson and Coulthard is that resistance, while absolutely necessary, is not sufficient. Taiaiake Alfred, whose early work on resurgence influenced the current generation of Indigenous scholars, wrote: "Many of my own generation of scholars and activists hold on to ways of thinking and acting that are wrapped up in old theories of revolution. Those theories centre on convincing the settler society to change their ways and restructure their society through the use of persuasion or force." He asks: "What if settlers never choose to change their ways?" (2008: 11). Resurgence "refocuses our work from trying to transform the colonial outside in to a flourishment of the Indigenous inside" (Simpson 2011: 17). Drawing on anti-colonial political philosopher Franz Fanon, who urged those struggling against colonialism to turn away from the colonial state and "find in their own decolonial praxis the source of their liberation," Coulthard discerns and advocates an Indigenous resurgence directed not toward recognition by the state but "toward our own on-the-ground struggles of freedom" (2014: 48). Rather than pathways for change that are contingent on changes in settler society, resurgence calls for a "turning inward to focus on resurgence of an authentic Indigenous existence and recapturing the physical, political, and psychic spaces of freedom." For Indigenous Peoples resurgence is about "indigeneity coming back to life again" (Alfred 2008: 11). This approach to change informs strategies that Indigenous Peoples can use "to disentangle themselves from the oppressive control of occupying state governments (Simpson 2008: 15). "Transforming ourselves, our communities and our nations is ultimately the first step in transforming our relationship with the state" (Simpson 2011: 17).

Decolonial change calls for "actions that engage in a generative refusal of any aspect of state control, so they don't just refuse, they also embody an Indigenous alternative" (Simpson 2017: 35). Where settlers need to innovate and create new systems and lifeways if they are to live in just and sustainable ways, Indigenous Peoples have existing knowledge, practices and systems that are being reinvigorated. In this way, the dual strategy is different for settlers than it is for Indigenous Peoples. This difference is critically important. To form powerful, counter-hegemonic coalitions across movements, activists need to see that different people are fighting for different things, based on different histories of struggle, different visions of liberation and different philosophies of change.

This section has explored the theories of change emphasizing the transformative power of changing *how we understand and what we value.* Personal transformation, education, changing the story, systemic analysis, amplifying the voices of those most impacted and Indigenous leadership all play important roles. But potential tensions are uncovered in bringing these different aspects together: If white settlers are still the ones holding the mic, then amplifying the voices of others is not transformative; personal transformation doesn't lead to collective transformation, it must be linked to collective action; facts on their own don't change people's minds; changing the story is important, but it matters deeply who is telling the story and who is listening.

Many common strategies in the movements stop at education, or stall in the realm of the individual, and it's important that movements move beyond these tactics to consider all of the dimensions explored here. But it's also important to remember that each of these dimensions, in themselves, can be enacted in ways that are transformative and in ways that are not — and each is not enough on its own. These approaches for change become more transformative when working in concert with and bolstered by the other approaches. And, of course, most importantly, changing hearts and minds will not lead to change if people don't take action. It is action we turn to next.

HOW WE TAKE ACTION

Along with context and how we understand and what we value, *how we take action* was another key dimension of activists' theories of change. This is where the fruits of changing hearts and minds hits the ground, translating values, concern and intention into concrete action and building power through collective action. It is how activists work to impact the systems, structures and institutions that drive the social and environmental crises.

Building Power from Below through Collective Action

There is broad agreement among the people I spoke to that for systems transformation to happen, there need to be masses of people coming together and forming collectivities to organize, mobilize, provide leadership and take action. Doing this while combining forces through coalitions with other groups is how we build people power from the bottom-up — from the grassroots. Building power from below doesn't just happen automatically when a bunch of people come together. Their numbers need to be translated into power. This happens though *organizing*. Building power also requires reaching beyond the choir and attracting many more people to our movements. This is the work of *mobilizing*.

Academic scholarship on change, especially social movement studies, also places much importance on how movements build power through collective action. How we pool and allocate resources is crucial. For social movements to bring about change, we need to mobilize, which means "bringing under collective control resources of various kinds, including most importantly human labour: the willingness of people to commit their own time to the movement. Mobilization requires social organization ... which enable[s] collective action to be sustained over time" (Carroll and Sarker 2016: 16).

Collective action is costly and as such requires decisions on how to allocate resources. "Effective movements create a configuration of alliances and reciprocal relations of mutual aid (facilitation), thereby lowering costs of collective action" (Carroll and Sarker 2016: 16). Since states, corporations and other centres of power may respond to threats to their power by attempting to raise the costs of mobilization and collective action, movements need to develop strategies for dealing with such repression (Carroll and Sarker 2016: 16).

Social movement theorists provide a warning that while organizing is necessary, movements need to be wary of how organization can lead to increasing layers of bureaucracy. Weber's analysis on the tendency of social organizations to move towards greater bureaucratization and routinization serves as an important warning to social movements. If, as he argued, society is moving towards the iron cage of bureaucracy, "it is highly likely that the same logic will paralyse social movements organized along those lines" (Buechler 2016: 34; see also Weber 1978). As Piven and Cloward argue, "effective protest emerges from popular disruption and mass action rather than from organized movements ... once organization appears, effective protest dies" (quoted in Buechler 2016: 39). This tendency, though strong, may not be inevitable (Lipset, Trow and Coleman 1956). A combination of bottom-up organizing, local autonomy, dense interactions, democratic culture and multiple leadership factions can maintain democratic organization (Lipset, Trow and Coleman 1956; Buechler 2016). That said, the danger remains that the move to hierarchical, complex organization in movement organizations (which tends to happen as we try to be more efficient with our resources) can render them ineffective in bringing about change. There is a fine line to be walked. We need to be organized, but we are well-advised to not get so bogged down by bureaucracy that we lose the ability to act together.

There is consensus among the people I spoke with that *grassroots movements engaging in collective action together is how transformative power is generated to drive change.* But there are important divergences among activists' theories of change in term of how best to wield this power. One organizer provides a very useful metaphor that helps us think through these divergences. He argues that change is brought about by directing "a firehose of people-power" at key targets (E#10). There is notable disagreement among the people I spoke with about where to point the firehose of people-power in order to most effectively bring transformative change.

For some people the pressure forged in collective action leads to change through influencing government decision makers and affecting electoral outcomes. Others, who place less faith in governments' ability and/or willingness to push for deep systems change from the top, contend that transformative change happens when movements point that firehose of people-power at actively delegitimizing and dismantling the existing systems, confronting the existing power structure that maintains the unjust status quo. Others argue that people-power needs to be deployed to create, live and promote new systems now, based on just and sustainable ways of meeting our basic human needs. Others argue that all three are necessary, but each of them is insufficient on its own.

Engaging with the Electoral System

The electoral system came up many times when people spoke about their theories of change, but in wildly different ways. Where some believe that the work of social movements is to influence government decision making and that change happens through this interaction, others argue that system change cannot come through governments because they will always serve to maintain the system.

It is clear that important changes can and do come through putting pressure on decision makers and that whoever gets elected has enormous impact on environmental and social outcomes. As some see it, social change usually involves "a very large social mobilization linked to a progressive political party" (S#33) and "mass movements pushing governments to change" (S#36). Policy and legislative changes happen when "politicians feel supported" to make those changes (Int#6). Arguing for social movement engagement with electoral politics, one person told me: "Fundamentally, we're trying to push the political system. And if we can't do that, we might as well go home and start drinking" (S#37).

That said, the conflicting views on this suggest important limits to seeking change through the electoral systems. For people who have been working to influence politicians for decades, the lack of impact is dispiriting:

> Organizing is something I've been doing for forty years. I feel lost. I recognize we have to challenge the state, but I don't know what the vehicle for that is. Relying on [political parties] ... I've lost faith in that. We need something beyond the [usual approaches to change]. We talk about this almost every meeting: How *do* we resist? (S#37)

People explained the limits to change through the political system in various ways: large-scale systemic change will not come through electoral politics, that is not its job; looking to the governments to do something they cannot do diverts our energies from creating the necessary changes ourselves; the incentives created by the political systems mean politicians need to care about short-term, narrowly focused issues; corporate influence hugely biases governmental decision making; we can't afford the lobbying and backing of candidates that the political right can, so we will always lose that battle; and lastly, we don't actually live in a democracy:

[People] buy into that myth that a political party represents our interests, but they really don't. They represent what's going to get them elected. We're recognizing that government can't rescue us … when it comes to figuring out how we are going to get through [climate chaos] and work together, it comes down to the people at the community level who can make change happen. So, we're not waiting for government. We're going to look to ourselves. (Int#37)

How do we make sense of these compelling arguments for and against engaging in electoral politics to drive change? On the one hand, engaging with the political system may be necessary for damage control and for slowing or stopping unwanted policy and destructive development. Some important reforms, such as legislation to implement carbon taxes and to subsidize clean energy, can only come through the political system. But on the other hand, other kinds of deeper change will not come about through politicians making policy and legislation. In terms of decolonizing Canada, for instance, it is unlikely that the federal government will ever willingly give up its power and control over Indigenous Peoples and their lands.

There are clear limits to what can be achieved through the official political process, but it also seems true that "no movement has the luxury of ignoring the electoral front" (E#9). "We need to use the full toolbox and we need to be constantly finding new tools. We can't be ruling anything out" (Int#16).

How do we devise theories and strategies that take all these divergent insights into account? We need strategies that neither completely disengage from the electoral process nor invest everything in it. And "that's hard to do. It's hard to hold both ideas in your head" (Int#16). Knowing that some changes can be brought about through electoral politics but not others and seeing that policy and legislative changes are useful at certain phases of transformation but not others, we begin to ask more nuanced questions: Which social or ecological crises can be addressed this way? At which stages of the long-term fight are engagement with electoral politics most likely to help reach movement goals? Which activists/groups in a movement are best positioned to engage on this front? How does fighting on this front fit into the broader ecosystem of change work happening on other fronts? Perhaps the most pressing question is: If the electoral system in its current state cannot bring about the urgently needed radical changes in our social, economic and political systems, what can?

Confronting and Dismantling Power

Where some activists argue that we build mass movements to put pressure on politicians and decision makers by demonstrating a broad public will, others argue that the purpose of movements is to build counter-power that can challenge the power wielded by the state. "We have to build a mass movement to bring about change. You can't beg for change; you have to demand it ... power will [not] yield without force" (Int#11). Several people spoke about how historically, social changes that were big enough to restructure political and economic structures came through revolution and war: "Slavery didn't end by slave owners deciding to be nice and free their slaves. It happened through civil war" (Int#2). From this view, all the tactics we use, from awareness-raising to mobilizing, should be part of a larger strategy that escalates in order "to force change.... This requires a diversity of tactics that include a confrontational stance" (Int#11).

Scholars of historical materialism corroborate this more confrontational view of social change. They position contemporary movements within the context of capitalism as a way of life, a mode of production that includes the "institutional arrangements and alliances that stabilize the dominant regime" (Kinsman 2006: 136). In neoliberal globalization we have been witnessing "a very effective movement from above" (Carroll and Sarker 2016: 28). From this perspective we see social movements from above and below engage in struggles over how society changes or doesn't (Cox and Nilsen 2014). "Exploitation and oppression are underpinned by powerfully organized forces who will resist all serious attempts at structural change and who will, in some form, need to be taken on and defeated" (Barker, Cox, Krinsky and Nilsen 2013: 20). "Movements from below must, if they are to be effective, address and ultimately defeat the sedimented power of movements from above" (Carroll and Sarker 2016: 48). In other words, "if we want a truly sustainable and equitable human civilization, then we have no choice but to directly confront the nexus of control that drives our current system of ecological destruction and human misery. We have to take power back" (MacKay 2017: 27).

As discussed in the section about how we understand and what we value, power functions in various ways, playing a "central role in both stasis and change" (Green 2016: 36). I discussed how hegemonic power is wielded in indirect, invisible ways, through the manipulation of culture, values and worldviews. And as many activists and land defenders argued, movements must also engage in these indirect, less tangible realms if we are to build counter-hegemony. But power also functions in more direct, visible and tangible ways as well. And so must movements.

Along with invisible power, British social theorist Steven Lukes (1974) identified two other dimensions of power: hidden power and visible power. Hidden power is what goes on behind the scenes, wielded by "the lobbyists, the corporate chequebooks, the old-boys networks.... Power is exercised in a 'hidden' way by incumbent powers attempting to maintain their privileged position in society, by creating barriers to participation, excluding issues from the public agenda or controlling political decisions" (Temper et al. 2018: 9).

Visible power, also known as institutional or structural power, is the world of politics and authority, policed by laws, violence and money

> manifested through decision-making bodies (institutions) where issues of public interest, such as legal frameworks, regulations and public policies, are decided (e.g., parliaments, legislative assemblies, formal advisory bodies). This is the public space where different actors display their strategies to assert their rights and interest. Visible power is also manifested through economic frameworks that shape economic activities and productive systems in society. (Temper et al. 2018: 8)

These more direct forms of power shape the ways that people are disciplined in societies; which rules apply to whom and how rules are implemented. Uneven power relations of class, gender and race intersect, shaping and structuring institutions and organizations (Collins and Bilge 2016). This kind of structural and disciplinary power institutionalizes and enforces relations of domination and social hierarchy, which determine social outcomes and conditions, which marginalize and oppress less powerful people while serving the interests of the powerful. In other words, the power of domination is exercised by people to "ensure that their interests and worldviews prevail over those of others" (Temper et al. 2018: 9). In these ways, social and environmental decisions are being made by a small elite group of powerful people in order to consolidate and build their wealth and power while driving staggering social inequality and threatening the viability of life on Earth. "A radical perspective on transformation calls for an explicit engagement with the issue of power.... It is precisely by impacting on hegemonic power structures that [change can happen]" (Temper et al. 2018: 8).

Transforming hegemonic power structures is inherently conflictual and requires confrontational strategies and tactics, such as blockades and work disruptions. Some climate activists focus on strategies that help garner broad support for climate action — letter writing and public protest — and so they discourage the kinds of conflictual tactics that would result in them losing the support of large swaths of Canadian society. Activists whose aim it is to dismantle capitalism, colonialism and the Canadian state, on the other hand, know they cannot accomplish these goals employing the kinds of tactics that will retain large-scale support from the Canadian public, and so they are willing to forgo public support in order to fight for the larger goal:

> I understand the nature of decolonial activism in Western society. At some point, it will lead towards conflict. Not because we want it. Not because it's our pursuit or even a by-product of what we want. Violence, force, conflict will emerge as we challenge the power, privilege and benefit of the elites. (Int#38 Mi'kmaw)

Coulthard argues that direct action is required for decolonial change. He advocates for "temporarily blocking access to Indigenous territories with the aim of impeding the exploitation of Indigenous Peoples' land and resources" or reoccupation of Indigenous land in an effort to disrupt or block "access by state and capital for sustained periods of time" (2014: 168).

To many of the people I interviewed, conflict and confrontation are required to transform the power structures and relations that are driving the crises. They discussed this in the following ways: "Legitimacy is the key, when you're talking about one of the powers of perception in Canada. You've got to challenge legitimacy" (Int#38 Mi'kmaw). "Rather than snuggling up to politicians and lobbying them to take seriously the movements' goals, instead activists can work to expose and call them out on their hypocrisy" (S#37). You need to poke holes in the "liberal double-discourse: 1) prove they're lying, 2) attack them" (E#9).

Along with delegitimizing elite power and governance, large-scale social change becomes more likely when movements work to polarize issues. "Revolutions have usually happened when you had a really big divide ... the tension builds up until people can't take it anymore and they take to the street" (Int#15). In the Canadian context, much of the injustice and inequality remain below the surface, hidden by liberal discourse. Conflict can take a problem, often hidden, and bring it to the surface. Through polarizing issues, you can take something that seems fuzzy and make it clear. Conflicts can "make clear that something is right/wrong/ridiculous/hypocritical" (S#37). Engaging in confrontational strategies helps polarize issues by showing that the state is willing to use force against people who are defending their lives and lands. This can help delegitimize the state, expose the "real nerve" of what is going on and encourage more people to take a stance (Int#10).

Social change requires that movements hold power to account and pose a real threat to that power. Indeed, "change happens when the powerful are the ones who have to concede. This happens when there is a very real threat to the powerful people and to the power structure. In the case of the civil rights movement, it was widespread riots" (Int#30). "If we make it impossible for them to make a profit or to stay in power, they are going to change their ways" (Int#14). There are various strategies social movements have devised and used throughout history to make change through applying force to power. They include strikes, boycotts, property damage, lawsuits, public shaming, blockades, sabotage, demonstrations and occupations. These diverse tactics are aimed at depriving corporations of their profits, challenging power and the status quo.

Transforming economic systems means costing the bad guys money. One activist called this tactic "punitive strikes," which are used to "actually punish the responsible parties" (Int#14). This can range from damaging a company's reputation in ways that can erode shareholders' confidence, to "spiking trees" in order to "deprive the company of the profit they would hope to get from [a logging] operation" (Int#14). Citing many success stories from anti-logging activism over the last thirty years, this activist told me, "my motto still is, 'we're down with any action that slows down the destruction or stops it even for a minute.' If it costs the company money, affects the bottom line ... they ultimately lose over the long run. Also, it is a lesson for others who might think they can get rich that way" (Int#14).

Confronting power requires direct action and civil disobedience. To bring about the massive transformation of decolonizing and decarbonizing Canada, there is the "absolute imperative to be engaged in struggle. This 150 years of colonialism has to be confronted" (E#19). This is both a moral and a strategic imperative. "Direct action gets the goods" (S#37). "Direct action has been the most effective way of stopping [unwanted] projects … people physically stopping projects from happening. The Unist'ot'en camp in BC, Elsipogtog in Mi'kmaw territory … physical blockades. That has been the most successful way to go" (Int#30). Acknowledging that there have been significant victories through lawsuits and court cases, one activist argued that these wins are made more likely when mass awareness is raised through "sustained direct action, blockades, lock downs and nonviolent civil disobedience" (Int#30).

The problem is that risks and costs associated with direct action and civil disobedience are high and usually borne by a few individuals. They face risks of police violence, arrest and incarceration, as well as legal fees, criminal records and more. Yet, if this form of activism is required to actually force change, we need to think hard about how to reduce the costs for people willing to engage in this way. We need to practise ways to "maximize or optimize the impact of direct action and negate the risks of it.… I think the answer is to collectivize that action and to socialize that risk … that's the formula whereby direct action can be translated into meaningful change: collectivize the action, socialize the risk, universalize the benefits" (TT#2).

Radically transforming Canada will require confronting the power elite and dismantling the power structures that be. However, these confrontational strategies, while necessary, aren't sufficient. It's not enough to confront injustice; we also need to build new systems and structures to replace the ones we seek to dismantle.

Creating, Living and Promoting the Solutions

Another key theme in the movements' theories of change is that change happens through innovating, promoting and living the alternatives and solutions to the problems we're working to address. This is another direction to aim that "firehose of people-power": we build collective power and take collective action to provide the labour for the hard work of building the infrastructure, institutions and relations that will comprise the world we want.

"We must find alternatives" (Int#17) and "more inspirational politics" (E#3). "When you're yelling 'Fire!' everybody can hear that, but they don't necessarily know what to do. It's not as potent as saying 'here's the pump, here's the water'" (Int#1). As movements, how can we not only yell fire, but actively help communities access the pump and the water?

"People often find it very hard to envision themselves in this zero-carbon world" (Int#35). How can thirty-six million people house, feed, employ, transport and otherwise organize and care for ourselves and each other in ways that are equitable and within ecological limits and work to reverse the climate destabilizing impacts our industrial capitalist system has created? How can we do this in ways that undo the extreme inequality between Indigenous Peoples and settlers? And how can we enact these solutions while settler capitalism remains the order of the day?

Systems theorist Joanna Macy refers to this dimension of change as the development of "life-sustaining systems and practices," which involves a rethinking of the way human societies are organized and function and how they provide for human needs. This work is the "creative redesign of the structures and systems that make up our society" (Macy and Johnstone 2012: 96). This can include green building, alternative energy systems, cooperative forms of ownership, new forms of governance, permaculture and agroecology, alternative transportation, ethical financial systems, skill shares and community teach-ins.

Activists and land defenders whose theories of change emphasized solutions explained why a focus on solutions is necessary for transformative change. One reason is that the *Yes* brings more people to the movement than the *No*. Showing people viable alternatives is a great way to engage people around a social or environmental problem. It can inspire rather than scare them (Int#1). "People are unlikely to support or mobilize for social change if they see alternatives as unlikely" (S#23). It's very easy to see the destructive and unjust status quo as inevitable, but "we need to show there are alternatives to the god-awful capitalist system" (S#28). In addition, having concrete solutions to point to can be impactful when lobbying decision makers about an unwanted development project. They can be more easily persuaded to support your position if they see a viable alternative available.

Another reason solutions are important is that resistance work is stressful and exhausting and often done under great pressure. Spending some of our movement energies living and promoting the solutions can help ward off activist burnout. Helping enact the solutions can be the inspiration and hope that fuel our continued resistance work (Int#10).

Feminist economic geographers writing under the pen name J.K. Gibson-Graham (2006) offer important insights on thinking past capitalism. They define alternatives as "practices, performances, systems, structures, policies, processes, technologies, and concepts/frameworks, practiced or proposed/propagated by any collective or individual, communities, social enterprises, etc. that usurp, challenge the capitalist mainstream and that reflect a diversity of exchange relations, social networks, forms of collective action and human experiences in different places and regions" (Temper et al. 2018: 12).

The solutions and alternatives can be practised on different scales. For example, at the individual level, we can change our lifestyles, livelihoods and home lives. We can take action by growing food on the balcony or buying food from local farmers. This scale of change is easiest to enact but does not have huge impact against a capitalist system. To render these transformative they need to be scaled up from individual- and community-level solutions to regional, national or systems level solutions, and experimenting with ways to do this can have powerful impact.

Solutions can also be enacted in different social spheres or dimensions. The most common dimension conjured up in conversations about climate change is around technological solutions, such as alternative energy systems. But it's clear to many that technical solutions are important but just the tip of the iceberg of what is needed. There is need for creating alternative governance structures and institutions whereby collective decisions are deliberated and made, and through which we care for ourselves and each other. "We need different institutions; you'd have a huge change if that occurred" (Int#34 Anishinaabe/Ojibway). We need alternative worldviews, ways to live, ways to govern ourselves and ways of relating that reflect the world we want to live in.

Aligned closely with Gibson-Graham's theory of change, which focuses on building alternatives, scholars of solidarity economy, such as Ethan Miller, emphasize that "the economy" is a social construction. He points out that there are no "economic laws," and as such there is nothing inevitable about capitalist economic relations: "We make our economies, and therefore we can make them differently" (2012: 12). For these and other anti-capitalist thinkers engaging with the solidarity economy movement, social transformation does not hinge on revolution, nor does it wait for capitalism to "hit the fan." "We can begin here and now, in our communities and regions, connected with others around the world, to construct and strengthen institutions and relationships of economic solidarity" (Miller 2010: 26). This process becomes transformative "through the accretion and interaction of small changes in place" as a movement of movements grows, connecting people and alternatives across different places and circumstances; "this is one way that (counter-)hegemony is enacted" (Gibson-Graham 2006: 196).

Scholars of transformation echo this call for both dismantling the old and creating the new. There is a need to navigate through phases of disruption, intentional dismantling or unintentional collapse of the old systems, ideas and structures. But we also need to be creating and propagating new systems, ideas and structures (Loorbach 2014). Seizing the transformative opportunities that open up when economic or other kinds of crisis happen requires that well developed, innovative alternatives must be available. This can help the system "tip" in favourable directions (Westley 2011).

Movements can, and many do, prefigure change, living now the values, relations and structures of the worlds they are working to create. They aim to "render the system redundant by withdrawing energy from its structures" (Day 2005: 124). Providing — food, transport, exchange, housing, energy and more — for ourselves and our communities can reduce our dependence on the state and its services. The colonial state maintains significant legitimacy and control by providing essential services for citizens. By relearning the skills to provide for ourselves, to make decisions together and govern ourselves, we build towards the world we want and we reduce our dependence on the state. This allows us more space from which to resist; it is easier to oppose and dismantle something when there are other systems to move towards.

A problem faced by resistance movements when they speak, for example, about "smashing the state" or "taking down capitalism" is that the government provides important social services, so many people are what MacKay refers to as "rationally averse" to destroying the current social order. "To overcome this reluctance, we have to believe that the movement seeking to overthrow the oligarchic power structure is more legitimate and a better guardian of moral community than the oligarchs" (MacKay 2017: 205). This means having the alternatives to offer people. Movements that could offer good jobs, affordable housing and healthy food would be powerful indeed.

Developing and promoting solutions and viable alternatives can build legitimacy for counter-hegemonic movements, but importantly, can also help take care of people's basic needs until more just systems and structures can be put in place. One activist argued that a crucial aspect of activism is helping provide for the basic needs of communities, ensuring their survival until a more just society is brought about. She told me: "I draw upon lessons from the Black Panthers. They had a saying, 'survival pending revolution.' They had breakfast clubs … and provided other community services … knowing that having their community survive was incredibly important" (Int#32). As one Indigenous leader told me: "Change in Canadian culture has to take place. It's not going to happen overnight. It's going to take a long time. But it is achievable. In the meantime, we do the best we can to survive until that is reached" (Int#9 Kanien'kehá:ka). In a society where many people's basic needs are not being met, helping those communities survive and be well is crucial work.

By focusing on the solutions, social movements can support communities on the front lines of extractive developments identify and build viable alternatives to the jobs and revenues on offer from extractive industries. It is a momentous challenge for communities facing immense poverty crises to turn down the revenue brought by polluting industry. Movement and community efforts to support the creation of alternative sources of jobs and revenue in front-line communities can be a very high leverage strategy for bringing radical change — we resist by enacting solutions. "Maybe [change] comes down to those sparks where people can say, we don't need the fracking, we don't need the pipelines. Because in actual fact, we've got lots of other stuff going on already. We don't need to sign up for that" (Int#2). And indeed, many of the beautiful alternatives being cultivated in Canada are on Indigenous territories, particularly at blockades, forged as both resistance to colonialism and resurgence of Indigenous practices, protocols and ways of life.

Resurgence of Indigenous ways of living with these lands and waters is happening on Indigenous lands across Turtle Island. Building Indigenous alternatives at blockades and occupations is, according to many people

I spoke with, the most powerful and promising force for radical change in Canada. The Unist'ot'en camp as well as the Tiny House Warriors (a group of Secwepemc women who are building small solarized homes, on wheels, along the path of the Trans Mountain pipeline in their territory) are good examples of interventions involving many approaches to change — resisting destruction, enacting the solutions and providing for the basic needs of communities: "Our idea is to start occupying our land. It's not just blocking the pipelines" (E#21).

Through the resurgence of "Indigenous political-economic alternatives to the intensification of capitalism on and within our territories" (Coulthard 2014: 171), Indigenous Peoples can "disentangle themselves from the oppressive control of occupying state governments" (Simpson 2008: 15). "Transforming ourselves, our communities and our nations is ultimately the first step in transforming our relationship with the state" (Simpson 2011: 17). It has the "potential to wonderfully transform Indigenous life on Turtle Island" (Simpson 2017: 49).

Central to many activists' theories of change is the transformative power of self-determination of Indigenous Nations. This is the collective power generated through community and culture and through connection to land. The theory of change here is that when Indigenous Peoples enact their own governance systems, lifeways and culture, colonial structures begin to lose power: "We have to [regain] control of ourselves, and we have to be able to form our own governments ... have our own decision-making process and our own leadership" (Int#16 Kanien'kehá:ka).

In my conversations with land defenders and activists, several people brought up problems and challenges associated with this solutions/alternatives dimension of change. One key point that several people mentioned is that the *No* is easier to galvanize around than the *Yes* (Int#34 Anishinaabe/ Ojibway). It may be easy to get wide agreement across movements that we are against the expansion of the tar sands; however, "we all have different visions of what the Yes means. It's hard to get agreement on what that actually is" (Int#35). While some activists argued that a focus on solutions is an important way to bring new people to the movement, being explicit about the alternative futures that we're fighting for can bring to the surface some of the tensions underlying our coalitions. For example, environmental groups and First Nations may join forces to stop a pipeline, but once the pipeline has been stopped the environmental group's goal has been met. Yet settler colonial capitalism and deep racial inequality are still firmly in place. It could be that our movements, in part, are more focused on resisting what we don't want than focusing on enacting what we do want, because there are real tensions raised when we turn our gaze to the different futures we seek.

Another challenge of the solutions approach to change is what one activist referred to as the "implementation bottleneck." "There are so many solutions and they are ready to go right now. The hard part is we are realizing that we are bottlenecked" (Int#37). For example, resources and capacity necessary to scale up community-based energy and housing projects are lacking. This is the kind of problem that could so easily be remedied by government funding, which is challenging to access through bottom-up, grassroots processes. One Indigenous activist emphasized that people-power generated by settler social movements should be used to "funnel money and support to the front lines" (Int#12 Anishinaabe).

This can be important work, but a lot of the work of building alternative housing and food systems, for example, takes place far from sites of community struggle, disconnected from other movements. This is a problem because alternatives on their own are not transformative social change. We must ask how those who are forging independence from the state (e.g., "back-to-the-landers") can remain connected to movements, to other fronts of the struggle (Int#17), actively supporting the resistance work on the front lines. And importantly, settlers need to ask whose land we are enacting the solutions on.

Most people who emphasized the need for solutions did so as part of a wider theory of change. As with many of the other approaches to change, making change through solutions is necessary but insufficient on its own. Many emphasized that the intersection of resistance work and building solutions can be powerful: "There's a real exciting overlap to me which is putting solutions in the pathway of the problem. Like the Tiny House Warriors, like putting solar panels along the XL route etc. ... to inspire people to do what's possible" (Int#39).

Like all the other forces and factors of change explored in this chapter, how we take action is hugely important but not enough on its own. What matters most is how all the different approaches raised in this chapter are brought together, how all of us working on different fronts of change, mounting diverse strategies, come together and combine forces to transform our systems. That brings us to the final overarching theme in the movements' theories of change.

HOW WE RELATE

Relationships were a recurring theme in these conversations with activists and land defenders about how change happens. As one person put it, "regardless of what kind of change you want to make, it all boils down to relationships" (Int#37). Another told me that his "theory of change is that relationship is the basis of everything, and then you go from there" (Int#16).

It is clear that there are many factors and forces involved in the complex process of large-scale social change, and none of us can engage in all of them, or do all of them well. That said, it is important to think about how all the different kinds of approaches to change and movement efforts fit together. How do we plan them so they are mutually supporting? It's not enough that we're all doing different things, we need to think about how all these different projects, campaigns and initiatives relate to each other and "think about new ways to bring it all together and leverage it.... How do we connect the dots ... maximizing the impact of what everyone is doing?" (S#37). Many people's theories of change emphasized that change happens when different groups and communities coordinate together; that building power happens when movement groups work well together, sharing resources and information.

Rather than seeking the next new thing, we should look around at what exists now, and in order to "reinforce what each other is doing ... it would be helpful to develop a shared roadmap so that we're all heading in the same direction" (S#37). What we need is to devise ways to synergize our efforts more, without increasing administration, bureaucracy and meeting commitments. What might that look like? It has to begin with actually knowing each other and understanding the work we each do. We must build relationships within and across movements, across sectors, across borders.

Change happens by "creating solidarity between social movements" (Int#24) and "doing cross-sectoral organizing ... bringing these groups together. That is powerful" (S#37). This can be especially powerful when relations of solidarity are built between unlikely allies who aren't as yet working together, such as public sector unions and First Nations or the environmental movement and the Movement for Black Lives. Building these relationships can "create cross-opportunities and forge new ways of looking at the issues" (S#37). As we organize together, we build relationships. "You can't really quantify it, the relationship building that goes on. And the shared understanding and the trust that builds up over time. That translates into better decisions" (Int#33).

As one white settler activist explained, to make change "we need to work as closely as possible with First Nations, people of colour, artists and culture creators and Elders, help overcome divisions, build solidarity and energize people to persevere through a long, difficult struggle" (S#18). Fostering relations between the diverse justice movements — "reproductive justice, water justice, migrant justice, environmental justice and climate justice" (E#21) — is important. Furthermore, we need cross-border strategies: "We need to connect the struggles across borders" (E#18). "I think probably one of the things that we need to be most mindful of is expanding our allies ... strengthening our allyship among much broader political, personal, ethnic differences will allow for this movement to expand exponentially, not linearly. It's the multiplier effect" (Int#23). "Together, we are all stronger" (E#18).

Activists and land defenders spoke to me in many different ways about the need to build more and better relationships. Some spoke of the need to build on existing networks and developing stronger relations of mutual support among different front-line Indigenous communities: "Bringing all the front lines together is critical for the success of all the front lines" (E#12). "Much power would be built by creating a network of mutual support among Indigenous communities all facing similar threats. This could help them share information, strategies, resources and infrastructure" (E#14).

People also spoke about the need to build better relationships between activists and communities. Systems change requires that activists work well with communities on the ground, such as those facing pressure from extractive industries. But these relations are not always navigated with care. "We have to meet communities where they are at. We can't go into a community and talk about climate change and talk about fossil fuels as if these communities are the bad guys.... We are in this crisis and as a result of pushing so hard, we end up pushing people into standing more firmly rooted in their opinions" (Int#37).

Industries, including the fossil fuel industry, are also aware of the importance of relationships and, increasingly, they too have been using relationship-based strategy: "The LNG [liquified natural gas] industry came in super early and they started sitting down with hereditary chiefs and band councils, and they started creating relationships. So, it is relationships that creates change in either direction. Whether we agree with it or not, it is relationships" (Int#37).

Several people's theories of change pivot on people relating to others who are different from themselves: "We change the world by talking to people who don't think like we do" (E#10). "At a strategic level … people need to meet people who are different from them … and talk about things that are hard. And that's the foundation of everything" (Int#28). Activists can help create spaces where we can "have these conversations to break down barriers … that transcend political allegiances" (S#37). We need to connect across difference:

> Mostly people want to feel like you understand what they're saying. And even if you don't agree with them, if they feel that you've understood their perspective or where they're coming from, it makes a world of difference … that feels like the heart of the transformation, that's transformative capacity there … the heart of what makes a good relationship. (Int#37)

In addition, several people emphasized how important it is to build relationships in person: "What we have to do is have lots of conversations with a lot of people. And not just on Twitter. We have to talk to *people*.… Bringing people together face to face is crucial for building relationships. There's a lack of civil space where we can talk. We do it online and that's dangerous" (S#37).

Underlying all these different calls for building better relationships within and across movements is the shared conviction that if we can work together more, and in better ways, we can be more powerful in pushing for systems change. And indeed, according to academic theories of change, one of the various ways power functions is through relations. Intersectional feminist scholars argue that power is inherently relational (Collins and Bilge 2016), and Foucault also conceived of power in relational terms, moving through networks, flowing or shared between institutions or people (1971). Temper et al. refer to this as *relational* or *associative* power (2018; see also Long and Van Der Ploeg 1989).

Rowlands (1997) provides another framework for understanding different forms of power. To her, there are four forms: power within, power with, power to and power over. Where *power over* is the power of domination and hierarchy, *power with* — the power of collective action, of organizing together, of acting in solidarity with others — is how people combine individual power such that they begin to grow their shared capacity to influence social outcomes (*power to*) and to resist and oppose *power over*. Building people-power through relations and collaborations is how we build counter-force to the hegemony of those who are working hard to maintain the destructive and unjust status quo.

Building counter-hegemonic force requires overcoming the divisions and fragmentations of the left, created by divide-and-rule politics of the elite, and forging strong alliance politics of the left (Harvey 2014). Unity across struggles can be forged, forming coalitions that make possible "a coherent, counter-hegemonic alternative to the dominant order" (Epstein 1990: 51). Despite this need for alliance, in Canada movements remain fragmented, rendering us less able to build counter-hegemony powerful enough to bring about social transformation (Carroll and Sarker 2016). To overcome this, we need to be asking ourselves how forces for transformation can be strengthened through "widening and deepening relations of solidarity across differences" (Carroll and Sarker 2016: 47).

One answer to this question links back to the discussion earlier in the chapter about systems analysis; understanding the systems of colonialism, capitalism, patriarchy and white supremacy and how they intersect helps us see how different struggles are connected. Understanding how different struggles connect can help us to forge relations between movements and to devise strategies and solutions that address as many forms of oppression as possible, leaving no one behind. Intersectional analysis and organizing is the promise of a movement of movements capable of creating a counter-hegemonic, transformative force. Intersectionality is an analytical and strategic tool developed by women of colour in social movements in the 60s and 70s and developed further by Black feminist scholars in the 90s (Collins and Bilge 2016). It analyzes the ways class, race and gender (and other systems of domination) relate and intersect, as well as how to forge links between these oft-disparate movements.

Indigenous resurgence scholars Simpson and Coulthard also emphasize the power in aligning across different anti-oppressive movements. Simpson writes of the need for Indigenous movements to oppose not only "dispossession and settler colonialism" but also "the violence of capitalism, hetero-patriarchy, white supremacy, and anti-Blackness that maintains them" (2017: 10). Coulthard argues that any strategy for decolonization must "account for the multifarious ways in which capitalism, patriarchy, white supremacy, and the totalizing character of state power interact with one another to form the constellation of power relations that sustain colonial patterns of behaviour, structures, and relationships" (2014: 14).

Simpson envisions networks of communities resisting as "constellations of co-resistance" (2017: 218). Through these reciprocal relations she sees the promise for radical change. She writes: "When the constellations work in international relationship to other constellations ... movements are built, particularly if constellations of co-resistance create mechanisms for communication, strategic movements, accountability to each other, and shared decision-making practices" (2017: 218).

In settler scholarship on change, relational power is generally framed around building social power through networks of humans. Indigenous scholarship on change, on the other hand, frames relationships in less human-centred ways, conceptualizing powerful networks of relations with non-human others, with waters and with the land itself. In my discussions with activists and land defenders, relationship with the land was understood to be deeply important: "The connection to the land will be the answer to climate change" (E#18). Connection to land and to water then connects communities and movements and brings change. "This water that we're fighting to protect, all across from the east to the west, is what connects us. And the impacts that these destructive projects are having on our water also connect us. That's how we're going to create a big strong force — those connections" (E#17).

"Now, then and forever" Alfred states, "the fight is for the land" (2008: 10). Land is central to Indigenous struggles and to Indigenous theories of change. Coulthard describes land as "a mode of reciprocal relationship" that can teach us about "living our lives in relation to one another and our surroundings in a respectful, non-dominating and nonexploitative way" (2014: 60). Relationship with land, what Coulthard calls grounded normativity, provides crucial guidance about the goals and strategies for change (2014). Stories, ceremonies and "the land itself are procedures for solving the problems of life." In this way, "theory is generated from the ground up." In trying to sever Indigenous Peoples' connection to land, "colonialism has strangled our grounded normativity." Reconnecting to land-based knowledge, through resurgence, is the mechanism for their continuance as Indigenous Peoples (Simpson 2017: 23–25).

A final point made in these conversations about relationships is that the ways power inequities continue to play out in movement spaces are hindering our capacity to form strong links and collaborations within and across movements. In this way, forging just relations is central to building powerful movements for driving systems change. Relationships between Indigenous Peoples and settlers are critical for transforming Canada. These are important but deeply damaged relationships. Settlers have a way of carrying power and colonial relations into their collaborations with Indigenous Peoples. Alfred writes that "settlers have very serious difficulties thinking thoughts that are outside foundational premises of their imperial cultural backgrounds. Very few of them can overcome the ingrained patterns of authority and dominance that are the heritage of empire and colonialism" (2008: 10). The power inequalities that exist in movements have implications for their effectiveness in bringing about change (Carroll and Sarker 2016). Some environmentalists have been working to build these relationships over the last few decades of anti-logging and now anti-pipeline activism, but have often done so in ways that reinforce rather than heal the oppressive dynamic and mistrust that exists (see Clapperton 2019; Stainsby and Jay 2009).

We need to do better.

Andrea Smith envisions alliances built not just on a sense of shared victimization but on a deep understanding of the ways we are complicit in the victimization of others: "We would check our aspirations against the aspirations of other communities to ensure that our model of liberation does not become a model of oppression for others." She writes that this requires "vigilance in reflecting about how we internalize and replicate oppressive logics in our organizing practices" (2016: 69).

We cannot have strong relationships with people we have power over, or who have power over us. As such, we must undo relations of domination in our movement spaces. Where colonialism and capitalism have taught relations based on competition and domination/subordination, movements and communities must learn just relations:

> It's about painting the vision that this "other world" is not only possible, but we're going to do it together. To do that, you need to be fucking solid in yourself, because so much of what we see, the left exploding on itself — eating each other alive because we're so quick to judge and reproduce these [relations of domination] and not examine where we fuck up.... The solutions are in our relations with each other, as we learn to be better with each other. (Int#10)

Solid, just relations within and across movements create a foundation that can help strengthen the other dimensions of systems change discussed throughout this chapter. The strength of the relationships we build affects our ability to mobilize, to coordinate strategies, to change the story, to build people-power. All these are done much more powerfully and sustainably within strong relationships. As one person put it, our work as activists is "drawing people into living in a way that puts dignity in all their relationships with all ... with self, others, planet" (S#37).

THINKING ACROSS THE
DIFFERENT DIMENSIONS OF CHANGE

This chapter has explored the many ways activists in these movements understand and articulate their own theories of change. The overarching themes of context, how we understand and what we value, how we take action and how we relate provide a framework for seeing the many factors and forces that shape how change happens. This collaborative theorizing teaches us that systems change is a complex matter, and that as such we need to complexify our approaches to activism and nuance our theories of change.

We need to be attentive to context and timing as events and crises change what is possible. We need to help shift understanding and values and engage with this through personal transformation, education, changing the story and systemic analysis. But we must do all this in ways that amplify the voices of those most impacted and follow Indigenous leadership. All of this attention to context, understandings and values is vitally important, but it is not sufficient on its own. It's important that we take action and enact change, and it's important how that's done. We build power though collective action and then direct that people-power to influencing policy change and election outcomes, and to confronting and dismantling power. We use that people-power for innovating, promoting and living the solutions and alternatives — and become the world we want. All that is absolutely critical for transforming Canada. But if groups and individuals do things in isolation from each other and in ways that are in conflict, making each other's goals harder to achieve, our efforts are rendered less transformative. So how we relate is central. We need to coordinate efforts, sharing resources and information in order to strengthen the overall force for change we can build together. To do this, we need to build strong relations of solidarity within and across movements. But this won't happen if we allow relations of domination, the legacies of colonialism, racism, classism and sexism that we carry with us into movement spaces to continue to shape the ways we organize. We must unlearn relations of domination.

As has been pointed out again and again, not any one of the specific approaches to change (direct action, changing the story, coordination, etc.) is itself enough. Systems change is forged through a convergence of many or all of the approaches chronicled above. Systems change requires "a lot of people and groups doing a lot of different things" (S#24). As one person said, change is "part education, part disruption, part interrupting the colonial narrative, raising consciousness, providing platforms" (Int#36). Another said that it's

> through convergence of tactics and strategies that we build political power at different levels (grassroots, civil society, sometimes government) that slowly evolve social norms and/or that create pressure for change from different angles. It sometimes relies on fortuitous timing and combination of events. It is always grounded in long-term, patient, under-thanked/-paid/-recognized work. (S#32)

It's the ways that different forces for change build on each other that renders them transformative. There are many examples of this and many lines of synergy we can draw between different themes presented in this chapter. Developing a shared *systemic analysis* helps activists know where to aim the firehose of people-power. Once they've *built power through collective action*, they can then most effectively target the root causes of the climate and inequality crises. *Changing the story* about what is wrong and what can be done about it, while also *offering real viable alternatives,* can bring significantly more people to the movements, increasing our ability to *build power from below*. When *crises* occur, people are more open to hearing *new stories* and *practising alternatives*. These new stories and alternatives can be most transformative if they *amplify the voices of those most impacted* and follow *Indigenous leadership. Confronting power* through *direct action* can help create *crises* that make space for *alternatives* and new *relations* to take hold. *Undoing relations of domination* in our movements makes *building the links between different movements* much more possible, as more people find shared movement spaces where they feel valued and welcome. With this movement of movements, we can build unprecedented *power from below through collective action*. There are endless examples of how all the different factors and forces for change work together synergistically. Thinking about how they work together informs our collaborations and can help us imagine new ways of combining strategies and tactics to increase impact.

That said, there are also important ways that these different factors and forces for change are in tension. In certain ways and under certain circumstances they can work against each other. It's important to understand these dynamics as well, if we hope to do our work in ways that do not hinder the efforts of others.

In bringing all these many theories of change together we access a wider view than each of us may hold, but the wider view also exposes tensions, conflicts and debates that exist in these movements. It's important to *develop strong relations* and *coordinate* within and across movements, but working in coalition and having to make decisions with large groups of people can hinder our ability to respond as *context* changes and as *events* occur that open up windows of opportunity. *Engaging with the electoral system* can be extremely useful in winning certain policy and legislative changes, but can also serve to reinforce the state and thus be counterproductive to *confronting and dismantling power*. *Direct action and civil disobedience* are powerful tactics that have won significant changes for social movements through history, but these confrontational approaches can make it harder to win the support of the masses of people you may need to win an election, and thus counter-productive to strategies centred on *engaging with the electoral system.* These debates and tensions over conflicting theories of change are alive in the movements and among the activists I spoke with. These tensions are discussed further in Chapters 6 and 7.

This wide diversity in theories of and approaches to change stems in part from the fact that the people converging to resist oil and gas pipelines come from many kinds of backgrounds. From anarchist punks to popular educators to policy analysts to Indigenous land defenders, we all bring with us different values, worldviews, social change goals and theories of how to get there. The urgency of the climate crisis and the ongoing push to expand the tar sands have been a catalyst for many different people and movements coming together:

> I think that the real opportunity we have with the climate movement is to organize behind one cause, and there's many solutions. The real beauty of all of this is that it's such an urgent issue that no one action is enough, and all actions are necessary, and so whatever people can bring to this movement.... We need everybody. (Int#23)

"We need people inside and people on the outside. We need people at the grassroots and people at the top" (S#37). We need radical change and incremental steps for getting there: "The fact is that different parts of the movement need each other and work together whether they actually work with each other or not" (Int#19). So, "we need movement theory that overarches and sees where people are at ... where there's a role for everyone" (Int#32).

Finding ways to bring the diverse efforts for change into one "heterogenic front" (Int#19) is promising. But at the same time, there are "some ways that things are irreconcilable. Theories of change are different, politics are different. Trying to make everyone work together all the time ends up watering down messages until they are palatable for everybody" (Int#19). Indeed, we need to find ways to work across difference that neither ignore debate nor erase difference. And we need to work with the diversity that exists in ways that are synergistic and don't undermine each other's efforts. Indeed, "how do we make sure that what we do is in solidarity with the others' tactics?" (Int#32).

There is much to be done — and on a very pressing climate deadline. The overarching theory of change that emerges from these conversations is that we'll transform this country as we become better at thinking and working across difference. There is no one right way of making change. We are all necessary but individually insufficient to bringing change. "I think that it's really important that we understand that one tactic isn't going to do it (E#16). "Diversity is what makes us strong — in nature and in the movement" (S#27). We need to develop and embrace sophisticated and multi-pronged approaches to making change. And to find ways to do that together, without erasing the important differences between us.

One person I interviewed told me that "if anyone knew what the answer was on how to make change, things would be very different … no one has the answers" (Int#11). I close this chapter by proposing that, as individuals, we indeed may not have the answer to *how change happens,* but together, I believe that we do.

CHAPTER 6

TAKING STOCK OF WHERE WE ARE AT AND WHAT STANDS IN OUR WAY

The people who control the money want to keep the system as it is. — Int#10

What would be most threatening to the corporate political structure in Canada is if all the activists got together.... But we are going the opposite way. — Int#14

Thus far in this book, we've explored how activists and land defenders in these movements understand the climate and inequality crises and how they envision the socially just and ecologically viable future that they're working hard to create. We've also delved into the understandings in the movements about how large-scale systems change happens or can happen. Now we move to discussing where we are at: what's working and what's not working in the movements we are part of, and the barriers, the obstacles, that stand in our way.

WHAT'S WORKING AND WHAT'S NOT WORKING IN OUR MOVEMENTS

What's Working

Encouragingly, there are many things that activists report as going well in their movements. Some people feel that groups and organization across the country are working together more and "building networks that extend beyond the [usual] people that show up" (Int#5). Pipeline fights have connected people "from coast to coast ... mobilizing on so many fronts" (Int#27). And the environmental movement is learning to think and organize more intersectionally, which is helping create the capacity to build coalitions across diverse movements.

There is also a sense that "people are understanding the issues more and more" (Int#29); more people are starting to understand climate change, racism, colonialism and other issues and the ways these are connected. That is a "huge shift in Canada" (Int#32). The climate movement has been getting better at centring Indigenous Peoples and their struggles and voices: "Making space for Indigenous leadership has been a cultural shift. It's not perfect but the space of Indigenous leadership is like wildly different [than it was in the past]" (TT#3). Fights like the one against the Trans Mountain pipeline have given NGOs the opportunity to practise taking leadership from front-line Indigenous communities. There are also more women and people of colour in leadership positions in the movements. "There's a real willingness to do things differently ... being intentional about who is speaking and when. And about who needs to step back to make that space" (TT#3).

Movements are changing in other ways too. Direct action, for example, is becoming more widely accepted "as an effective way of attacking extraction projects" (Int#37). Indeed, "direct action and land defence have been working" (Int#14). It is no longer something that "just radicals do" (Int#30). Divestment campaigns are also seeing enormous success, spreading across Canada and the world and offering a real challenge to fossil fuels. Several people mentioned that the movements' collective capacity for strategic thinking as well as our ability to navigate the challenges of working together are slowly improving. We're seeing a willingness to really reflect on what's working and what's not: "In some of the movements people are like, 'we're losing, we're failing.' It's a wake-up call. We need to reassess and that has been liberating. There's this big external crisis, so people are willing to talk about what can change" (Int#28). Honest reflection on what's not working creates space for important discussions about changing our approaches to activism.

What's Not Working

People spoke to me about what is not working in the movements they are part of. One activist described how the crises we seek to address are accelerating, but our tactics may not be keeping up:

> Everything is challenging right now. It seems like there is a lot of backlash of the gains that have been made in the last fifty years on most fronts, from the initiatives for climate change in the US, to equality between races and sexes worldwide. Violence against women is increasing. Poverty is increasing. The divide between rich and poor is greater. Environmental degradation is accelerating. [We need to] start with a realistic assessment that we are not winning, [old tactics] may not be adequate to the challenges that we face now. (Int#14)

This same activist went on to explain: "We're not losing because our analysis is wrong. We're not losing because our politics are not moral enough. We are losing because we are overpowered" (Int#14). Others agreed that indeed, "the movements just have to get so much bigger" (Int#16). And that this reality of being out-numbered is even more so "if you are an activist of colour. If you are Black or Indigenous you are a minority in a minority" (Int#7 Kanien'kehá ka).

We are not doing well enough in growing our movements: "Groups spend a lot of time talking to their supporters but there's still the 95% of Canadians that don't really know or care and that's a big challenge" (Int#33). "I don't think people know how to build broad-based movements" (Int#36). "There are new allies and we need to absorb them. And that's a particular challenge. We need to bring in and train more people, to help take the pressure off … to avoid burnout" (TT#3).

We need more people, but we also need the right people: "The huge problem with the climate movement is that we're still very Western-centric and very white" (Int#6). There are white settler groups that are not doing well enough in educating themselves about colonialism and Indigenous issues: "There are people with years of doing climate change work and they desperately want to be allies with Indigenous Peoples and have them in their movement but … they don't know the actual history.… It's a real lack of knowledge" (Int#20 Michif Cree). This places an unfair burden on Indigenous Peoples to educate settler activists: "There is a lot of pressure we are under ... it gets really old and tiring to teach successive waves of activists" (Int#7 Kanien'kehá ka).

Others pointed out that the movements are not organized enough and we're using our energies inefficiently, spreading ourselves thin: "Everyone is too busy" (Int#21). When we don't coordinate efforts "the danger is to spread out the energy" (Int#17). "We need to be smarter and more strategic" (Int#14). "Industry and government do a lot of strategic planning. And we're up against that and we're not doing anything to counter that" (Int#38 Mi'kmaw).

The most common answer to the question of what is not working in these movements is that we are fractured and at times we're pushing against each other rather than pulling together in the same direction: "What would be most threatening to the corporate political structure in Canada is if all the activists got together ... if all these groups linked up into one powerful network.... But we are going the opposite way" (Int#14).

Despite all of these challenges and shortcomings, many of the activists found hope in the increasing willingness to come together to acknowledge these issues and imagine how we can make our movements bigger and stronger. "We are in the process of working together, trying to understand each other in our different strategies" (Int#27).

> [In the past] building good interpersonal communication and moving through conflict wasn't something that was valued. Now we're seeing that to be able to do coalition work, we need to be able to work with people who are not the same as us ... we need to be able to work in large, diverse groups. That requires time and ways of communicating that are healthy and that help us to get through differences and conflicts. There is a shift towards valuing this, understanding that we need to work on this, we need to take time for this. But, it's so hard to think like that when shit is hitting the fan. (TT#3)

THE BARRIERS TO DECOLONIZING AND DECARBONIZING CANADA

Closely related to these discussions about what is not working, people also talked about what they see as the biggest barriers to the change they are trying to make. There was a wide variety of answers to this, both external and internal to the movements. External refers to the forces and phenomena that exist outside of the movement spaces, within Canadian society or the world more broadly, and which the movements have limited control over. Internal refers to the dynamics and situations within movement spaces, which activists have more responsibility in shaping. Although the people I spoke with discussed a number of barriers both internal and external, there was slightly more emphasis placed on the internal barriers. We turn first to the external barriers.

External Barriers to Change

With a lack of public will, corporate influence on the political system, the prevalence of false solutions and the ongoing criminalization of anti-pipeline activism, these movements are up against some substantial external barriers. Naming and understanding these obstacles help us confront and overcome them.

The external obstacles to change centre around several key themes: the economic system (capitalism), lack of public will, corporate influence in the political system, the legal system and criminalization of dissent, false solutions and false understandings, lack of alternatives and fear of job loss, and the state. Figure 6-1 shows the relative frequency with which each theme was raised in these conversations.

Figure 6-1: The Number of Times Each External Barrier Was Mentioned

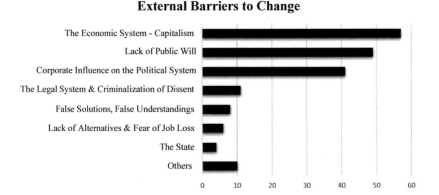

External Barriers to Change

Lack of Public Will

There's a general acknowledgement that our movements are still too small, that the mass public engagement needed to steer Canada to justice and sustainability is just not there. This lack of public will is a significant barrier to the kind of changes we're trying to make.

For some, the lack of public will is rooted in public apathy, the idea that people are informed and yet don't feel compelled to act or that it takes suffering to inspire action and most Canadians are not "suffering enough to make change. They haven't felt it yet" (Int#7 Kanien'kehá ka). Others talked about how facing the realities of crises like climate change "can be paralyzing" (Int#13). "People are not apathetic because they don't care; they're apathetic because they are overwhelmed or scared" (Int#37). Others were more pessimistic. People don't believe that change is possible (S#11), don't believe we have the power to change things (S#19). "People have forgotten that the rights we now have were won through struggle by activists before us" (S#25).

Over the "last fifty years of consumption — of the 'century of the self' — capitalism has done a very good job of getting people to opt out" (Int#11). The lack of public will for change also lies in "the confusion and demoralization that decades of neoliberalism have created" (S#13). People are both disengaged and distracted: "It's hard to make information on complex issues resonate while competing with all of the rest of the internet click-bait" (S#31). Some see the lack of public will to meaningfully address climate and inequality crises as stemming from disconnection from each other and the non-human world (Int#27). This makes it hard for people to feel the urgency and to have empathy for people for whom the situation is urgent. Most of us don't feel directly impacted by climate change or pipeline leaks, nor do we feel connected to the people who are impacted by them (Int#5). This disconnection from each other and from the Earth contributes to "the mass mental health crises in the West and it is also a major inhibitor to movement building" (Int#5).

And many people are busy just trying to get by: "It's tough to ask people to be involved, when they work so hard to support their family and they are tired. It's normal, they have kids, debts" (Int#18). "The pressures of life: you work, come home and barely have time to reflect on your life and your position in society, you're just trying to make it to next month. It's designed to distract you from your bigger connection to this state apparatus and from seeing that we're all enabling these systems to continue" (Int#21).

Expectations around the standard of living was another explanation for the lack of massive public will to transform Canada:

> People have grown up with steadily increasing expectations ... that we can just fly wherever we want.... They are not going to embrace a transition unless it enables them to keep everything and get more. It makes it hard for people to want to attack the problem. People know that they are attacking their own interests. (Int#2)

Indeed, many of the people I spoke to recognized that the security and wellbeing offered by an extractive economy (at least in the short term) — secure jobs, easy access to food, technological innovations — is a significant barrier to gaining mass public support for social transformation. There is a sense that most Canadians believe that their lifestyles will not improve from decolonizing and decarbonizing Canada. One person told me: "The biggest problem is that in the first world we don't have that much to lose. No, I should say that differently — we have a lot to lose — and that is privilege" (Int#30). Most people are unwilling to give that up (S#2, Int#30).

All these many factors — apathy, pessimism, disengagement, disconnection, lack of time and standard of living — work together to limit the public will for systemic change in Canada.

Lack of Alternatives and Fear of Job Loss

Some people spoke about the lack of alternatives to these systems as a substantial barrier: "We lack a coherent economic analysis and plan that could offer an alternative to capitalism" (S#19). One way that the lack of alternatives is playing out on the ground is that "many Indigenous communities across the country have very, very few economic options" (Int#2). For many, the options are to work in extractive industries or to collect social assistance. As one person said, "We really need to come up with a third option" (Int#2).

A perceived lack of alternatives also has implications for fossil-fuel sector workers: "Many workers will support new pipelines because they do not see any viable alternatives to the kinds of jobs and pay levels the pipeline jobs represent" (S#25). There is considerable opposition to both moving away from fossil fuels and respecting Indigenous rights and sovereignty, galvanized by the fear of loss of jobs, loss of revenue and loss of economic growth. This is an understandable fear given that many of the solutions currently on the table are admittedly wholly inadequate for dealing with the crises we face.

Perhaps real, compelling solutions that could transform the economy, provide for people and the planet, undo inequality and offer meaningful work to all would reduce the fear of change. These do not yet exist at anywhere near the scale necessary, largely because the perverse incentives created by capitalism are hindering them from scaling up and out. For example, the profit motive, central to capitalist logics, drives corporations to continue to propose and build projects despite the projects being deeply harmful to people and the planet. And to make matters worse, the dependence on endless economic growth that is also inherent to capitalism drives decision makers to approve and subsidize new oil and gas projects that make no sense at this moment of the mounting climate crisis. These perverse incentives serve to strengthen the status quo and channel resources away from investing in new energy systems and other alternatives.

False Solutions and False Understanding

False solutions refer to market-based solutions such as carbon trading or techno-fixes such as carbon capture and sequestration. They are false because they "reinforce the status quo by supporting the power structure which benefits from the status quo and as such continues to defend it (Charman 2008). Mainstream solutions to the crises in Canada are ineffective at best, and can even be counter-productive, because they strengthen the systems that are driving the crises. For example, market-based instruments like carbon taxation and trading mechanisms constitute the primary strategy Canada is using to reduce GHG emissions in this country. Yet, these instruments reinforce the capitalist ideology that markets can solve all. Climate change should be causing us to deeply question such ideologies, not to look to them for solutions. These kinds of strategies "will not bring the change" (Int#18). Mainstream climate action and reconciliation do not target the root causes that are driving the crises; instead they offer only "band-aid solutions or false solutions that continue to perpetuate the root causes" (Int#32) while not threatening the status quo. The kinds of "half measures being presented are hindering the movement" (Int#39).

To make matters worse, false solutions can also amplify existing social injustices (Sharife and Bond 2009). An important example of this globally can be seen in how carbon trading mechanisms such a REDD+ have pushed Indigenous Peoples off their territories in the name of protecting the carbon sequestered in their forests (Beymer-Farris and Bassett 2012). In Canada, the move to further develop natural gas, which has been marketed as the clean fossil fuel and a solution to climate change, has been a driving motive for the violation of Indigenous rights and the violent repression of Indigenous land defenders and water protectors. We have seen this happen in the conflict over Coastal Gaslink Pipeline in Wet'suwe'ten territory, fracking exploration by Corridor Resources in Mi'kmaw territory of Elsipogtog in New Brunswick, Alton Gas storage caverns in Mi'kmaw territory in Nova Scotia and many others. In this way, "solutions" aimed at decarbonization perpetuate colonization.

Another barrier that activists identified "is that a lot of the discourse [on climate solutions] is so individualized" (Int#30). Transformation on the scale needed requires massive collective action. Mainstream focus on individual action, like driving less and eating less meat, ignores the scale of collective action needed to transform economies and communities.

Activists also note that the solutions being presented mistakenly understand the issues as separate and compartmentalized: "When I think of politicians in power and the platforms they propose, they're still putting 'environment' in a box rather than promoting policies and solutions that understand the interconnections between climate crisis, poverty, inequality and racism" (Int#39). For example, as mentioned above, industry and government alike have been touting natural gas as a climate-friendly fuel. Yet, not only does natural gas contribute to climate change and lock in fossil fuel infrastructure (Howarth 2015), these unwanted projects also violate Indigenous rights, threaten livelihood practices and deeply divide communities. Whereas opposition to oil pipelines has been strong, "a unifying force for the entire coast" (Int#33), LNG has been a hugely divisive conversation: "Families have broken up over whether or not to go with LNG. A couple of the organizations have come close to dissolving over this" (Int#33). False solutions are not only ineffective, they divide communities and organizations. "This idea of we can have economic growth *and* save the environment — that's not the vision of the world I want to see. Economic growth forever is not sustainable" (Int#13). Not only will the false solutions offered by capitalism not work, they are wasting precious time and diverting people's energies (Int#36).

It's not just false solutions that are barriers to transforming Canada; it's also false understandings — a lack of accurate and sufficient understanding of the problems. There is a lack of education on "the dangers of climate change" (S#6) and a "lack of knowledge about the realities of renewable energies. [This allows] fossil fuel companies to rig the tenders or laws to promote gas and disseminate false information" (S#15). There is also a huge deficit in understanding about Indigenous issues: "There is a population that is born in Canada, and people who migrated here, who are never introduced to anything to do with Indigenous rights. Climate and colonization are major issues here, and growing issues in this country, yet most people know so little" (Int#26). "The biggest barrier ... is ignorance of the legitimate problems we face, the scale of these issues and how they intersect. This translates into apathy" (S#31).

This barrier, this lack of understanding, is reinforced by "human arrogance. It hinders our ability to learn. We need humility" (Int#12 Anishinaabe). Ignorance and false understanding are also made worse through privilege: "I think we've been very sheltered in Canada. [Many] white people are extremely sheltered ... people who are less privileged, they have a more realistic assessment of the world politics" (Int#14). "There's such a self-satisfied, self-deluded narrative in Canada. There's so much colonial, racist, sexist baggage to unlearn and undo" (S#32).

The lack of understanding is further exacerbated by the media and corporate influence over the media (S#9, S#24, S#22): "The media trains people how to think" (Int#25 Dene). "Media colours our view ... it's an arm of neoliberalism ... they propagate racism and fear of each other. When you cut the links between people, you can more easily manipulate them. When people are scared, there will be less solidarity and less beautiful things will be created" (Int#27). "Our whole political system is challenging right now, and the information, and the fake news, and the era of Facebook running political campaigns makes it tougher" (Int#32).

The Economic System — Capitalism

The most common external barrier discussed in these conversations is how the economic system — captive to capitalist logic — is actively working against ecological sustainability and social justice. "The domination of society by capitalist relations of production (interlocked with sexism, racism, settler colonialism, etc.) is the fundamental barrier to changing society" (S#3). Chapter 3 made clear that capitalism is driving the climate and inequality crises, but it also acts to hinder our efforts to meaningfully address those crises: "We're never going to have climate justice or any sort of sustainable energy system under capitalism. Capitalism is a system that necessitates infinite growth. Globalization completely locks that in" (Int#20 Michif Cree). That system "is not there to serve us. It's there to serve a few. People are sacrificed all the time to state and corporations" (Int#14). Additionally, "the way that capitalism has structured our social systems and lives is not conducive to mass mobilization. People are working beyond their limits, working too hard at jobs doing work they don't like because they have to" (Int#18).

Under capitalism, "corporations and other special-interest lobby groups wield an anti-democratic influence over our political system" (Int#11). This locks in counter-productive incentive structures (Int#33). For example, industries that need to be quickly phased out are instead given huge subsidies (Int#2). Under globalized capitalism, despite the fact that oil and gas pipelines make less and less sense, trade deals create the imperative to build them anyway:

> We've reached capacity, we don't need new pipelines. Industry is still pushing for them because they have contracts signed to ship the oil. Whatever happens, the shippers still have to pay the pipeline companies. The companies really don't care about how much oil is produced, they want to build the pipelines, so they can get the money. (Int#8)

These perverse forces and incentives created through globalized capitalism make it very hard to quickly transition away from the fossil fuel industry.

Under capitalism, only false solutions are on the table: "There is far too much emphasis on carbon pricing as a panacea. For some, all you need to do is get the prices right and it will take care of itself.... This view fails to see that markets are out of control" (Int#35). There is a "lack of analysis on how to diversify the economy and identify competitive advantages and economic opportunities outside of fossil fuel development and plan/ prepare for the transition away from fossil fuels" (S#26).

This survey respondent went on to explain that politicians and the oil industry are promoting a low carbon economy and decarbonization as possible without production declines. Federal and Alberta governments are approving new fossil fuel projects, locking in greater dependence on fossil fuels, while claiming this is in line with the Paris Agreement. The pervasive influence of capitalism on national and global decision making means that

> climate policy is currently completely disassociated from project approvals and until we recognize our responsibility not only for production emissions but also for the development of fossil fuel supply, we will continue to extract more carbon than the world can safely burn. We need our national interest determinations and economic analysis of projects to be consistent with a global market scenario of staying well below 2 degrees. (S#26)

By assessing projects according to business-as-usual market demand, which capitalism promotes, governments are approving projects that will lead to disastrous climate impacts (S#26).

Countries like Canada and Norway are trying to reduce domestic emissions while simultaneously developing fossil fuels, because capitalist logic promotes the idea that everyone has the right to compete in the world market. "We need countries like Canada to acknowledge that this pathway is leading to an unsafe climate and that the market-driven changes — demand-side policy and carbon pricing, etc. — will not happen quickly enough to constrain supply" (S#26).

In the examples above, we see the capitalist logic creating problematic incentives on the macro level, but it does so on the micro level as well. For example, the financial and credit systems also act as barriers to change. One organizer in BC told me a story of an Indigenous community that was forced to sign an LNG pipeline benefit agreement because their preferred plan, which was to develop a geothermal energy business, failed when they could not secure a start-up loan from a bank: "They were refused because reserve land, held in common, cannot be considered as collateral assets that can be seized if they do not repay the loan" (Int#68). The financial system of growth and debt drives the climate and inequality crises while hindering just and sustainable solutions from taking root.

Capitalism promotes competition among people and as such can be divisive to communities and movements trying to collaborate towards change: "There's only so much money to go around and we fight over the same pools of money to keep ourselves going, and that just creates a lot of bickering" (Int#31). "You know what's not effective? Bringing people together around money. There's an external barrier!" (Int#28). Under capitalism, funders are generally only willing to fund activism that doesn't threaten elite vested interests: "Funders are still funding a failed strategy" (Int#4). Organizations that are funded by foundations and government are unlikely to denounce capitalism and are unlikely to devise strategies that tackle root causes because "there can be threats to that money" (Int#19).

The economic system, dominated by capitalism, acts as a barrier to change by insisting on continuous growth over justice and sustainability, creating perverse incentives, locking in fossil-fuel dependence through market logics and global trade deals, offering only false solutions, promoting competition among people when we need to be working together and funding only the kind of social change that doesn't threaten the status quo.

Corporate Influence on the Political System

The deeply problematic influence of capitalism on political decision making is another key dynamic people raised when I asked about barriers to making transformative change in Canada. The people I spoke with described it in various ways: "The most significant barrier is the power of big business" (S#20) and "powerful fossil fuel lobbies" (S#8), and they noted that the current capitalist system and the anti-democratic influence that corporate lobby groups have over our political system is at the root of what's holding the country back from transitioning away from fossil fuels (S#21, S#27). This phenomenon exists across the political spectrum as "both Liberals and Conservatives are greatly influenced by big business especially oil and mining interests" (S#6). And it is not just corporate influence over political decision making that stands in our way; corporations also wield massive "control of media" (S#24).

One activist explained that "the most significant barrier is that there is not the political will for the kinds of transformative changes that climate change and social justice require. Decades of neoliberal rule have empowered the wealthy and corporate class. This is the force we are up against" (S#10). This hinders transformation in that "the powers that be are profiting too much from the status quo" (S#34), or to put it differently, "the people who control the money want to keep the system as it is" (Int#10). As such there are "extreme political and economic forces" working to maintain the status quo and they have disproportionate access "to loudly and repeatedly have their views and ideas aired in the public realm" (S#22). To put it bluntly, "the elite [are] fighting dirty to hang on to their power and ill-gotten wealth," and that is a massive barrier to decolonizing and decarbonizing Canada (S#18):

> These entrenched financial interests are incompatible with decarbonizing our society. Some of the largest companies in the world, their entire business model is made on the combustion and processing of fossil — the discovery, the processing, transportation, the selling and the combustion of fossil fuels. Financial interests that are entrenched in this industry are the same ones that are entrenched in the political process. The inability of these companies to diversify their business model has hampered them in adapting to this changing political environment where we see the necessity for decarbonizing our society. So, because their business model has been entrenched in this carbon intensive industry, it makes their business model now incompatible with what we need to do. Why have they been resistant to change? Because their entire business model is based on the extraction of fossil fuels and their stock value is only valued by what they have in reserves. These companies are realizing "wow we're really in trouble." They're putting all their chips into obstructing justice and influencing the political system. (Int#23)

There is ample evidence to support the activists' and land defenders' claims that corporate influence on the political system is a massive barrier to the transformation needed in Canada. For example, a study conducted by researchers at the Canadian Centre for Policy Alternatives and the Corporate Mapping Project — drawing on data from Elections BC's Financial Reports and Political Contributions (FRPC) System, and a database of fossil fuel corporations — found "a remarkable and disturbingly close relationship" between oil, gas and coal industries and the BC provincial government (Graham et al. 2017: 4). This relationship is manifest through two main mechanisms: *lobbying*, through which corporations secure access to key political decision makers, and *corporate donations to political parties*, whereby corporations provide financial support to political parties whose policies are favourable to the corporation's interests. Donations help corporate actors gain access to politicians, ensuring that their views on particular issues have influence. The report concludes that this relationship "not only contradicts the province's stated aim to fight climate change but also undermines democracy and the public interest" (Graham et al. 2017: 4).

A report released by the Pembina Institute in 2012 exposed how Canada's dependency on the tar sands as the prime economic driver is, to an important extent, a result of corporate involvement in public policy and how policy is designed and implemented by the Canadian government. The report explains that

> the corporations involved in the petroleum industry and their ability to influence the country's political leaders and bureaucracy has changed the political landscape in their favour ... industry players are enthusiastically lobbying for and actively designing friendly public policies that will hasten industrial development, through the speeding up of approval processes and the weakening of environmental regulations. (Cayley-Daoust and Girard 2012: 1–2)

These views from activists, land defenders and researchers alike make clear that the egregious corporate influence on the political system is a formidable obstacle to transitioning away from the fossil-fuel based energy and economic systems in Canada. All this has powerful implications for movements determining strategic targets and developing effective strategy.

The Legal System and Criminalization of Dissent

These aforementioned ways that Canada's economic and political systems serve to maintain, rather that help transform, the extractive status quo can also be see in Canada's legal system.

Some people put much of their change efforts into pushing for legislative change: "With one stroke of a law, they can change everything all at once" (Int#6). Although there have been some important wins in Canadian courtrooms — key cases where Indigenous rights have been affirmed and where the fossil fuel industry was impeded — some still see the legal system as more of a barrier than a pathway to change. A predominant example of how the legal system hinders social change efforts is through the criminalization of direct action and land defence.

In a political system based on capitalism and compromised by corporate interests, representative democracy often fails as a way for citizens to influence decision making. In a failed political system, direct action can be the only way to push for more just and sustainable decision making (TT#2). But the legal system was not designed to protect activists taking direct action for justice: "Our laws are created to protect people that own things, ownership, privacy. The rules are very vague and they permit officers to arrest anyone in almost any situation" (TT#2). "A lot of people still treat activists like we're a bunch of criminals disrupting Canadian business" (Int#26). Instead of law and governance that can defend the rights of communities, ecosystems and the people fighting to protect them, the current legal system is regularly employed to watch, arrest and criminalize activists:

> There is a conflict between companies and Indigenous Peoples ... to the point that ... if you're a native then you are a terrorist. If you look at how policing is used against activists and environmentalists, it's fucking disgusting. [They justify it by] painting us as wack jobs ... crazy people, not like everybody else. They try to make us out like we don't know what we are talking about, like we're not part of society. (Int#7 Kanien'kehá ka)

It was understood by many people that I spoke to that criminalization of activism is done "to discourage the protesters. That is certain. To discourage you from returning to the street" (Int#17). As a result, people are afraid to protest. "To keep the pool of protesters and to find and mobilize other activists is difficult. Many people feel it's discouraging to do direct action" (Int#17). "The state apparatus has done a wonderful job maintaining the complete monopoly of violence and bringing in the heavy guns ... it's becoming normal for the military to come to protests and make mass arrests. It has had a long-term paralyzing effect on us.... That's the main hurdle, that's what's holding us back" (Int#11). "This closes the space for open expression and the ability to denounce unwanted projects. This is an enormous injustice" (Int#18).

Indigenous land defenders face more risk of arrest and criminalization than do settler activists (Monaghan and Walby 2017), as can be seen in the fact that Indigenous Peoples and people of colour are disproportionality overrepresented in Canadian incarceration rates (Owusu-Bempah and Wortley 2014; see also Maynard 2017):

> When it comes to Indigenous Peoples defending their own territory, there is a history of law enforcement escalating quickly. This is not a new thing, this has been happening for a long time. It is a racist system playing out ... white supremacy that is keeping Indigenous Peoples in fear because either you're going to get shot, the military is going to be called, or you're going to be facing life in prison. So, it's not the same story when it comes to a bunch of white people in kayaks blocking the freighters.... For Indigenous Peoples it's our lives that are at stake when it comes to defending the land and the water. (TT#2 Anishinaabe)

There are special forces trained in Canada to counter Indigenous resistance. As one person told me: "Since Oka, the military and the police have been practising at taking down Indigenous blockades" (Int#38 Mi'kmaw). That Indigenous resistance is criminalized more than settler activism is a matter of politics, not a matter of law: "It's important for us to acknowledge that every act of enforcement is an exercise of discretion. It's a political choice" (TT#2). "What they actually want to do is to criminalize political dissent. They want to create such a condition of fear that even people who are acting under moral necessity or democratic justification think twice before they engage in their action. It amounts to an attempt to criminalize Indigeneity itself" (TT#2).

In response to the Idle No More movement in 2012, the RCMP set up Project Sitka to monitor and track Indigenous protests and activists (Nikiforuk 2019). This has been part of an ongoing increase in the criminalization of environmental and Indigenous activism in Canada. Monaghan and Walby (2017) explain how, as with other countries, security agencies in Canada are now classifying environmental activities as domestic terrorist threats. This categorization has mobilized considerable national security resources to monitor movements. They trace the development of the use of the concept of "critical infrastructure protection," which is used to justify domestic surveillance. In the 2018 book *Policing Indigenous Movements*, Crosby and Monaghan investigate how policing and other security agencies have been working to surveil and silence Indigenous land defenders and other opponents of extractive capitalism. They make the case that the expansion of the security state and the criminalization of Indigenous land defence have been allowed through the norms of settler colonialism.

The legal system, like the political and economic systems discussed earlier, is failing to address the multiple social and environmental crises we face. Instead, it is monitoring and punishing those who are fighting for their communities, their land and waters, defending justice — and life itself.

The State

For some people I spoke to, it's not just capitalist and corporate control over politics, the economy and the legal system that we're up against. To them, the biggest barrier we face is how all these forces are linked together. The state itself is the barrier:

> The main barrier is the bureaucracy in the Canadian government. Indigenous Peoples are one of the most legislated peoples in the world. Jody Wilson-Raybould [former federal justice minister and first Indigenous person to hold that position] recently said UNDRIP could not be implemented. And she's right. Because Canada is a bureaucratic state. It'll take a lot of work to get rid of all that regulation. (Int#9 Kanien'kehá ka)

> These structures that have been built are so powerful. It would be really hard and really destructive to try to overthrow those systems.... The centralized systems of power. (Int#20 Michif Cree)

> The external barrier is the fact that on the other side what we're fighting against is an extremely well organized, extremely large, extremely well-financed enemy — the monolith of the state. They are aware that we exist and have been planning against our challenges. They're increasingly good at it. This doesn't make it impossible. But we need to realize that we're up against pretty big odds. (Int#5)

Social movements in Canada are up against some formidable barriers indeed. As these conversations have explored, a general lack of public will keeps the movements small and less able to create a critical mass to build counter-hegemony against an economic system that incentivizes social and ecological destruction and allows corporate interests to drive public decision making. All of this creates incentives for those with a vested interest in the political and legal systems to maintain the status quo. At the same time, criminalization of activists and land defenders disincentivizes the direct action needed to force change. The state and its many layers of bureaucracy ensure that dismantling unjust systems becomes an arduous task, at best. Meanwhile mainstream focus on false solutions and the lack of widespread roll-outs of real alternatives lead to fear of job losses and increased investment in the status quo. All this works together to obstruct the paths of decarbonizing and decolonizing Canada. And that's just the barriers stemming from outside the movements.

Internal Barriers to Change

Many of the conversations about barriers to change centred on obstacles that are internal to the movements. I have categorized the types of internal barriers that activists and land defenders identified into eight themes — relational tensions, NGOization, fractured movements, activist culture, centralized/hierarchical structures, activist burnout, lack of financial resources and bias/self-interest/privilege. Figure 6-2 offers a visual overview of the number of times each theme came up in the interviews and surveys. As the graph makes clear, relational tension is by far the most

Figure 6-2: The Number of Times Each Internal Barrier Was Mentioned.

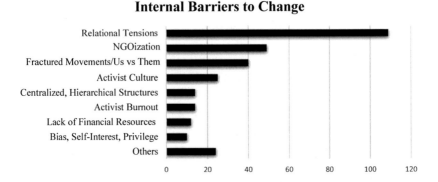

Internal Barriers to Change

common internal barrier to change identified by the people I talked to, but, in order to explore the overlap between the various barriers, we will first explore lack of financial resources and activist burnout.

Lack of Financial Resources and Activist Burnout

According to one person: "Right now, in Canada, the most significant barrier is the lack of financial support for front-line communities and organizations opposing fossil fuel development" (S#26). As will be explored below in the section on NGOization, there *is* money in the movements, but it's mostly held and used by the NGOs. This is despite the fact that the most transformative work is being done by front-line communities and grassroots movements. "There is a handful of groups who have money but there is not a whole lot of money around for activism for Indigenous land rights and for shutting down the tar sands" (Int#26).

Many of the communities on the front lines of unwanted oil and gas development live in very remote areas, and there is huge geographical distance between them and their supporters, and between various front lines: "These distances are difficult ... it requires financial resources" (Int#17). The capacity is "limited because we don't have money to pay to get people to be in the right places" (Int#26).

But it's not just the money required to get the word out and the support to the front lines. A very real barrier is a lack of financial resources within Indigenous communities, which makes refusing and standing up to extractive projects very challenging: "They either need the jobs or just don't have the resources to fight (Int#25 Dene). Communities that want to build alternatives to extractive industries on their territories often "don't have the money upfront to invest" (Int#37). And while resisting through the courts has sometimes been an effective strategy for Indigenous Nations opposing the violation of their rights and destruction of their lands and waters, this is a "very expensive strategy. The costs are huge, and many communities just can't afford that" (Int#31). Similarly, and harkening back to the external barrier of the criminalization of dissent, communities that take a direct-action approach to resistance often face extremely high legal fees in cases where arrests have been made and charges laid. As such, there is a need to find "some reliable economics that would make it work for people so that [activists and land defenders] can continue to do their work ... something that provides a livelihood...."

With some real funding you could have armies of people doing incredible work" (Int#2).

There's a clear sense that a major obstacle to scaling up much of the work being done is the lack of the financial resources available to make that happen. Activists and communities are compensating with their labour but are tired and burning out. Indeed, one person told me: "The biggest threat I see is people getting burnt out" (Int#19). Burnout, is something that activists and others experience as a debilitating and long-term condition of mental exhaustion (Schaufeli and Buunk 2002) and can result in losing the drive to work for social change (Pines 1994). Activists described the "emotional fallout from doing this kind of work" (Int#14) and spoke about the intense and difficult work of activism in which people "have no time for ourselves" (Int#27), take on too much and become exhausted (Int#18). As one land defender said, "colonialism is such a hard thing to fight against, it's very frustrating and a little isolating too.... We end up with a lot of mental health problems" (Int#13 Kanien'kehá ka). Losing people to burnout and mental health struggles is a barrier to building strong movements.

Research studies with social justice and human rights activists conducted by Paul Gorski, a wellbeing researcher at George Mason University, uncovered that around half of the activists who reported experiencing burnout ended up leaving their movements permanently (see Chen and Gorski 2015): "When you have so many people burning out and leaving, it really messes up the potential for these movements to be effective.... You're always mentoring new people, there's no consistency in who's engaged, and everyone's exhausted all of the time and snapping at each other" (quoted in Solis 2018).[11]

Activist Culture

Another internal barrier that arose in the conversations is about activist culture itself and how it espouses narrow notions of activism, thereby limiting its appeal. It is inward-focused, blocking communications outside our circles with the use of inaccessible activist jargon. Activist culture has also been accused of being overly critical and too focused on what it opposes. The over-criticality can make people cynical and more likely to disengage. These characteristics of our movement cultures limit our ability to bring in new people, burns people out and leads to loss in our ranks.

"We need to go beyond the activist subculture that exists.... Organizing is done around subcultures, and that can lead to insularity" (Int#5). According to one person:

> The direct action sphere has been dominated by a particular vision that tends to come with the "fuck capitalism, fuck the cops, fuck the man" mentality, which turns some people away. The more that you look like a weirdo and some sort of [radical activist], the harder it is to build a community of resistance. (Int#4)

"We are organizing in self-selecting groups ... we have no way to access the people who wouldn't choose to talk to us" (TT#3). One person reflected:

> We just really don't know how to talk to regular folks. We're much too deep in our bubble, in all this jargon that is super specialized.... We are mired in language that the rest of the world does not understand and so we create fairly inhospitable spaces for new people to come in. (Int#30)

People also suggested that many activist cultures are overly critical: "One of the biggest challenges that movements face is ... criticizing each other, endless critical thinking ... sharp sticks for everyone. Critical thinking is an absolutely necessary tool, but in what dose?" (Int#16). We critique each other over tactics, over flawed analysis, over how we should be structuring the movement and designing messages. "All these things are frustrating. It can make a lot of good people become cynical, throw their hands up and say, 'Fuck it'" (Int#23).

However, several people made clear that some critiques are very much needed, for example when marches are organized and led by white people, when voices of those most impacted are not included and are not heard. These are necessary critiques. But we mustn't allow criticality to be a defining feature of our movement cultures. We need to find ways to handle our relations with each other with care, creating spaces we want to stay in and where others feel drawn to join us.

Fractured Movements/Us vs. Them
Previous sections in this chapter reflected on the small size and marginal nature of our movements. From conversations about internal barriers, it

becomes clear that it's not just this small size that impedes our success; our movements are also fractured. Though there is a lot of great work happening, our efforts are dispersed and fragmented, our activism and organizing siloed and performed in isolation from each other. This fragmentation is stopping us from being able to build the counter-hegemonic force we need.

This fragmentation is happening within and across movements. "The biggest barrier I see is the lack of solidarity between movements" (S#14). "I see sparks, tons of small ones ... but we're very fractured ... super atomized" (Int#2). Our movements lack solidarity and consensus:

> In a lot of the movement work I do, there is no consensus among people. What is the plan? How are these different moving parts going to fit together, so that they all push in the same direction? It is kind of stressful watching and being part of it. [There is no] cohesive strategy of moving forward. (Int#14)

> Sometimes it's contradictory. (Int#15)

Some spoke about the tendency to fragment as resulting from the cognitive bias we humans have, driving us to divide the social world into "us and them" (see Green 2014; Choudhury 2015). Some grassroots people see NGOs as the "other," while some organizers working hard to reach mainstream audiences see disruptive radicals as the "other." There are all sorts of dividing lines like these in the movements that split us into ingroups and outgroups, "You see yourself; your identity is clearly on one side and then you see anarchists or people who talk to the government as the 'other.' You go towards the groups that resemble you the most" (Int#18). "Activists have a lot of anger toward the big enemy, but it can also fuel that us vs. them" (Int#15). The fire that we activists have inside can turn us against each other.

The fractured nature of our movements is not surprising given the incredible diversity and wide spectrum of people and groups involved. It's not surprising, it's not new and it's not unique to these movements. "This stuff has plagued movements forever. The right wing knows the left is fragmented. They bank on it. That's the difference between us. [The right] doesn't mind hierarchy — that allows them to choose one message and force everyone to stick to it" (Int#10). The radical left doesn't have the same hierarchical tendencies, which, though problematic from our perspective, are useful for fostering unity.

Diversity is a good thing, as is the radical left's aversion to hierarchy, but fragmentation is a problem when trying to build collective power. Part of this fragmentation is due to internal tensions, but also, our opponents actively work to divide and conquer the movements (Int#14). Government, industry and police use specific strategies to create tensions and divisions between activists (Int#8).

Elites use this divide and conquer strategy to provoke conflicts in order "to break down the relationships and unity between subjugated groups struggling for justice, freedom, and liberation, in order to maintain the status quo" (Aorta 2017: n.p.). This has all too often been "infuriatingly effective" in fracturing social justice movements who were not adequately prepared with counter moves to defend the solidarity which had been built up within and across movements (Aorta 2017: n.p.). Tactics used to divide and conquer include creating a narrative that blames each group for the other group's problems in order to spark mistrust between groups and to divert attention away from the systematic inequalities that link the different struggles. In another tactic, elites bribe some groups with access to resources, serving to align those selected groups with the elite instead of other marginalized groups. Threatening to withdraw needed resources or enact violence if the groups continue to ally with other groups is also used to create a culture of fear that profoundly impacts movements' capacity to work together to build power (Aorta 2017).

We can see these kinds of tactics being used by corporations and governments in Canada, for example in the all too common narratives that pits workers and environmentalists against each other, deeply weakening the power that could come from red–green alliances (see Russell 2008). And when pipeline companies "consult" some Indigenous leadership and not others, and/or offer significant amounts of money to some communities to approve projects and not others, divisions appear within and between communities. These tactics are also often used to create conflicts between more and less radical strands within movements, for example, by having infiltrators show up at an action and advocate for violent actions, sparking huge internal debates within groups over preferred tactics. In all these cases, attention, energy and resources are channeled away from communities and movements' focus on confronting elites and building counter-power. Instead we spend precious energy debating and struggling amongst ourselves. There are profound reasons to think hard about the animosities that have been provoked between us. And we can take heart in seeing this oft-used divide-and-conquer strategy as strong evidence that the potential alliances across movements deeply threaten the status quo. And that our opponents know it.

All that said, some of the divisions between us are of our own making. That needs to be acknowledged and addressed too.

Relational Tensions

These discussions of fragmentation, of criticality, of "othering" point to the relational tensions that, as Figure 6-2 so clearly shows, is by far the most significant internal barrier to change identified by the people I spoke with. Indeed, the quotes from interviews and surveys that I put together while analyzing relational tensions in the movement fill over eighty pages of text. Here I attempt to summarize a huge and very important conversation in a few pages.

The fracturing of the movements is driven, in large part, by relational and ideological tensions between people and groups. One person jokingly told me that she defines a coalition as "a group of organizations that spend 95% of their time arguing over the 5% of things they disagree on" (Int#33). One person named "horizontal hostility" (Int#14), and another "friendly fire from allies" and a "propensity to attack those who are (or who ought to be) allies" (S#1). One person told me that fighting inside the movement is burning him out more than fighting against big corporations because "you're fighting your own people" (Int#19). "I don't know why we eat each other. If we can't work together, we're fucked" (Int#28).

People raised many different sources of tensions — power imbalance, identity politics and unequal access to resources, to name a few. There are tensions over which social and environmental issues and change goals are being prioritized, and over conflicting theories of change and tactics. In Quebec, people also reported tensions between anglophones and francophones. But the relational tension most frequently raised in these conversations is the tension between Indigenous Peoples and settlers.

Problematic relational dynamics often result from the reproduction of power inequalities within our movements. When "women aren't given the platform to speak or the white people are dominating the conversation"

(Int#23) or "when it's white dudes being shitty" (Int#26). These power imbalances are always present (Int#23) and they cause relational challenges that need to be addressed. One woman said, "I've experienced them to be barriers. I have certainly walked away from many conflicts because I don't have the emotional energy to explain something to a white man that I've explained to countless other white men" (Int#28). And as one Indigenous organizer put it: "There are a lot of privileged white people in positions of power who don't want to be uncomfortable, who we've needed to work with" (Int#18). Power imbalances within and across these movements abound, reproducing the relations of domination we are trying to fight, and they are building tensions and driving wedges between us.

As activists try to figure out how to hold each other responsible for reproducing inequalities, some struggle to do this in ways that foster the sense that there is more than one right way to engage: "There's a lot of paralysis right now that comes from identity politics gone amok" (Int#11) because of "purity politics and the politics of denunciation" (Int#14). We don't always "have proper vocabulary for everything. Sometimes you say the wrong thing and people very quickly put you in a box and then assume your politics based on that slip up" (Int#21). This can make movement spaces feel "exclusive" (Int#23) and intimidating. One person suggested this is "reproducing carceral logic. You no longer belong in the community if you fuck up. The left [is] exploding on itself ... eating each other alive because we're so quick to judge" (Int#10). "It's making it hard to collaborate, it's hard to bring new people in" (Int#32).

That said, "we really, really, really do need to be called out. We have a lot of shit to change" (Int#10). But to develop non-oppressive, intersectional movements, we need to go deeper than merely learning to "say the right thing and use the right language. You know, that's shitty for all the folks who are on the front lines who don't say the right thing. That's not the work" (Int#32). The work that is actually required is in developing a shared understanding of the ways the many forms of domination intersect, and coming together to undo them all. We must do this without undoing each other.

As evidenced in Chapter 5, there are many differing, and sometimes conflicting, theories of change held by people in the movements. People reflected on the relational tensions created by these conflicting theories of change and about how these tensions act as barriers to change. For example, some believe "that working within the system is the only and most important way of affecting change," whereas others maintain "that working outside the system is the only way" (Int#10). Tensions exist between those who think change happens through conflict versus those who believe change happens through collaboration. People "get locked into a certain theory of change" (Int#31). "The problem often is that people don't question their own assumptions. They assume they know how to do change and that other people don't know how to do change properly. I see a major barrier there" (Int#3).

"There is a lot of fracturing in the movements because of ideology. Even a slight difference, where someone doesn't believe in a certain tactic and someone else does and so they won't work together" (Int#26). This plays out particularly between groups that believe in engaging with the electoral system and those that don't. Under the Liberal government, there has been a lack of cohesion in the movements as some people seek to influence politicians, while others consider that a losing strategy. As someone told me in the lead up to the 2019 federal election:

> With the upcoming federal election, I fear there is going to be a retreat to defend the lowest common denominator ... defend the carbon tax, or "don't hurt the Liberals too much because we're going to get worse." [It's going] to be very messy because some people are going to want to defend the Liberals' environmental programs and the carbon tax and others are going to be like "Trudeau sucks because of pipelines." (TT#3)

Tensions over tactics also play out between those who engage in direct action and those who don't approve of confrontational tactics. One activist told me a story of a direct action she engaged in while opposing a proposed pipeline project. She was arrested and charged. At the moment of her arrest she was more concerned with what other activists would say about her than she was about the legal consequences to herself. She said: "We want a diversity of tactics, but we have a lot of difficulty in applying that. We put so much energy in judging each other. That energy could be used much more effectively against the [pipeline] projects. It creates the lack of solidarity" (Int#18). She told me: "We need to be careful, mindful of our dynamic within the movement. And we need to be in solidarity with those willing to take risks" (Int#18).

One person said that the deepest divisions are between Indigenous and settler activists over the fact that each is facing very different strategic conditions. These different conditions call for very different tactics, which can be in conflict with each other. Many settler groups' strategies are based on garnering mass mobilization: "To mobilize masses of people, you have to create very, very powerful appeals, you need to have a broad appeal" (Int#38 Mi'kmaw). This land defender went on to explain that climate movements have a chance of being broadly appealing because the majority of Canadians may be able to see climate action as in their self-interest. But Indigenous Peoples fighting for self-determination and decolonization must design strategies that do not require mass mobilization, because their goals will never resonate with most Canadians:

> As Indigenous Peoples, we know there is no mass mobilization. We have a strength in direct resistance. We have a strength in exposing the levels of repression the state is willing to go to, through violence and force, to preserve industry … that's what we have to work with. There is tension between non-Indigenous activists and Indigenous Peoples because the non-Indigenous activists come in trying to impose their strategy or ask us "why aren't you doing this tactic?" They tell us: "your Indigenous tactic is undermining my tactic of social mobilization for the masses." So, when [settler activists] are trying to win over the masses in Canada they are in effect doing nothing to support an Indigenous strategy. Their reformist strategies work well for mass mobilization, but they can be very counter-productive to Indigenous Nationhood … all they do is re-entrench colonialism. (Int#38 Mi'kmaw)

In these ways, settler and Indigenous strategies and tactics can be directly in conflict.

"There are some contradictions hidden within the environmental movement. We don't all have the same end" (Int#8). As explored in Chapter 4, these movements involve people with a wide variety of change goals that range from reducing GHG emissions in Canada to taking down capitalism and reinstating Indigenous sovereignty over the lands and waters known as Canada. Sometimes efforts towards one goal can work against efforts towards other goals. Conflicting end goals cause relational tensions too.

In Quebec, for example, the people aiming for decarbonization and those working on decolonization are not aligned nearly as much as they are in BC. Quebec sovereignty and rights to its land and resources are at the heart of francophone Quebec culture and politics. This stands in stark conflict with the movement to acknowledge that Quebec is stolen Indigenous land and for the defence and promotion of Indigenous rights: "People in Quebec feel that they are the colonized people" (Int#10). "Quebec is doing really poorly on the whole decolonizing issue. Really worse than the rest of Canada and Canada is just getting started" (Int#15). This is exacerbating existing tensions in movements in Quebec over language, tactics and activist culture.

Difficult relations between Indigenous and settler activists was by far the most common kind of relational tension that came up in these conversations. The environmental movement in Canada has a long and sordid past of problematic relationships between environmental groups and Indigenous communities. This legacy is alive and continually navigated in the anti-pipeline, climate justice and Indigenous land defence movements currently in Canada. When I asked a Mohawk Elder about how settlers can actively be supportive of the change he wants to see, he told me: "Get out of our way. We appreciate the support, we appreciate the sympathy, but don't try to tell us what to do. Don't try to speak for us. We can speak for ourselves" (Int#9 Kanien'kehá ka).

There are deep differences in worldviews and knowledge systems: "[For settlers] everything revolves around money and [Indigenous Peoples] don't necessarily see it the same way. We see land as life. We value life more than we value money" (Int#9 Kanien'kehá ka). "There's this [difference] between the reason [settlers] want to stop climate change and the reason that Indigenous Peoples want to stop climate change" (Int#20 Michif Cree). Where settlers learn from science that we should protect nature because we may need it to survive, Indigenous Peoples have long held nature as sacred, as kin, as having inherent worth: "There's just a lack of legitimate effort on behalf of many settlers to actually understand that (Int#20 Michif Cree). "The most annoying thing about collaborating with 'environmentalists' is that white folks have this concept of 'the environment' as its own issue. All of the sudden you just separated environmental from social justice, from human wellbeing. In Indigenous worldviews it's not separate" (S#37). "If you're creating parks, you are saying you need to protect the land from yourself, which is an admission of failure and you need to think about that." This vastly different sense of "what environment means" plays out constantly in our collaborations, exacerbating difficult relations (Int#33).

There are many tensions that form from unjust relations between settlers and Indigenous Peoples in these movements. Many environmental groups seek to work with Indigenous communities because Indigenous rights are powerful tools for protecting lands and waters, but the environmental groups often end up co-opting the message, tokenizing Indigenous Peoples, financially benefitting from the relationship and not being accountable or transparent: "First Nations people don't want to be used just because there is a perception that they have certain veto power over projects. They want more fundamental self-determination, free and prior informed consent" (Int#36). There are many problematic reasons why settlers seek collaborations with Indigenous communities. "Settlers should not be reaching out to Indigenous Peoples out of a sense of guilt; it should come from a place of shared understanding that colonialism and oppression is fucked" (Int#21).

There are also ongoing tensions inherent in living on stolen land. One settler organizer in BC told me: "I know that I live on unceded territory. I know I have received something that was stolen. And I know from just basic morals and ethics, if you receive something stolen it is your duty to give it back. Except I don't want to give it back. I really like it here. And I can't afford to just give back all this stuff I have paid and saved for. There is this tension that is really ugly" (Int#37).

There are genuine conflicting material interests present in the relations between Indigenous and non-Indigenous activists. Allyship between Indigenous and settlers can only go so far if settlers want to hold on to the benefits and privileges that colonialism has bestowed on us, namely power and land. We often avoid discussion of land. As one Indigenous organizer told me: "Even white allies with the best intentions won't give up power. The minute you talk about land suddenly the limits of allyship presents itself" (Int#38 Mi'kmaw). These real conflicting interests are constantly present in movement spaces and make for shallow or strained collaborations at best.

"There's power imbalance between Indigenous and non-Indigenous communities. That's a huge barrier" (Int#34 Anishinaabe/Ojibway).

"Historical and ongoing inequalities have brought us here, and there is a lot of the damage done and traumatic relationships between the people who are living together on this land" (Int#28). This is true in Canada in general but also true within social movements. "One of the huge challenges that Indigenous Peoples have faced is that [settlers] have tried to use them instrumentally to advance their [social change] goals. We've learned that good intentions can sometimes be very, very damaging" (Int#34 Anishinaabe/Ojibway).

Part of this process of building better relationships is for settlers to really understand historical and ongoing colonialism:

> The occupier of Indigenous territory has to hear a story that they don't want to hear. A story of how they are the villain. They are not the hero, they are not the saviour.... In these relationships with Indigenous Peoples, this truth is being exposed. And that's a hard thing for them to swallow. (Int#38 Mi'kmaw)

> There's a lot of fear both in the Indigenous and non-Indigenous communities around these kinds of engagements. People don't trust one another. (Int#34 Anishinaabe/Ojibway)

In many collaborations within the movements, settlers still hold the reins of power and this continues to damage relationships. As one Indigenous land defender put it: "This has been the problem for five hundred years. We've been forced under their agenda" (Int#38 Mi'kmaw). There is a huge need for accountability and trust to be built if we are to begin to heal these relationships.

NGOization

The second most common internal barrier identified is the dynamics between large NGOs and other groups/actors in these movements. These dynamics are one of the relational tensions, but NGOization came up so often I have given it its own section. According to one activist: "One of the big barriers is NGOs. There are many ways that NGOization is decimating the movement" (Int#32). These critiques come from interviewees who work in NGOs as well as those who don't.

In their 2013 book *NGOization: Complicity, Contradictions and Prospects*, Choudry and Kapoor define NGOization as the process of institutionalization, professionalization, depoliticization and demobilization of movements and struggles (see also Armstrong and Prashad 2005; Kamat 2004). NGOs are "not in touch with grassroots and marginalized movements" (S#14), and they have the "impression that they're the ones doing the most and the most important stuff" (Int#10). The collaborations they do have with communities and grassroots groups are often instrumentalizing: "The NGO wants to control the messaging — they're creating a container that they want people to fill" (Int#23). "They'll make their grand master plan, then just be like, 'You grassroots people can just be the bodies in our master plan'" (Int#13). "It's really presumptuous, this model of 'we'll do the thinking and you do the doing'" (Int#32).

"Big NGOs often will talk to the people who agree with them in Indigenous communities and use those viewpoints to further their goals for the environment without supporting Indigenous sovereignty in itself. Co-option is a big problem" (Int#13). "They are just so good at co-opting our language and resources and then deciding what to do with them on behalf of everyone else" (Int#32). NGOs will enter into coalitions with grassroots and communities, agreeing on certain goals, and "then the NGO all of a sudden pulls a 180," changing the goal without consulting the broader group (Int#16).

There are critiques of NGOs co-opting movement efforts as well as watering down goals and messaging. They tend to have narrow framings of the problems and don't take on systemic analysis or strategies: "NGO's suck up all the oxygen and actually don't fight systemic issues" (Int#36). "We want to change the roots of the problems and NGOs just focus on the surface of the problems; they never go into the structural, the roots of the problems" (Int#18). Having "bought into the system" (Int#33), "their frameworks are so in line with capitalism and asking the government to do things. At the end of the day, I don't believe that will ever bring about wide-scale change" (Int#38 Mi'kmaw). NGOs are constrained by their relationship with the funders:

> If you work in the system, in the structure, like an NGO or the government, it makes it harder to talk about the structural problems. It's more difficult to make this kind of change because you are constrained. But what's going on in these movements is that the people who are constrained in their analysis are the ones

who have the resources. It's that closeness, working within the system, that allows them access to such resources. It's a barrier to systemic change that the people with the radical analysis and the goal of changing the system are not the people with the resources and access to put towards this kind of systems change. (Int#18)

"There is so much money that goes into these large organizations who are not capable of delivering the goods" (Int#19). In fact, "NGOs historically were created specifically with the aim to take the teeth out of the movements, to make them less of a threat" (Int#30). Similar arguments have been made about NGOs in Arundhati Roy's, *Capitalism, A Ghost Story* and *The Revolution Will Not Be Funded* by INCITE's Women of Colour against Violence.

People I spoke with explained that NGOs' funding structure renders them timid and risk-averse in their strategies, and therefore ineffective: "NGOs keep their messages moderate to keep funders happy … people with money want to keep the system as it is … funders won't be excited about radical messages" (Int#10). "The reason they get the most resources is because they are not as threatening as the people who are advocating for system change" (Int#20 Michif Cree). They end up focusing more on maintaining their organization, building their base and fundraising than actually working for social change. As they become "mainly concerned with their survival as an organization, a lot of the actions that they do are done in the end to produce victories — even though those victories might be hullabaloo — so they can take those victories to their funders and they can get more funding, so they can keep going" (Int#30).

Many NGOs tend away from direct action and sometimes denounce those groups that do engage in direct action. "The biggest downfall in that movement as a whole, I think, is the tendency of those larger NGOs to actively discredit people doing direct action in order to save their own capitalist, liberal legitimacy in the view of the public and the funders" (Int#20 Michif Cree). "It's a very big challenge for social movements to not be co-opted and to maintain the radical demands, and not co-opted into something short of that, because human survival is at stake" (Int#16).

NGOs tend to be structured hierarchically, espousing a top-down structure within the movements they are part of. They are often not accountable to the grassroots groups, communities and others in the movement, and some collaborate with government and industry, sometimes cutting deals behind closed doors. Different NGOs are often in direct competition with each other for funding and media attention, creating tense relations between the organizations: "Because they are direct competitors, they are a less effective force for change" (Int#33).

NGOs need to be held to account for hoarding resources, for using others instrumentally, for co-opting movements, for paying high salaries to CEOs while front-line communities struggle to survive the very crises around which the NGOs craft their careful messages. "How do we hold them to account effectively without being divisive? I don't know. That's a barrier" (Int#16). All these dynamics make for very challenging collaborations, hindering effective, powerful coalitions. They represent a significant barrier to the kind of collective action that can foster radical social change in Canada as envisioned by the people I spoke with. The imbalance of power between large NGOs and others in the movement makes for tense and unjust relations.

These observations and critiques of NGOs are grounded in the specific dynamics of these particular movements, but they reflect a wider phenomenon that has been discussed in many different movement contexts and by various scholars. Work by Kamat (2004) and Piven and Cloward (1979) corroborate the activist views above that the funding structure of NGOs, whereby they must show managerial and technical capacity to administer funding and prioritize the financial survival and organizational maintenance, tends towards diverting efforts and resources away from pushing for actual structural change. Choudry (2010) compiles other critiques of NGOization, which include the failure of NGOs to name and address the root causes of the issues they aim to address. Not only do they fail to name capitalism, their work can serve to obscure capitalist assumptions underlying their approaches to change, as well as obscuring the organizations' complicity with these underlying systems:

> This frequent failure to name capitalism, imperialism and colonialism, alongside commonly articulated NGO platforms on participation, fair trade, sustainable development, vaguely defined claims about democracy, rights and justice, and sometimes a kind of stylized, "respectable" militancy, also helps to obfuscate the ways in which many of these organizations are implicated in

ruling relations, forms of discursive and practical organization which coordinate these activities and actors in the interests of the state and capital. (Choudry 2010: 20)

Others have written specifically about NGOization in the Canadian context. According to the 2014 article "NGOization: Depoliticizing Activism in Canada" by Dru Oja Jay, there are hundreds to thousands of grant-dependent, mission-oriented organizations in Canada, all drawing from a comparatively small pool of funders. While there is a wide diversity of organizations, the foundations that fund them tend to share certain characteristics:

> Almost all funders prefer solutions that don't question prevailing neoliberal policies or capitalism. When they tolerate questioning, effective mobilizing is strictly forbidden. Funders demand centralized control and accountability in the form of regular and extensive reporting, and often direct oversight. Funders avoid grassroots organizing that directly empowers people whenever possible, preferring structures that provide tight, centralized control. (Jay 2014: n.p.)

Examples of the ways that the NGOization has been playing out in the environmental and climate movements in Canada are offered in the 2009 report *Offsetting Resistance*. Using as case studies the Great Bear Rainforest deal in northwestern British Columbia and the then-emerging North American Tar Sands Coalition, the authors contend that these cases demonstrate a track record of corporate- and foundation-funded environmental NGOs making closed-door, backroom deals with industry and government, serving to concentrate decision-making power, ignore affected communities, develop abstract policy proposals and work at odds with actual effective community-led resistance efforts. The lack of transparency, absence of democratic structures, questionable sources of funding and other deeply problematic issues in the ways NGOs do their work call for an open and informed discussion (Stainsby and Jay 2009).

Furthermore, Lee (2011), drawing on the 2010 Canadian Boreal Forest Agreement case, argues that NGOs play a role in perpetuating colonialism in Canada. When NGOs partner with First Nations governments (which were established expressly to serve Canada's interests), the partnerships end up legitimizing the state's control over Indigenous Peoples and strengthening the state's claim on Indigenous territories and resources while acting counter to Indigenous rights and title and their own responsibilities to the lands and waters.

Together, these activist and scholarly discussions make clear that NGOization is a significant barrier to transformative change in Canada. Though it's important to note that not all NGOs are guilty of all the things described above, and many are working to counter these tendencies, many are working in ways that perpetuating uneven relations, weakening the potential to build counter-hegemonic force in Canada.

Centralized, Hierarchical and Top-Down Structures

Another barrier that came up in these conversations is the barrier of different and sometimes conflicting organizational structures. Where NGOs tend to be organized in centralized, top-down hierarchical structures, many community and grassroots groups organize themselves non-hierarchically. Some people feel that top-down structures are inherently non-transformative and therefore constitute barriers in and of themselves, while others reflect on the barrier created by the tensions between groups, over incompatible organizational structures. One activist in Quebec told me of the large coalition she is part of:

> We're stuck. It's not going well. The movement is split 50/50 over whether we should structure ourselves in a centralized or decentralized way. The more radical folks want decentralized — it empowers more people. Whereas other folks are like, "It's urgent!" so we need a small pocket of people to make those decisions. There's a sense that there's not enough time for horizontality or that we'll do it [hierarchically] because we've always done it this way. (Int#15)

There is a sense that though horizontal, non-hierarchical decision making might be better in some ways, hierarchical, top-down decision making ensures decisions are made faster and more efficiently. But to some, this sense of rush and competitiveness is part of capitalist ideology. If we want to transform our worlds away from capitalism, we need new, non-capitalist ways of relating, and that means finding ways to work together and make decisions together where everyone's voice matters. We need "spaces that can allow us to take the time to explore new ways of relating and new ways of structuring our relations" (Int#18).

In horizontal structures, you

> recognize the value of all the competencies of each person and ... believe that everyone has something to contribute to the struggle and making social change. If we are not able to recognize that, we lose the opportunity to have a diversity in our ways of reacting, our ways of bringing social change. (Int#18)

> That's how you spread power, you create spaces that allow communities to reshape the power, reshape the context of control, according to their own culture of values, according to their own practices. (Int#21)

There's a shared sense among the more radical strands of the movements that organizing ourselves in horizontal ways can help undo power imbalance and prepare us for the world we want. Decentralizing governance is both the means and the goal of transformation. It is in developing non-hierarchical, decentralized movement structures that we begin to prepare for and live the futures we want, now. "Canada does not need another NGO; we need something else. We need some other model of organizing that can help coordinate but in a bottom-up, horizontal way" (Int#33).

Bias, Self-Interest, Privilege

According to some folks I talked with, underlying many of the other barriers is bias, self-interest and privilege, all significant obstacles to social change towards justice. The resistance to giving up the privileges and personal benefits of extractive colonialism makes it very hard to bring the masses to the work of radically transforming Canada.

There are two really tough discussions people need to have within the movements, and in Canada in general, about power and land:

> What will provoke the Canadian, non-Indigenous Canadian society to a point where they are willing to give up power and land? ... 97% of the population benefits from the existing condition. This makes it extremely difficult to get them on board. How do I

get potential white allies on board, when they feel it's not in their interest? (Int#38 Mi'kmaw)

Basically, if we want revolution, we need to convince people to [remove themselves] from positions that are upholding the system. [Their unwillingness to do that] often comes from a deep fear that they won't be secure. (Int#10)

The — understandable — desire to preserve privilege and self-interest makes it hard to bring large numbers of Canadians to the movements. It also makes it hard for activists in the movements, with all the different positions they hold, to align around truly radical and just goals. Many of the tensions around different theories of change, about strategies and about the end goals discussed in previous sections are not just about personal preference or ideology. They are rooted in internal biases and self-interest (Int#38 Mi'kmaw). It's not enough to recognize that there are different doctrines, end goals and theories of change: "A better part of the analysis is why people choose these. They choose them not based on the merit; they choose it based on the preservation of self-interest" (Int#38 Mi'kmaw). According to this land defender, people who benefit from the status quo are more likely to hold more shallow reformist tactics and theories of change, while the people most negatively impacted are more likely to hold radical approaches to change: "The tensions that exist aren't usually just based on the relative merit of different approaches to change. They are based on people's biases and self-interests ... these biases are the real roots of the tensions in the movements" (Int#38 Mi'kmaw).

Craig Fortier explains that, over and over throughout history, the revolutionary potential of social movements has been blunted by the ways that many white people, even poor white people, fought for political gains and political power *within* the settler state, rather than aligning with Indigenous Peoples and others *against* the settler colonial state. Since even those least well-off within white settler society share the benefits of land and resource theft in Canada (as well as global capitalist exploitation abroad), most movements and coalitions in Canada fail to coalesce around shared goals of dismantling settler states, challenging white supremacy and resisting imperialism (Fortier 2015).

The creation of relationships of solidarity between different groups of people who are negatively impacted by these processes of domination through displacement, enslavement and dispossession would pose a serious threat to settler colonial states (Fortier 2015). However, over and over, this "potential has been thwarted in the history of settler left struggles, whereby the potential solidarity with insurgent Indigenous, African, Asian, and other oppressed and exploited people was mitigated by the ruling classes through the promise of land and the doctrine of white supremacy" (Fortier 2015: 80).

It's important to see the relational tensions and barriers described in this chapter within a larger historical context in which movements have perpetuated, and continue to perpetuate, the structure of settler colonialism. It's important to see that the anti-Indigenous racism that happened at the Montreal climate march in September 2019, the story that I opened the book with, was not an isolated event, but represents very real, ongoing ideologies, worldviews and politics that are dividing movements and weakening the potential to build a more just and livable world. As Eriel Deranger has made clear: "While the climate justice movement is working hard to address the legacy of white supremacy and colonialism within environmental and conservation movements, it is a work in progress" (Deranger 2019: n.p.).

These kinds of conversations about what's not working and the barriers that are in our way are necessary if we are going to learn to work together to confront and overcome the obstacles. I feel a spark of hope that this revolutionary, radically transformative potential — real solidarity across class, race and sex — can begin to materialize as settler activists and organizers let go of the benefits and privilege settler colonialism has afforded them and really align with Indigenous Peoples and people of colour against the settler colonial capitalist systems, structures and relations that are at the root of the climate crisis that threatens us all.

Everything is a stake and we have no time to waste in movements weakened by the divisions among us: "If we can't work together, we're fucked" (Int#28). It's time to stop fucking around. That means *rallying together around the needs, voices, visions and end goals of the people most impacted* by the unjust and unsustainable systems we are trying to change.

Note

1. Gorski has compiled this list of resources to help activists ward off burn out <https://wellbeing.gmu.edu/resources/thriving-activist>.

CHAPTER 7

OVERCOMING THE BARRIERS AND BUILDING MORE POWERFUL MOVEMENTS

Diversity is what makes us strong — in nature and in the movement. — S#27

We need movements that, not just theoretically, but in practice embrace different people. — Int#24

Chapter 6 laid out a daunting collection of internal and external barriers that these movements are facing, painting a bleak picture for the prospect of transforming Canada. Movements are up against powerful structures and very challenging internal dynamics. Examining all the barriers together paints a demoralizing portrait of what we're up against. However, the people I talked to saw these barriers as daunting but not insurmountable. And the conversations did not end there. Much of the time I spent talking to activists and land defenders across the country was spent strategizing, brainstorming and dreaming up ways to confront, dismantle and overcome these barriers and build bigger, stronger, more powerful movements. In this chapter I present the many different ideas that were raised and then focus in on one key theme that underlies all these conversations, a theme that came up again and again across these chapters and across the many conversation I had: that building stronger, more just relations within and across movements is deeply important to social transformation. And to build the kinds of relationships called for, we need to get much better at thinking and working across difference.

CONFRONTING AND OVERCOMING THE EXTERNAL BARRIERS

Conversations about confronting the external barriers — the lack of public will, the economic and political systems that serve the unjust status quo, the criminalization of dissent and others — centred around a few key themes. These include building power by growing our movements, expanding the scope of what activism (and activists) look like, changing the narrative and generating and supporting alternative livelihoods.

The conversations made clear that to build the necessary counter-force we need to bring many more people to the movements: "We need to adopt a movement-building framework within our organizing" (Int#5), widen the scope and learn what it is "to organize millions of people" (Int#28). This means making the "space and time to actually connect with others" (Int#11), creating spaces that make it easy for people to get involved and providing concrete tasks that make sense given their skills, interests and availability (Int#29). We need to help people "see how they can make a difference, remind people that they have agency to shape their world and to be a part of history" (S#24).

Activists spoke about the need to develop new organizing and mobilizing structures that help grow movements quickly. How can we organize through work places, communities and other existing social groups such that we can tap into the transformative potential of people where they are, as opposed to waiting for self-selecting people to come to us? We should seek out and create mobilizing structures that can "nourish grassroots organizing at every level" (Int#16). And to attract and hold many more people to our movements, we need "more spaces, more activities, more actions that bring more happiness inside the movement … that will bring more people to join the movement" (Int#19). There is a need for "more participatory and celebratory events and practices [to] help build trust and bonding" (S#18) and make movement spaces warm, supportive and just. We need to be "really thinking about how to embody just, equitable and supportive values as we organize" (Int#28).

We talked about "doing direct action trainings in neighbourhoods with people outside of activist circles, making everybody activists" (Int#10). We need to widen conceptions of activist and activism (Int#10), because "we're still a niche bunch of weirdos. We need middle-aged church ladies blockading shit. Then we'll be unstoppable" (Int#4). To do this, we need to divorce the radical message from the radical activist stereotype (Int#10). "We need to speak in more accessible terms and clearly show how these important issues intersect" (Int#16). We need to get outside of our issue boxes and "engage in a bigger social imagination" (Int#33), helping others see viable "alternatives to capitalism and deliver these messages in ways that can reach people" (S#13).

Many people emphasized that to build movements we need to talk with people we don't usually talk to and with people we don't necessarily already agree with. This means being attentive to people's needs, ideas and worldviews and relating to them with respect: "To reach people who are not already on side, we need to figure out communications, strategies and tactics that reach people and that make it safe for them to engage" (Int#37). "People need to meet people who are different from them and talk about things that are hard" (Int#28). This involves "making our arguments in unfriendly forums.... Especially those of us that are in situations of privilege, we have to do that. We need to routinely and specifically speak in places where we're pretty sure it's not going to be welcome. That's where we need to speak" (TT#2).

Really communicating and working across these differences means actually caring about people. "You need to go where people are at and always offer a helping hand. That's really an important part of how you grow the movement.... Be super respectful. Don't shame people for not having the same views" (Int#19). "We need to be having really respectful, non-shaming relationships with potential allies" (Int#23).

Many people emphasized that it's not just about bringing new people to the movements; key to building more powerful movements is building the connections across different social movements, "expanding our circle of allies.... Strengthening our allyship among much broader political differences will allow this movement to expand exponentially" (Int#23).

The work of bringing new people to the movements and the work of forging links between movements both require compelling narratives that help people see what is at stake and what else is possible, that help people see the structural links between climate change, racism, colonialism, violence against women and other forms of injustice. We need the kind of narratives that inspire people to see how these struggles are inextricable, that make clear that we need to fight together. Much environmental messaging over the last four decades has done little to explicate the connections between environmental destruction and social injustice. Doing so, making the links clear, can help many more people see a place for themselves in these struggles and help different movements see the benefit of working together to push in a common direction.

We also need to change common conceptions of what constitutes wellbeing and self-interest. As more and more people begin to feel the existential threat of climate chaos, and as this leads them to fundamentally rethink wellbeing and what is in their self-interest, new common ground is built: "Creating a narrative based on a common problem — direct threats to people's lives — this can help bring people to the movements" (Int#4). "At the end of the day, we all want a safe, dry place to live, and we all want to be able to turn on a tap and drink water. Part of the social change is finding that commonality. If we all can agree that water is life and we need that to live, that will pull different peoples together" (Int#12 Anishinaabe).

All that said, it's very important to acknowledge that transformative narratives and visions need to be supported materially. It's not enough to offer visions and narratives of a better world; we need to be "changing on the ground practicalities" (Int#2). "People need livelihoods.... To transform this country, the livelihood issue has to get addressed" (Int#2). When the extractive industries come to town, what if our movements showed up with resources to help communities build ecologically and economically viable, culturally appropriate, scalable livelihoods? What if these alternatives were not only climate-friendly, but also addressed colonialism, poverty, inequality and other issues? "An environmental justice movement that offered alternative, meaningful livelihoods, that would be powerful" (S#37).

Movements that actively help create alternative systems and structures are how we overcome the external barriers to the change we want to see. It's also about mass movement building, reaching beyond the choir, reaching people where they are at and meaningfully engaging with them while creating welcoming, inclusive and just spaces that people want to be part of. It's about allying across movements and across sectors to build power to hold government and industry to account. According to the people I spoke with, all of this is important to overcoming the external obstacles we face.

CONFRONTING AND OVERCOMING THE INTERNAL BARRIERS

As for the many internal barriers we are up against — fractured movements, relational and ideological tensions, NGOization, insular activist culture, burnout, a lack of financial resources and bias, self-interest and privilege — these too were considered daunting but not insurmountable. When I asked people how to confront and overcome these barriers, they offered strategies for making our movements more internally cohesive and powerful. Some people focused on movement education, training, celebration and being explicit about tensions, while others emphasized the need to redistribute resources and decision-making power from the NGOs to the grassroots, to get funding to the front lines and to fund the work that is tackling the root causes of the crises. The most common theme, by far, that came up in these conversations about overcoming internal barriers, however, was building better relations within and across movements and developing our collective capacities to work more effectively across difference.

To strengthen our movements, "we need more trainings, more education. We need to get a sense of history of the movements, how to fight, what happened, what can go wrong, what can go right" (Int#19). This sense of history is important, we need to acknowledge that we're not "the first revolutionary, radical, activist, social justice organizer who is thinking through these things" (Int#11). We must "know [our] Elders. There are many great [movement thinkers] over the last 150 years. Don't let that history become forgotten. It's important to keep those ideas alive" so that we're not wasting time and effort "reinventing the wheel" (Int#11).

Others emphasized that keeping our movements strong and warding off burnout "will require celebrating victories" (S#13), whether big or small. We need to be celebrating the "big lofty things but also celebrate having coffee with somebody from another movement or eating from your garden" (Int#6).

One person advised his fellow land defenders to

> get good at your skills. Get damned good at your skills, because the way to overcome the asymmetrical relationship in this conflict is not through quantity, it's through quality. And quality means training. I don't care if its passive, legal resistance or civil disobedience, but get damned good at it. Because then that will

start to offset the advantage that the opposition has, in terms of resources. (Int#38 Mi'kmaw)

There was a shared sense that we need to develop better skills at strategic planning:

> We all know how to state a goal — eradicating capitalism, for example — what is harder is developing the plan to get there. What is lacking in activist circles is real strategic capability.... We don't have to out-muscle our opponent, we have to out-think them ... If there is a secret weapon to defeat colonization, capitalism, industrialization, all that, it's the weapon of strategy ... without it we are taking shots in the dark. (Int#38 Mi'kmaw)

Part of being "smarter and more strategic" (Int#14) "is studying the industries we oppose, [getting] better at identifying their weak points" (Int#8).

Strategy means asking ourselves: "Who are the allies we should be working with? What is our capacity? What are our strengths? What are our weaknesses? What are the targets? What kind of tactics and strategies do we want to engage in and why?" (Int#14). To work towards a synergizing of movement efforts in ways that are not top-down and centralized, we need "more people who are strategic minded, that have the ability to develop plans ... a council of strategic thinkers. That's our force multiplier" (Int#38 Mi'kmaw).

Related to this idea of decentralizing strategy and decision making, many people offered reflections on how to address the problem of NGOization. Indeed, "NGOs were created. We can un-create or remake them to be better" (Int#32):

> One of the problems with NGOs is that it's not clear what their role is in the broader movement — it's vague. They need to know their place and let that determine what they do. If an NGO is there to give support for movement building than it should know what that looks like and organize from that place. (Int#32)

If people in NGOs can be honest and explicit about the ways they are constrained by their need to reach broad audiences and to secure funding, efforts could be made to help mitigate the problems. "For NGOs there's going to be these kinds of constraints, these kinds of pressures," so, they need to ask "what you can do to keep your vision strong and how you can avoid becoming corrupt" (Int#28).

Several people expressed the contention that if NGOs are serious about wanting to help strengthen the movements, they can only do that by actively supporting grassroots groups and communities: "In order to find better and more ethical ways of doing things, NGOs need to constantly ask themselves how what they are doing will impact the most vulnerable people and most impacted communities. And they need to ask how [they] are taking leadership from those folks" (Int#32).

People spoke about how decision-making power needs to be more fairly distributed within movements, as does funding and access to resources in general. One person stated: "We need to democratize the finances of environmental groups" (Int#19). "When you look at the salaries that especially the executives in the NGO take in, it's gargantuan ... imagine putting that money towards grassroots direct actions campaigns, for people who are actually willing to fight." We could transform Canada "if those resources were available to them instead of these high-paid executives" (Int#16).

Overall, "the NGOs' role in the movement should be giving resources to [community and grassroots organizers]" (Int#18):

> I think the paid person in the room should be the person who does the most boring work and supporting trainings, providing the resources. The best of NGO staff, they don't see themselves as the activists, they see themselves as supporting activists.... Imagine the resources of NGOs being used to set up a resource hub for community organizers, with a print shop and child care, etc. NGOs should be doing that. Not strategy. (Int#32)

> Community organizers and land defenders should always be calling the [shots strategically]. (Int#18)

The lack of financial resources in the movements, or perhaps more accurately, the concentration of funds by NGOs who are too risk-adverse to push for radical systemic change, is a clear barrier to organizing. In response to this, many people spoke about ways to get funding to the front lines and to the people doing the most transformative work: "People need to put their resources in things that are working. If you are an organization that has a million dollars, and you have staff, perhaps you should look at the landscape and consider where that money can go to speed up, strengthen, leverage and help the overall movement" (Int#28). "What is the ideal role for NGOs in the movement? One thing, straight up, is redirecting resources" (Int#10). "NGOs have big fund-raising power and big ability to coordinate things, good infrastructure and good money and that should be used for grassroots things ... redirecting funds for land defence" (Int#10). "NGO budgets are enormous.... With a certain percentage of that money distributed to groups who have nothing, but accomplish a great deal and do miracles with nothing, that could make an enormous difference for the movement" (Int#19). For this to happen, we need to make it socially unacceptable for NGOs to pay their executives such high salaries: "We need to create a social cost for doing that" (Int#16).

There is a decent likelihood that, regardless of the transformative power of this kind of redistribution of resources, NGOs are not going to hand over their money, so people discussed other ways of getting resources to the front lines and the people willing to push for more radical change:

> It's always been the folks on the front lines that risk it all, because they don't have a choice. My work is about getting privileged, liberal, sit-on-their-ass white people to get to the point of feeling like that they too don't have a choice. And if we can find a place where white, privileged people realize that we are in fact in need of liberation, I think there's a much better chance that the waves of action that are necessary are going to come about. (Int#4)

How do we help convert the growing awareness about white settler privilege into action and the mobilization and redistribution of settler resources?

One way to do this is through grassroots funding: "I think we can raise some serious grassroots funds. Standing Rock showed that there's a lot of support available ... millions and millions of dollars in donations were sent.... But we need to create these kinds of funds ahead of time, not just in these moments of crisis. Perhaps through monthly donations?" (Int#4). How about an "Adopt an Activist" initiative whereby well-meaning people who are too busy to engage in activism could fund a grassroots activist to do that work? (S#37). "How to get the money is less important than making sure it is available when people on the front lines need it" (Int#8).

Another person suggested reconciliation reparations as a way to fund transformative front-line work:

> If Canadians are really into reconciliation ... only 0.02% of the lands in Canada belong to Indigenous Peoples today.... So why don't we put a 0.02% tax on every piece of land that's sold in Canada and put this into an Indigenous World Bank and then rebuild our communities, pay for lawyers, things like that. Put the money — that settlers owe for living on stolen Indigenous land — in the Indigenous World Bank. And let's think about whether that can be expanded to include any of the revenues from resources that are extracted from Indigenous territories. People could apply to the Indigenous World Bank — with requests like "I need $10,000 to help defend my people [from this pipeline, or this mine]." (Int#25 Dene)

There is a need for redistributing resources in Canada in general, as well as within movements: "Strengthening the movement means trying to invert the power dynamic of who has the resources" (Int#13).

Underlying this conversation about redistributing resources more fairly is a broader theme that came up again and again: the need to coordinate our movement efforts more effectively and get information and resources where they need to be so that we can build collective power that's able to transform the systems and structures driving the crises. According to many, coordination within and across movements is key to confronting the barriers constituted by the ways our movements are fragmented, our efforts dispersed and the ways we sometimes work against each other.

To begin with, if we want to be able to work together in much more powerful ways, we need to practise talking openly about the internal tensions and power asymmetries that exist in our movements. One activist told me that "the tensions are always there.... When I've experienced them to be barriers, it's been because they are unnamed.... We need to be making issues explicit" (Int#15). "Acknowledge it all, that helps" (Int#28). We need to talk about "our complicated alliances so that we can move forward. Name the tensions" (Int#40).

To overcome the fragmentation and internal tensions that are weakening our efforts, we need to learn to collaborate better across difference:

[We may] be uncomfortable with each other's ideas, but it's better done in coordination than not … ideally all of the people in
the movement would sit down together and disclose what each
is doing. We could disagree and push back on each other and
think about the diversity of things being done that can play off
each other in a good way. (Int#10)

Having strategic times where we all come together to support
each other, that's how we build the mass movements. (Int#11)

At the very least, a starting point for forging mutually beneficial relations should be a commitment to avoid publicly denouncing each other:
"Can we stop stepping on each other" (Int#40) and "not talk shit about each
other?" (Int#20). Indeed, some groups have made explicit mutual nonag-
gression pacts between themselves, promising "that we won't denounce
each other" (Int#26). But we can aim for more than just non-aggression:
"How do we [coordinate efforts] so that they become mutually beneficial
to each other? Mutually supportive?" (Int#39). How do we work together
to "overcome divisions, build solidarity and energize people to persevere
through a long difficult struggle?" (S#18).

Collaborating across differences is not easy: "There are going to be
things that we wholeheartedly disagree on, so we need to figure out, how
do we move forward in a way that allows us to disagree, and still move
forward?" (Int#37). If we're going get ourselves out of this crisis, we need
to learn how to make decisions and work together. The way to get there
is "taking action, doing things, building, trying, screwing up, apologizing,
trying again" (Int#28). "I think what we need to do is to figure out how
to break out of that mould and find and rediscover or revitalize or invent
modalities of action that are self-organizing and self-directed within a clear
container and frame. That's the only way we can go exponential" (Int#4).

But there are costs associated with coordination: it takes time and it
can add layers of bureaucracy. As one person told me, "as someone who
sits for fifteen hours of meetings every week, I see the limits of [coordina-
tion]" (Int#39). Coordination can be cumbersome and hinder movement
groups from being nimble and being able to respond quickly to moments
as they arise. Coordination can replicate Western managerial forms and
calcify change processes that are inherently messy and emergent.

There are other limits and problems associated with coordination: it is often done in top-down, centralized ways which are problematic and involve imposing strategy on others and using them instrumentally. "[Coordination] tends to be centrally spearheaded and run more or less tightly from the top" (Int#4). And "trying to make everyone work together all the time ends up watering your own messages until they are palatable for everybody" (Int#20). "If we're going to collaborate it needs to be true collaboration, which means just and horizontal" (Int#13).

If fragmentation in movements is a barrier to change, then forging more coordination and unity within and across movements is called for. This needs to be done in ways that do not replicate power-over relations, nor managerial, bureaucratic processes that hinder our autonomy and ability to respond quickly. What do bottom-up forms of communication, of connectivity, of synergizing the efforts of fractured, siloed movements look like?

Bottom-up coordination means making sure it's not always the same people convening; it means "building trust between groups" (Int#28). Instead of coordination being imposed from on top, it should emerge organically through responsiveness, through active solidarity across groups and movements. We need to be looking outwards enough to see and respond when there is support needed elsewhere in the movements. "Know what solidarity is and be prepared to stand in solidarity. Solidarity is the antidote to factionalism, and solidarity means that sometimes you stand in solidarity with people you don't like" (Int#14). "The work we do creating solidarity between social movements is our best way to build revolution and new systems of governance" (Int#24).

Many people spoke about building strategic alliances across various differences: resistance projects, geographic locations, legal cases, approaches to change and end goals. There is so much amazing work going on across the country, with people taking action in all kinds of ways. How can we link them up and combine all forces into something more transformative?

The most common kind of answer I got when I asked people how we can overcome the internal barriers we face was about finding new ways to coordinate our efforts, to understand where each of us is best positioned to contribute to the movement, to value the rich diversity that exists and to use it to build our collective power to make change. Several people referred to this as movement ecosystem perspective, the key question of which is how we can work with this diversity that we're currently struggling with. Can each group, community and organization do its work without counteracting or pushing against others in the movements? "How do you make it work so that we're not hindering each other's work?" (Int#15).

"I look at it as an ecosystem ... different groups with different skills" (Int#40). "There is not one set of strategies and tactics. You can't look at what one group is doing and say 'this is systemic change'.... I don't think you can look at a set of tactics and strategies in isolation from what others are doing" (Int#39). It takes many different groups doing many different things to bring about systems change. All this diversity will become more effective as the relations and communication between diverse groups are forged and strengthened: "Like an octopus with many arms moving in different directions and doing different things ... each arm knows what the other is doing" (Int#39). "We need to map out the relationships. Who knows who? And who is doing what? How do we actualize those relationships and release the power that is inherent in those relationships such that we effectively make shit happen?" (Int#16).

This movement ecosystem approach can help us see ourselves as part of a greater whole and approach our work in ways that strengthen the whole movement rather than merely perpetuating our own specific group, organization or community. This approach prompts us to ask: What are the goals of the movement and where do we fit in? What are our strengths? What are our resources? How can we best serve the overall movement? "Know where your place is and do your part well. Be part of a larger movement context" (Int#32). Can we get to the place where the different groups in the movement can identity as a necessary but insufficient part of a system? "It's a tough one — putting aside self-interest in favour of the greater good" (Int#33).

"There will always be and should be a diversity of approaches in the ecology of the movement" (Int#4). "There are so many different people doing different things on different issues. It's like biodiversity, the stronger the diversification is, the stronger the movement. You cannot cut the head off the movement because it's going to grow something somewhere else" (Int#19). The more diverse we are, the stronger we are. But diversity is not enough. The diversity needs to be coordinated (Int#40).

The diversity that exists within these movements, the end goals, ideology, tactics, etc., is a strength but it is also a source of tension and division. It is a barrier to change because the diversity is in many ways blocking collaboration and coordination. How do we transform this diversity from a barrier into a strength?

> We have to approach it with a lot of humility and see it as a team sport. Think of the movement as a hockey team. You can't have one person on the ice the whole game, it doesn't work. Not everyone can play forward. Not everyone can be the goalie. You have your goons, and you have delicate artistes with the puck. You have the grinders who are just going to get in there and tough it out. They have to play different roles. (Int#16)

"People need to see value in each other" (Int#15), and "we all need to be really humble about what our role is. None of us can win without others. The question becomes — what is the kind of relationality that's going to make us do this better?" (Int#16). Thinking about movements as ecosystems may be a kind of relationality that can help us do better.

Can each group, community and organization in the movement understand where it's constrained and where it's powerful? What does collaboration look like when taking each other's constraints and strengths into account? Clearly, grassroots groups are constrained by a lack of resources, but they're unconstrained in terms of what they can say and the tactics they can engage in. NGOs, on the other hand, have more access to resources but are constrained in what they can say and what tactics they can use. A movement ecosystem perspective could help nurture a humility that allows us to see that each of our favoured approaches to change is necessary but not sufficient. It can help us see the whole and identify how "we can do what they can't do, and they can do what we can't. It becomes more of an organic support system, where we're all trying to raise the bar" (Int#31).

"People should look at their aptitudes and gifts" (Int#4) and, based on our respective strengths and constraints, determine which strategies are most helpful in developing our "strategy within the larger ecosystem" (Int#3):

> George Lakey may be responsible for the concept of movement ecology. He explained that in the large ecosystem of change there are reformers, the people who work in the system to make change, there are people who are working in opposition to the

system, and then there are people who are working outside the system. (Int#10)

"There's a role for the healers and for the teachers and for the direct-action organizers ... in a movement ecosystem" (Int#32). "All of those things are valid, and we should just be encouraging other people to do the things they like to do. This pretending it's one way or the other is not helping us" (Int#20 Michif Cree). You need both the

> good cop and bad cop. If you don't talk to people who are in power, they're going do what the hell they want. You need the good cops who will speak to the people in power. But you also need people who are out there on the streets saying, "This does not make sense!" There is room for both. (Int#15)

Which groups are best positioned to have an impact on the system? Where and how can the various forces work synergistically? "Everyone takes their place in the fight. Each has their specialization. Everyone has their role" (Int#16). "We need movement theory that overarches and sees where people are at, that there's a role for everyone" (S#27):

> How social change happens is a question of seeing at which times you need which strategies and who is in the position to best use those strategies. It's never going to be only just one, it's got to be a mix of those strategies ... blockading, marketing campaigns, negotiations, demonstration projects, court cases, pilot projects.... But you need to figure out who else is in the mix and put that whole package together. (Int#33)

There is a need for more coordination between different niches of the movements, more synergizing of the efforts. There is a shared sense that top-down coordination doesn't work. What do horizontal or bottom-up linkages look like? The ecosystem metaphor can help us here. Forest ecosystems build health and resilience by sharing information and resources, getting things to where they need to be, to keep the whole of the system strong. How can movements share information and resources more effectively such that everyone's transformative capacity is increased because of the relations we have?

Movement ecosystem does not mean we're all in "formal coalitions.

Coalitions can be awesome, and they can drive you nuts" (Int#33). We don't need to be formally working together, but we'd be well advised to look to the diversity within the movements we are part of and ask ourselves:

> Where's the energy? Where's the power? What are the different points of leverage? What's the economic leverage? What's the sort of creative energy that can be unleashed? What's the imaginative energy? What's the cultural values that are already there to be leveraged? All those things. Just look at all the resources that are available in the broadest way and then figure out how to make them accessible. And then figure out a plan for creating the relationships that are necessary to put all that together. I think a lot of it just comes down to relationships and common understanding. (Int#16)

Again and again in these conversations, people spoke of relationships as the basis of building collective power, and of movement building as "the long, hard work of building relationships with people" (Int#5). "It is relationships that create change" (Int#37). "The more we work on our relationships the more we arrive at new ways of organizing ourselves" (Int#18). "Capitalism has weakened community ties. If we can rebuild these relationships, we can better share the risks and share the responsibilities" associated with social change (Int#5). Relationships can bring more people to the movements and can be the antidote to burnout and keep activists engaged for the long haul. Relationships need to be fostered and cared for, and we need "more spaces where people can recharge their batteries and be surrounded by love and people" (Int#19).

Building regional relationships is key to strengthening our movements, as is strengthening our relationships to place: "Remembering where we belong on the planet ... happens through experience and relationship to place" (Int#33). "Connection to land will help foster better decision making in the future" (Int#37). But for settlers, relationship to land and place needs to be done with care:

> You don't have rights and title. But [you have] responsibilities. If you live here and you accept those responsibilities, change how you walk in this world, and help other people come to that recognition. It's not about ridding yourself of that tension or absolving

yourself of that guilt, it's about changing how you make decisions, changing how you look at things. (Int#37)

In movements, we work with such a sense of urgency that we often put aside care for ourselves and each other. But this kind of care is needed if we are to build relationships that will be the foundation of collective action: "We're so productivity-oriented that at times civility goes by the wayside. But we have to take care of each other" (Int#11). "We need to learn how to be better with each other.... It's important to feel [we] can count on [each other]" (Int#10).

> It's about trying to operate from our higher selves ... genuinely being mindful when we're in movement spaces ... that I will make mistakes and the person in front of me will make mistakes, but we're here to do the best we can. Remember that people are trying ... tread gently in the collective tango that we're doing. There is no perfection. There's a lot of trying. (Int#11)

To strengthen our movements, we need to learn to listen better: "Non-Indigenous people need to learn to listen and to really listen well" (Int#25 Dene). "That listening feels like the heart of the transformation, of transformative capacity. That's the heart of what makes a good relationship" (S#37). "Being really good allies, that's the only thing that matters" (Int#33).

These visions of a vibrant, healthy, diverse movement ecosystem of multiple, intersecting, mutually beneficial relationships are inspiring and compelling, but as the discussion on the internal barriers to change makes clear, this is not where our movements are at currently. We are struggling to work together across the many division and tensions and to find ways to turn the diversity into a strength, rather than something that divides and weakens us.

In these conversations, and in parallel discussions going on in academic and activist literature, again and again I hear a call for relational approaches to movement building and activism. By weaving together activist and academic conversations, I will begin to sketch out what such relational approaches to social change may be based on and what they might look like.

RELATIONAL THEORIES OF CHANGE AND
RELATIONAL APPROACHES TO MOVEMENT BUILDING

> What seems to cascade across the accounts is a rendering of collectivity itself as a theory of change — E. Tuck and K.W. Yang, *Youth Resistance Research and Theories of Change*

In Chapter 6, we saw that the relational tensions that exist in these movements are understood to be the most significant barrier to change, hindering our efforts. But these tensions and fragmentations are not unique to these specific movements. This tendency in movements is "a public secret," widely known but not easy to talk about (Montgomery and bergman 2017: 23). These tensions "exist across the broader left, where sectarianism has been a disastrous and weakening force" (Dixon 2014: 233). They hinder the creation of widespread and strong collaboration, and inhibit our ability to envision strategies and futures together. As Naomi Klein put it: "The intellectual fencing has constrained the progressive imagination for so long it's lying twisted on the ground" (2017: 263). In these and other social movements, deep ideological and other rifts are "rendering much of our work useless" (brown 2017: 62). We need

> more developed ways of avoiding rigidity in theory and practice. Left political currents, despite their best intentions, are a treasure trove of ideological dogmas, idealized models, fetishized practices, and sectarian conflicts.... We need to cultivate fresh thinking that begins not with rigid formulas but rather with hard questions grounded in the dynamic, complicated circumstances in which we struggle. (Dixon 2014: 222)

Capitalism, colonialism and heteropatriarchy have damaged our relationships with each other and with the Earth. These damaged relationships hinder our ability to think across difference and forge powerful alliances strong enough to radically transform our world from one of destruction of people and planet to one of healing, justice and mutual flourishing. We need to learn and practise new ways of relating.

At some point during the winter of 2017, while reading Indigenous theories of change and reading through and coding the interview transcripts, I began to see the theme of relationships come up again and again.

It slowly became, to me, the key lesson of this project. Relationships are central to social change, while fraught relations in our movements are holding us back from being as powerful as we can be. As I thought, read and had many conversations with fellow activists about all this, what I heard loud and clear is that building stronger movements means working together better — working better across all kinds of differences and tensions that currently fragment us and weaken our power.

I have come to believe that underlying the interpersonal tensions and ongoing debates in the movements is the tendency in Western thought and culture to reduce the world into rigid compartments, dividing rich complexity into simple binaries and dualisms (Plumwood 2002; Escobar 2018). As discussed in Chapter 3, Western worldviews tend to break the world into hierarchized binaries, which undergird systems of domination such as racism, sexism, colonialism and destruction of nature by humans (Plumwood 2002; Collins and Bilge 2016). These dualisms have not only led to the social and ecological crises we face but also serve to constrain human responses to these crises (Moore 2016; Head 2016). Indeed "our sense of social hierarchy as natural, undermines our ability to create movements for social change that do not replicate the structures of domination we seek to eradicate" (Smith 2017: 153).

Dualism constructs "devalued and sharply demarcated sphere[s] of otherness" (Plumwood 2002: 41). Within this worldview, difference becomes interpreted through the lens of good/bad, inferior/superior. It is a worldview that drives disconnection and oppression (Escobar 2018: 65). Dualism does not just divide up the social world into hierarchal difference, but it also divides up our conceptual worlds in these ways. As I will argue in more detail below, this kind of thinking fosters oversimplified conceptions of change, where we reduce the complexity of social change into rigid ideas that change needs to come, for example, from the bottom up, *not* the top down, or from outside the system, *not* from inside the system; that we need radical, *not* reformist change; that change must come from collective, *not* from individual action. Though each of these contentions is pointing to important issues that we do need to attend to, they are also missing some of the rich, complex nuance about change and the social world that we may benefit from engaging with more. Dualistic thinking also nurtures this tendency to hierarchize different issues and struggles. To some, climate change is so urgent that we must raise it above the social crisis of inequality. To others, people are dying right now due to racism and sexism and that needs to be prioritized over the more distant problem of climate change. This move to raise one issue above the other, to rank struggles according to relative importance, is ethically problematic, makes it difficult to forge strong relations of solidarity across movements and keeps us from combining forces to push together for a more just and ecologically viable world.

"Efforts to transcend capitalism in any egalitarian and broadly sustainable fashions will be stymied so long as the radical political imagination is captive by capitalism's either/or organization of reality" (Moore 2016: 3). Thinking from within the dualisms that are inherent to capitalism constrains our ability to develop adequate anti-systemic strategy. In other words, the worldviews that are driving the current crises are not likely to help us confront and solve them (Moore 2016).

Dualistic thinking is a characteristic of the Cartesian, reductionist worldview that sees life and all phenomena as made up of separate, individual things. This reductionistic way of seeing "assumes the pre-existence of distinct entities whose respective essences are not seen as fundamentally dependant on their relations to other entities — they exist in and of themselves ... independent objects interacting" (Escobar 2018: 100–101).

To transform reductionism, hierarchy and dualism and the ways they constrain our thinking and structure relations of power, we need to replace them with non-hierarchical ways of navigating difference (Plumwood 2002). Undoing dualism requires a "recognition of a complex, interacting patterns of both continuity and difference" (Plumwood 2002: 67). Relationality can help us understand life and movements in a non-dualized way. Intersectional feminism, Indigenous ontologies and nature itself can help us explore this idea of relationality.

In contrast to reductionist, dualistic understandings, relational ontologies understand things and beings *as* relations; individual things do not exist prior to the relations that constitute them. In contrast to a world made of independent individuals, relational worldviews see individuals as interacting, interdependent and *mutually constituted,* meaning that things exist because of their dependence on other things: "Nothing pre-exists the relations that constitute it. Life is interrelation and interdependence through and through, always and from the beginning" (Escobar 2018: 101).

Intersectional feminist scholarship about activism offers important insights into fostering relational thinking:

> The either/or binary thinking that has been so central to Eurocentric social thought is less relevant for intersectionality. Instead intersectional projects look at the relationships among seemingly different phenomena ... strive to go beyond oppositional thinking carried out by Eurocentric binaries and attempt to forge a complex and interactive understanding of the relationships between history, social organization, and forms of consciousness, both personal and collective — in short, relational thinking. (Collins and Bilge 2016: 195)

Rather than either/or binary thinking, intersectionality embraces a both/and frame, helping us to see social phenomena and various axes of oppression as interrelated and co-constructed, exposing the relationships between race, class, gender and other systems. This perspective expands intellectual and political potential, helping to find common ground across what may seem from more reductionist perspectives as disparate, unrelated social struggles and movements (Collins and Bilge 2016).

Many Indigenous ontologies and epistemologies are deeply relational, understanding all beings — humans and non-humans, living and non-living — as related, as kin, as profoundly interdependent (Kimmerer 2013; Simpson 2017; Atleo 2011). Although it is crucial not to homogenize Indigenous cosmologies and ways of knowing, as there are many diverse cultures and peoples represented when we say Indigenous, it is clear that Indigenous ontologies have much to teach non-Indigenous people about relationality.

In *Principles of Tsawalk* (2011), E. Richard Atleo points out that the Nuu-chah-nulth worldview sees "creation filled with mutually interdependent life forms that require mutually acceptable protocols in order to maintain balance and harmony" (37) and that "all of reality is considered to be a universe of relationships" (46). Atleo also sees the global environmental crisis as fundamentally about relational disharmony. Re-establishing healthy relationships is a major aim of many of Indigenous resistance and resurgence movements (Coburn 2015: 25). Alex Wilson emphasizes that "we, each of us, have responsibilities for healing relationships with all our relations in the human, natural and spirit worlds. This means justice is not conceived in the mainstream, colonial language of autonomous liberal individual (or human) rights. Instead justice appears as a matter of fulfilling responsibilities towards all relations (paraphrased in Coburn 2015: 44). Cherokee scholar Jeff Corntassel explains that Indigenous resurgence "at its core" is about "spiritual and relational responsibilities that are continuously renewed" (quoted in Coburn 2015: 33).

Leanne Betasamosake Simpson writes: "My Ancestors didn't accumulate capital, they accumulated networks of meaningful, deep, fluid, intimate collective and individual relationships of trust. In times of hardship, we did not rely to any great degree, on accumulated capital or individualism but on the strength of our relationships with others" (2017: 77). Writing about her Nation, Betasamosake Simpson describes this ontology as a

> web of connection to each other, to the plant nations, the animal nations, the rivers and lakes, the cosmos, and our neighbouring Indigenous nations ... an ecology of intimacy. It is an ecology of relationships in the absence of coercion, hierarchy, or authoritarian power.... It is relationships based on deep reciprocity, respect, non-interference, self-determination, and freedom. (Simpson 2017: 8)

Across Canada and around the world, based on close ties with and fierce love for people and land, Indigenous communities are resisting destructive development. They are "defending relational territories and worlds against the ravages of large-scale extractivist operations" (Escobar 2018: 67). Indigenous relational ontologies that centre reciprocity and respect offer alternatives and indeed the counter-force and antidote to extractivist worldviews (Kimmerer 2013; Simpson 2017; Klein 2014). "The economic alternatives these movements are proposing and building are mapping ways of living within planetary boundaries, ones based on intricate reciprocal relationships rather than brute extraction" (Klein 2014: 451).

What is needed is for many more people to cultivate worldviews "embedded in interdependence rather than hyper-individualism, reciprocity rather than dominance, and cooperation rather than hierarchy" (Klein 2014: 462):

It's understandable that we associate these ideas today with an

Indigenous worldview; it is primarily such cultures that have kept this alternative way of seeing the world alive in the face of the bulldozers of colonialism and corporate globalization. Like seed savers safeguarding the biodiversity of the global seed stock, other ways of relating to the natural world and one another have been safeguarded by many Indigenous cultures. (Klein 2014: 443)

And Nature too has much to teach us about relationships. In the book *Braiding Sweetgrass*, ecologist and member of the Potawatomi Nation Robin Wall Kimmerer writes that pecan tree groves teach us that "there are no soloists ... the trees act not as individuals, but somehow as a collective.... What happens to one, happens to all. We can starve together or feast together. All flourishing is mutual" (2013: 15). She describes how trees in forests connect to each other through fungal networks underground: "These fungal networks appear to redistribute the wealth of carbohydrates from tree to tree.... They weave a web of reciprocity, of giving and taking. Through unity, survival. All flourishing is mutual" (Kimmerer 2013: 20). Kimmerer explains that lichens too are made of relations of mutualistic symbiosis, partnerships in which both members benefit from their association: "When conditions are harsh and life is tenuous, it takes a team sworn to reciprocity to keep life going forward. In a world of scarcity, interconnection and mutual aid become critical for survival. So say the lichens" (Kimmerer 2013: 272).

All flourishing is mutual. What would change if this phrase became a central guiding principle in our movements? What would it look like if we knew that our power and survival lie in our relations and our mutual aid? How can we learn from the natural world around us about how to best collaborate, about how to shape change? (brown 2017). How can we "be movements like flocks of birds" with "underground power like whispering mushrooms?" (brown 2017: 23)?

Capitalism needs us to bicker amongst ourselves and fracture our efforts; it seeks to divide and conquer. Solidarity is a commitment to mutual flourishing. It is how we reject and release capitalism's grip on our relationships and lives. Caitlin Cahill and David Alberto Quijada Cerecer offer what they call a powerful "crazy glue theory of change." They write:

Our commitment begins with a commitment to each other ... a crazy glue theory of needing each other and having each other's backs ... love like social change is collectively produced, evolves, requires guidance, and daily reminders that we know how to love like we know how to dismantle oppressive conditions through our shared participation in the world. (quoted in Tuck and Yang 2013: 135–136)

Relationship is power. Power is relationship. Or as Collins and Bilge put it: "Power is better conceptualized as a relationship than as a static entity.... Power constitutes a relationship" (2016: 28). Temper et al. (2018) too describe power as relational. They write that transformative power is built through social connections and networks and through breaking down the walls that separate struggles, seeing the links between issues and creating stronger alliances. Through active solidarity, we begin to figure out power without domination (brown 2017). It is by transforming power-over to power-with that we may be able to generate a force strong enough to tear down the barriers we face. There is much promise in our, as yet untapped, capacity to build power through our relationships — within and across movements, and between activists and land defenders and those yet to join the fight.

What if we apply relationality to building bigger, stronger movements? In the next sections I explore this in two ways: by applying a relational approach to thinking across different understandings of change and different approaches to change. I then I apply a relational approach to thinking across the most prevalent dualism of all — us vs. them.

Thinking and Working across Difference

When we think about change, we think about change within the constraints of what we already know — Kai Barrow, quoted in Chris Dixon, *Another Politics*

In the movements I am part of we talk about intersectionality and we raise up Indigenous ways of knowing, but in many ways we are still relating to each other and understanding change in binary, hierarchical ways. As I've argued, the legacy of Western, reductionist thought is one of the forces driving divisions, tensions and our difficulties in thinking and working across difference. I have noticed a pervasive tendency to assume that our preferred approach to change is *the* most effective — dare I say the superior — way of doing activism. As adrienne marie brown, a women's rights activist and black feminist from the US, has observed about the movements she is part of: "There is a practice of narrowing down, identifying one path forward, one strategy, one way, one agenda, one leader, one set of values etc., reducing the wild and wonderful world into one thing that we can grasp, handle, hold onto, advance" (2017: 155–156).

Those who tend towards confrontational, direct action tactics argue that this is what is needed. Those who engage in electoral politics emphasize that this is the only way we'll make the changes that are needed. This tendency is completely understandable — of course we engage in the ways we think are most effective. But underlying this dynamic are over-simplified, reductionist, binary ways of understanding change that divide up the movements along many lines. These dividing lines include reform vs. radical, inside the system vs. outside the system, top-down vs. bottom-up, resistance vs. solutions, confrontation vs. collaboration and individual action vs. collective action.

Although these divisions point to important questions that we must ask ourselves about effective strategy, I believe that in some ways they also constitute false dichotomies. These dualized conceptions of change may be constraining our willingness to collaborate across difference and are likely constraining our ability to develop adequately complex approaches to dealing with complex problems. These ways of understanding change reinforce conceptual and relational silos and divide and weaken our movement efforts. We value diversity in theory, for sure, but in day-to-day organizing, we tend to want to work with people who share our political analysis, theory of change and preferred tactics. Indeed, "this pretending it's one way or the other is not helping us" (Int#20 Michif Cree). Though we're all attached to our idea of what constitutes effective social change, "no single organization mode, type of organization, or strategic model works across all circumstances. Treating any practice, structure, or approach as infallible is thus a dead end; it shuts down our abilities to think and act innovatively" (Dixon 2014: 228).

Though not all approaches to change are created equal, we could generate more power in our movements if we get past these dualized notions and instead think about how we can work across these differences in ways that are generative. As Ethan Miller says about the social movements he is part of:

We cannot afford to divide ourselves along these lines, and we must cease to participate in a culture of activism which tries to place final judgments on the importance, effectiveness, or "radicalness" of our diverse forms of work. We need each other. We need each other's differences. We need the many different things that each of us has to offer. This is about relentless humility: we do not know how to make the changes that we need to make, and we will only discover the paths together. (2012: 18)

The kind of working across difference that I envision "is less about adding up movements as if they could be unified, and more about illustrating the productiveness of their difference; like combining different tones and rhythms to see how they resonate" (Montgomery and bergman 2017: 34). It's not just bringing together different kinds of people who don't usually work together, although that is part of it. It's also about bringing together, merging, cross-pollinating different strategies and tactics that usually happen in isolation from each other. And seeing what happens.

The Zapatistas articulated the concept of the pluriverse, a world where many worlds fit (Escobar 2018). I am thinking about movements where many approaches to change fit, "weav[ing] together our strengths" (brown 2017: 66). Borrowing from Collins and Bilge, who were talking about intersectionality, I want to see how we can work in ways in which our "heterogeneity [is] not as a weakness but rather ... a source of tremendous potential" (2016: 204).

Ecology and permaculture theory speaks of the "edge effect," whereby there is more diversity and richness where two or more ecosystems meet. I think this is true in social systems too. Though "we naturally gravitate to those who are like us and with whom we can have more or less fruitful conversations ... the most useful work takes place on the margins, in networks with those who are not quite like us" (Cox 2017: 612). Another way to put this is that "possibilities light up at the intersections" (brown 2017: 175). adrienne marie brown reflects that her best work has happened during her most difficult collaborations "because there are actual differences that are converging and creating more space, ways forward that serve more than one worldview" (2017: 159). Working at these edges can be powerful, but they are not easy. "We often reject that chaotic, fertile reality too soon, as if we can't tolerate the scale of our own collective brilliance" (brown 2017: 156). I am really curious about this capacity for collective brilliance that can emerge when we step outside our dichotomous notions of change.

Chapter 5, on the movements' theories of change, offered the insight that change happens through a convergence of many forces and factors and that different approaches to change can be brought together to build power. I seek to apply all that important insight here, in envisioning how the false dichotomies and lines of division can be reconciled as we learn to work at the edges and across difference.

The systems that we seek to transform are complex and processes of transformation are themselves complex. And so, we need complex strategies that take into account and resist the many forms of injustice simultaneously, that put pressure in different ways, that take aim at multiple targets, strategies that shift and morph as the conditions change. We need approaches that make use of the rich and diverse skills and insights that the many different people and groups and communities in the movements have to offer. We need more holistic conceptions of change and approaches to activism that account for the complex nature of what we are trying to do. It is these more nuanced, complexified, messy and lively approaches to change that I've come to believe can really transform the political and economic status quo. What follows are many frameworks, which I gathered through reading and through conversations, that can help us think across the many different approaches to social change.

Joanna Macy's "three dimensions of the great turning" framework offers the insight that there are three main approaches to bringing about systems change. Firstly, there is *holding actions,* which "aim to hold back and slow down the damage being caused by the political economy of Business as Usual" (Macy and Johnstone 2012: 94). The goal is to defend what is left of our natural systems and our social fabric. Tactics include blockades, boycotts, legal proceedings and protests. These are crucial, but "vital as protest is, relying on it as a sole avenue of change can leave us battle weary or disillusioned" (2012: 94). We also need to create and live and promote alternatives, solutions and new systems. She calls this dimension *life-sustaining systems and practices*; this is a rethinking of the way human societies are organized and function and how they provide for human needs. This work is the "creative redesign of the structures and systems that make up our society" (2012: 96). This can include green building, alternative energy systems, cooperative forms of ownership, new forms of governance, permaculture and agroecology, alternative transportation, ethical financial systems, skill shares and community teach-ins. However, on their own, these are not enough. "These new structures won't take root and survive without deeply ingrained values to sustain them" and thus a shift in consciousness is needed too (2012: 96). *Shift in consciousness* is the third dimension of Macy's framework. Though it may seem esoteric to many of us, this kind of change comes from shifts taking place in our hearts, our minds and our understandings of reality. Changing the deeply held stories we tell ourselves and each other about what's wrong, what's possible and what's important inspires us to act. Telling new stories "gives fuel to our courage and determination. By refreshing our sense of belonging in the world, we widen the web of relationships that nourishes us and protects us from burnout" (2012: 96).

Each of these dimensions of change is necessary but insufficient on its own; they are mutually reinforcing. Many activists and other agents of change tend to gravitate towards one of these approaches over others. This is fine, but three important points can be made here: People and social change groups focusing on one approach should acknowledge the importance of the other two approaches as also necessary but insufficient. Communication and collaboration across the three approaches can help leverage change efforts and change initiatives that do all three at the same time may be particularity effective.

Ethan Miller's framework of "the four wings of transformative movements" emphasizes that to bring about a transformation away from capitalism, we need to link the various forms of transformative work that exist. He refers to these as defence, offence, creation and healing (Miller 2012: 18). He argues:

> We must connect the work of *defending* our lives and communities from colonization and injustice, the work of actively *opposing* oppression in all forms, the work of *healing* together from trauma and hurt, and the work of imagining, *creating,* and building alternative ways to live together and meet our needs as integral parts of a holistic movement for transformation. (2012: 18)

Gibson-Graham offers another framework, arguing that social change necessitates imagination, self-change and collective decision making. Our *imagination* allows us to expand our visions of what is possible. *Self-change* is a dual path in which changing the self is a path towards changing the world and transforming one's environment is a mode of transforming the self. Finally, *collective decision making* involves experimental projects and the decisions people in communities make together (2006: xxxvi).

Habermas's theory of change emphasizes both defensive and offensive work — defending the life world from further colonization by the system while also working to "conquer new territory for equality, justice and communicative rationality" (Carroll and Sarker 2016: 38). Carroll and Sarker argue that building counter-hegemony requires three things: confronting and opposing the existing status quo and its legitimacy, creating alternative understandings of society that "pose a challenge to the dominant bourgeois-led view" and creating alternative structures that prefigure a socially just and ecologically healthy world (2016: 48). This involves three kinds of tasks: building community, meeting needs and mobilizing and engaging in collective action (Carroll and Ratner 2001). In yet another framework, Kevin MacKay (2017) argues that to transform society away from oligarchic control, movements need to focus on four strategic areas, arguing that resistance, education, solidarity-building and alternatives-building are all required for bringing about radical change. And finally, according to social ecologists, radical change requires that movements work on three levels. They must develop critical praxis and self-education, be oppositional and resist, and create alternatives (Tokar 2018).

Many of these frameworks and many of the other theories of transformation emphasize this need to link the processes of *resisting* the status quo with the development of *alternatives* to it. Temper et al. emphasize Paul Robbins' concept of the "hatchet and seed" approach, which involves the dual task of deconstructing the old systems, relations and ideas, and creating the new (2018: 14). Transition scholar Loorbach (2014) argues that there is need to navigate through phases of disruption, intentional dismantling or unintentional collapse of the old systems, ideas and structures as well as the creating and diffusion of new systems, ideas and structures. Loorbach contends that, ideally, we can work to manage the descent of the old at the same time as the ascent of the new in order to minimize disruptions and suffering. Critical scholars also see the need for this dual strategy. For them, social transformation means opposing the systems of domination and destruction as well as creating just and ecologically viable alternative forms of livelihoods and relations (see Gibson-Graham 2006; Miller 2012; Allard and Davidson 2008).

Indigenous scholarship on change frames this dual strategy somewhat differently. Decolonial change calls for "actions that engage in a generative refusal of any aspect of state control, so they don't just refuse, they also embody an Indigenous alternative" (Simpson 2017: 35). Where non-Indigenous people need to innovate and create new systems and lifeways if they are to live in just and sustainable ways, Indigenous Peoples have existing knowledge, practices and systems that are being reinvigorated. In this way, the dual strategy is different for settlers than it is for Indigenous Peoples.

To my mind, the most exciting strategic intersection, or edge, is where resistance and solutions meet. Generally, the people working on the solutions and building the alternatives and those enacting resistance to the destructive systems are working separately. Over the last few years in Canada there has been a new and powerful strategy for transformation emerging in Indigenous communities opposing ongoing oil and gas development; they are building solutions in the pathway of the problem. The Healing Lodge and permaculture gardens at the Unist'ot'en camp in BC, the Treaty Truck House at the Mi'kmaw protest camp against Alton Gas in Nova Scotia, the Tiny House Warriors fighting the Trans Mountain pipeline in Secwepemc territory and the Watch House on Burnaby Mountain are all examples of Indigenous Peoples building low-carbon, beautiful, culturally-grounded alternatives and placing these alternatives strategically to block the way of proposed oil and gas projects being pushed into their territories. These alternatives are offering inspiration by making clear that there are other ways to build economies. At the same time, they are enacting Indigenous sovereignty and lifeways. This new strategy of placing the alternatives in the pathway of the problem has been changing what environmental justice organizing and protest looks like in Canada.

I can imagine much more of this. I envision permaculture and urban agriculture practitioners at the front lines, working with environmental activists and land defenders to develop *direct action solutions*, whereby instead of just standing at demonstrations and protests with placards listening to speeches and yelling slogans, we have a three-hour work party where people plant seeds and trees, install solar panels, guerrilla garden, skill-share or glean from unpicked fruit trees and then march through the streets, with placards and slogans, distributing food to folks who need it. In this way, we are learning the solutions to capitalism while we gather in the streets to protest the things we don't want.

This kind of *thinking across* approaches to change can be applied in many different ways. In the conversations with activists and land defenders, many people offered frameworks for thinking and working across the many differences that exist in our movements. In order to figure out how to work across difference, it can be helpful to be clear about what kinds of *tactics* you're willing to engage with. Knowing each group's *doctrine* can also help determine how different groups' work can fit together: "A lot of us have very different doctrines. Doctrines are how you fight; the kinds of tactics you are willing to engage in. Once I know your doctrine, I know where you can fit" (E#12). Different phases of social change campaign strategies call for different kinds of tactics, and so knowing the end goals and doctrines of different groups helps us determine where their work can best support the overall movement (Int#38 Mi'kmaw).

It's also helpful to think about how different kinds of actions and different kinds of leadership make sense at different phases of a fight. As one person explained to me: "There are shaping actions, the actions that make it possible for people to revolt. Sustaining actions which allow people to continue to revolt. And then there is decisive actions, where you win" (Int#14). Different groups have different positions and skills and this can determine who is best equipped to take the lead at different stages in a campaign or fight.

One person provided the following way to think about the different roles that need to be played in a movement and to identify where we can best position ourselves to contribute:

> Imagine there's an earthquake and there's a group of people who are being impacted and the government isn't bringing aid to these people. What do you do? Do you a) go to the government and do lobbying, are you a *lobbyist*? b) Do you organize a demo, are you a *mobilizer/organizer*? c) Do you go to the site where the people are impacted and give direct support, care, water? Are you a *front-line helper*? Or d) Do you shut down a highway until the government acts … are you a *rebel*? Lobbyist, organizer, front-line help or rebel? All necessary. (Int#10)

This is a helpful way to think across the inside vs. outside and reform vs. radical debates in that some of these roles need to be played by those with access to formal power (lobbying) and others by those on the periphery of the systems (rebels). This too contributes to nurturing a sense of valuing the diversity in how we approach activism.

Another person identified four different strategic approaches that are needed in a movement:

> There is *facilitating change*. That's your planning process, where you sit down and figure things out together. There is *enabling change,* which is more advocacy, creating space for new solutions. Which can be legal work or political advocacy. There is *demonstrating change,* which is the pilot project model, which shows that something is possible, because you have just done it. And then there is *forcing change*, which is more the court cases or the market campaigns. (Int#33)

All these frameworks help us think about different approaches to change and work towards a more relational, inclusive approach to movement building while also weakening the old debates over the right tactic. It is not to say that all groups have to engage in all these approaches to change: "Not all groups can or should move between those. Some groups are really specialized and have real skills and talents in particular approaches. Having groups that only do one thing, that can be powerful, but you need to figure out who else is in the mix, to put that whole package together" (Int#33).

It's important to note that all these frameworks and efforts to embrace diversity and differentiated roles should not be interpreted to mean that all approaches to social change are equal. It is not a call for strategy free for all. There needs to be some mechanism for determining which approaches to change are called for when and under which conditions, and to make sure we can think about how and why certain strategies and approaches become problematic. Specifically, "we need to make sure that in such diverse tactics, there are not unintended consequences to marginalized communities." We need to "take leadership from those front-line communities that are the most at risk.... These are the kinds of power calculations that require an in-depth analysis on anti-colonialism, anti-racism and anti-oppression. It's really critical" (E#16).

Here we begin to see how thinking about different end goals can help us think through which approaches to change make sense in which context. There are people engaged in these movements for whom the end goal is stopping a pipeline. For others, it's reducing greenhouse gas emissions. For others, the end goal is the return of land and self-determination to Indigenous Peoples on Turtle Island. For some, it is the end of all forms of domination. What your end goal is can really shape your approach to change and who you're willing to collaborate with and why. So many of the relational tensions in these movement spaces are about how we approach change, but underlying those debates are tensions over different end goals and how these may or may not be in line with each other.

For some radical change goals (like eliminating all power inequities) it may be that collective action, from the bottom up, is necessary. Whereas maybe for more incremental, reformist goals that don't threaten the power structure, top-down, insider strategies may indeed work best. If we can be more explicit about our end goals, we can lay them out and see where shorter-term goals, such as stopping a pipeline or getting a left-leaning politician elected, can help support longer-term end goals, such as Indigenous self-determination.

To be able to see how we can all work as a common force, even if towards different ends along the way, we need to be explicit about our end goals:

> Maybe your strategic goal doesn't match ours but it's along the way. Maybe your strategic goal goes as far as our intermediate goals. And that's fine, let's find a way to make those goals work together and support each other. We want to see where everyone is at and start to see how a possible overall strategy can start to be assembled. (E#12)

"What can happen is when people start to understand the strategic goals, each group can take their responsibility in the way they see fit" (Int#38 Mi'kmaw). This can help us in building decentralized transformative power, but it requires that "everybody is coalesced around a strategic long-term objective" (Int#38 Mi'kmaw). That is the key point here. In order to build a common force that is not only powerful but also doesn't replicate oppressive relations, we need to be coalescing around the end goal, the long-term objectives, of the people most impacted by the status quo, those with the most far-reaching, most radical change goals. In the case of these movements, we are talking about Land Back, we are talking about a fundamental redistribution of land, power and wealth. Again, this does not mean some climate groups can't work on other interim goals, such as energy transition and climate policy, but if we want to build a movement of movements powerful enough to transform this country, we all do need to make sure that we are working towards our short-, medium- and long-term goals in ways that help rather than hinder the end goals of those on the front lines.

This is what solidarity means. This is what a relational approach to movement building means. If your goal is creating democratized, renewable energy, ask yourself how you can work towards this goal in a way that supports Indigenous sovereignty. If your goal is transforming food systems, ask how your work and the solutions you are developing can be put to the service of front-line land defenders who are putting their lives on the line to stop pipelines and defend their lands and waters.

We talk about intersectional analysis and intersectional organizing, but we also need to think about *intersectional solutions*. How can we design alternatives that help address as many forms of injustice as possible? Often solutions and alternative are being innovated and practised on small scales, away from urban centres and in cultural niches. To scale these up and render them more powerfully transformative, solution innovators must look beyond their niches and be on the front lines so they can ensure they are doing their work in the service of those most impacted. I see permaculture practitioners providing labour and materials to help construct infrastructure at pipeline blockades. I imagine permaculture water treatment systems being installed on First Nation reserves that haven't had clean drinking water in generations. Think of radical mycologists practising myco-remediation, using mushrooms to clean or transform toxic soil, in communities of colour dealing with the alarmingly high levels of toxic pollution from environmental racism, such as Aamjiwnaang, Ontario, and Shelbourne, Nova Scotia. I see engaging high school students to help provide the labour necessary to do this kind of ecological remediation on a big scale and to train a new generation in how to build just and sustainable systems. These kinds of solutions and alternatives can be refined and scaled up to the point where they become sources of revenue for the local community.

Many of the solutions or alternatives that are being enacted currently in Canada address only one problem or one dimension of a problem. For example, solar energy systems being installed help reduce greenhouse gas emissions from household energy use, but do they create local employment? Do they help reduce poverty and racism? How can solutions be designed to have many co-benefits, addressing many social and ecological issues simultaneously.

Another useful conceptual tool for thinking about how different approaches to change can work together, combining force and pushing in a common direction, is *non-reform reforms*. Reformism usually refers to initiatives that are dealing only with the symptoms of the problem, where as radical change digs to the roots of a problem, seeking deeper, systemic change (Temper et al. 2018). The debate between reformist and radical approaches to change is one of the more enduring and heated debates in movements. This ongoing debate is a source of tension that hinders collaboration withn and across different movements. Indeed, "what looks like victory to a reformist can easily appear as betrayal to a more radical mindset" (Green 2016: 231):

> That is one of the greatest tensions when we sit and talk with white allies ... tensions arise when we talk about the question of reform or revolution ... anti-pipeline activism can be very reformist.... Some people would be happy with the Liberals and Conservatives as long as they change their policies on pipelines, right? It's an extremely reformist goal. (Int#38)

Indeed, stopping one pipeline in one place does not change the colonial capitalist system.

Where reform tactics, such as petitions and awareness-raising, may be genuinely useful in the early stages of a campaign, more radical tactics, such as civil disobedience, become more appropriate as the situation escalates. In theory, reformist approaches and radical approaches to change *can* co-exist and be mutually reinforcing, but that is usually not the case. Reformism can often reinforce the systems and structures that make radical change harder to achieve. Duncan Green, author of *How Change Happens*, sees in these tensions a more fundamental dilemma: "expediency versus long-term transformation. Does signing off on limited reforms legitimize the current distribution of power, forestalling deeper change?" (2016: 231).

Non-reform reforms (see Walia 2013; Bond 2008; Gorz 1964) refers to the process of designing more incremental, reformist strategies in ways that create the conditions for more radical change to happen further down the road. "The challenge is creating a radical vision of change that is far-reaching but also identifying steps along the way that are achievable and head us in the right direction without being merely incremental" (S#26). How do we design reformist strategies so that they are steps in a revolutionary strategy? One of the people I interviewed asked: "Are there ways you can work with people who are working within the system in reformist ways to choose strategies that slowly weaken the current system and make room for a different system?" (Int#15).

What might some non-reform reforms toward decolonizing and decarbonizing Canada look like? Carbon taxes are regularly criticized for being a reformist strategy that is incapable of bringing about the kind of change we need and may even be counter-productive. But let's envision what a non-reformist reform carbon tax could look like: Imagine if the carbon tax revenue was used to install community-owned and -operated solar energy systems on First Nations reserves, for example. It's a bit of a stretch to imagine a federal government agreeing to this type of program, but imagine if we had some insider agents of change pushing for it, doing feasibility studies and initiating pilot projects, while at the same time people in the climate movement put pressure on politicians to pass the legislation. This illustrates that transcending the "change from the inside vs. change from the outside" dichotomy, too, can be generative in opening up new ways to build power to push for change. Though bureaucrats and activists may not seek out collaboration with each other naturally, "interesting things happen when unusual suspects join forces" (Green 2016: 228). However, with this particular example we'd also have to ask how a government-implemented carbon tax scheme might reinforce state control and settler colonial power in Canada. Perhaps truly transformative approaches to funding community-led energy transition have to be generated in ways that are not state-dependant. These are the kinds of questions we need to be asking as we build movements based on relationships across difference and in solidarity with those on the front lines.

Thinking and working across difference are essential to the creation of a movement strong enough to make change in the world. If the forms of activism that are generally done in isolation from each other are brought together we would be a force to be reckoned with. I don't have a blueprint for the strategies, or combination of strategies, that would be transformative, but I am calling for an approach to activism that is less constrained, more open to trying new things and more willing to work with others who do activism differently. At this point, "there is no reasonable response but for us to experiment ... shifting from the skeptical world of 'no' to the open and creative world of 'let's give it a try'" (Miller 2012: 13), developing "fresh, non-dogmatic thinking and practice" (Dixon 2014: 233).

To devise and deploy these innovative, intersectional, hybrid strategies that undo the false dichotomies that have kept us siloed, we'll actually need to work with people we're not used to working with; we'll need to get better at working across different forms of activism, as well as at relating across difference. This means transcending perhaps the most pervasive dualism of them all: us vs. them.

Working across the Us/Them Divide

> Without shifting our focus to repairing our relationships, our movements will rot from the inside out — E. Dixon, "Our Relationships Keep Us Alive: Let's Prioritize Them in 2018"

Chapter 6 described how the movements are not always positive and welcoming spaces. They are rife with interpersonal tensions that include but go way beyond the debates over strategies, end goals and approaches to change discussed above. Some movement thinkers, such as Montgomery and bergman in their book *Joyful Militancy: Building Thriving Resistance in Toxic Times*, observe that the ways activists relate to each other in radical movements act as a barrier to achieving the transformative change we seek (2017). As brown sees it, "we are so steeped in critique" (2017: 112) that "we have been growing otherness, borders, separateness" (2017: 33). "We are socialized to see what is wrong, missing, to tear down the ideas of others and lift up our own" (brown 2017: 5). This kind of "rigid radicalism ... makes us hostile to difference, complexity, and nuance" (Montgomery and bergman 2017: 20).

I've come to see these relational challenges as rooted, in part, in what cognitive psychologists call in-group/out-group bias. This is one way of understanding the dualist tendency to divide up social spaces into us and them. In the book *Moral Tribes: Emotion, Reason, and the Gap between*

Us and Them, Joshua Green argues that our brains and moral instincts evolved in hunter-gatherer societies whereby our survival depended on our capacity to cooperate with our "in-group" in order to defend against potentially threatening "out-groups." We have the tendency to split the world into people who are within our in-group and those who are not. We do so in multiple, shifting and somewhat arbitrary ways (Green 2014). "We all simultaneously occupy a variety of in-groups and therefore, out-groups" (Choudhury 2015: 86). We tend to be more generous, tolerant and self-sacrificing with people we perceive to be in our in-group, and "when dealing with those we perceive as 'not us' thinking frequently takes a backseat to feeling" (Choudhury 2015: 36). Green argues that these cognitive tendencies leave us vastly ill-equipped for current global problems that require cooperation across broad social divisions (Greene 2014). Capitalism has cultivated and encouraged this human tendency (Raworth 2017) and the Western worldview that divides up the world into hierarchized difference also exacerbates this:

> This in-group/out-group bias leads to *othering* which refers to any action by which an individual or group becomes mentally classified in somebody's mind as "not one of us." Rather than always remembering that every person is a complex bundle of emotions, ideas, motivations, reflexes, priorities, and many other subtle aspects, it's sometimes easier to dismiss them as being in some way less human, and less worthy of respect and dignity, than we are. (There Are No Others 2011: n.p.)

I see this cognitive bias reflected in the tensions in the movements. We "other" those who don't share our political analysis, or whose tactics are too reformist or too confrontational. As we cultivate in-groups in our movements and dismiss some as "other" we reduce the relational power we could be building through wide collaboration.

To forge strong movements, we need to be better at overcoming this bias and cultivating "soil that is fertile for relationship building," humbling ourselves to value others and other kinds of contributions (brown 2017: 39). Creating more space for other approaches to change and other kinds of people "means we can do, be, and create whatever we want to see, knowing that ours is one effort in the midst of many, and the multitude is where our power lies" (brown 2017: 116). To centre relationality in our movements and to build power through solidarity, we need "to listen to each other across all real and perceived divides" (brown 2017: 113). Compassion and empathy are essential in developing relational skills and developing more care and respect for the "other" (Choudhury 2015). Compassion and empathy are central tenants of a relational approach to movement building. We need to develop these capacities and let them dissolve the ways we "other" each other over the smallest difference. We need to stop tearing each other apart.

All that being said, it's often much more complicated than simply identifying cognitive bias as divisive. Often the relational tensions and indeed the tendencies to "other" are shaped by racism, sexism, classism and other relations of domination. The ways our brains are wired to see the world in terms of us and them "is compounded through the processes of being socialized and by ... power dynamics between groups" (Choudhury 2015: 8). "We are born with the bias hardware, while society provides us with the software" (Choudhury 2015: 63). "People coming into movements bring with them contradictions. Alongside liberatory aspirations we carry destructive views and behaviors that we learn by living in society" (Dixon 2014: 226). Activists can fall "back into modeling the oppressive tendencies against which we claim to be pushing. Some of those tendencies are seeking to assert one right way or one right strategy" (brown 2017, 8). In-group/out-group bias, dualistic thinking and systems of domination (racism, sexism, classism, etc.) all work in concert to hinder movement efforts towards systems transformation in Canada by blocking collaboration. All these need to be addressed.

"Radical empathy is required for change ... [it] is more than alliances, more than coalitions.... Radical empathy politics means that injustice anywhere is injustice everywhere" (Kelley, in Tuck and Yang 2013: 94). Radical transformation hinges on "our ability to extend empathy ... creating the possibility of true solidarity across social divisions created by gender, class, race, ethnicity and sexual identity" (MacKay 2017: 198).

Strong relationships cannot exist in unequal power. Trust cannot exist where some wield power over others. Only among equals can solidarity flourish. Equality in social movements is not just about how we perceive and treat each other and who takes up more space or has more influence. It's also about material reality; who has the resources to determine the strategy, to implement it, to shape the narrative. A relational approach to movements means a redistribution of power, resources and position within the movements. This means NGOs (and other groups and people currently wielding more power than others) relinquishing power and understanding that they do not have all the answers or even access to the best strategies. Indeed, there are "material, structural, and affective schisms we must tend to in order to win" (Walia 2019). With this in mind, let's explore what centring justice in this relational approach to movement building can look like.

CHAPTER 8

"WE GET THERE TOGETHER, OR WE DON'T GET THERE AT ALL"*

CENTRING JUSTICE IN OUR RELATIONS

I have been arguing that for our movements to be as powerful and transformative as they can be, we need to be better at thinking and working across difference. I have argued that underlying our challenges to think and relate across difference is Western reductionist worldviews and the ways they construct the social and conceptual worlds into dualism and hierarchy. And I've argued that relationality is the antidote. All this evokes a call for holism, making space for a wider diversity of people and approaches to change.

This vision of relationality as key to building a stronger *whole* evokes a call for unity, for wide inclusion. Talking about inclusion, mutual support, movement ecosystem and diversity is crucial but there is a risk that it can ignore or gloss over ongoing power imbalances that exist in the movements. To have strong relationships, we need to have just relationships. That means undoing inequality. But given the ongoing systems of oppression that exist within our movements and lives, it's not uncritical unity and it's not unconditional inclusion I am suggesting.

I am not proposing a kind of unity that ignores differences in power and privilege or pretends we're all the same. I am not advocating for building relationships with people who are racist, sexist, homophobic, transphobic or in any other way continuing to replicate relations of domination. I am calling for a *critical holism*, whereby we build more and stronger relationships based on a rich diversity of people who share a commitment to actively undoing all forms of oppression, in themselves, their communities and societies. Diversity is important, but the kind of diversity raised in these conversations does not include those who continue to enact these forms of power over others. "We need to be working together but we need to be working together in ways that reverse the existing power dynamics in our organizing" (Int#13).

The fight against climate change in Canada has brought together this diverse movement landscape that includes many groups, organizations and communities, some who are actively committed to undoing social injustice and some who are not. This *diversity* includes decolonial land defenders on the front lines, risking their lives to protect their territories from oil and gas pipelines, and it includes the white Quebecois climate activists who perpetrated racial violence against Indigenous youth at the climate march in September 2019.

Some environmental and climate groups and organizations do not concern themselves with issues of racism, colonialism and other forms of oppression; they focus on environmental goals as separate from social justice. I did not interview such people, so their views have not been included in this book. Yet they are implicated in these movements. How do we make sense of all this in thinking about how to strengthen the movement ecosystems? And what does it mean for creating effective, just and mutually supportive relationships? Does my movement ecosystem include environmental groups that do not centre justice, that refuse to do land acknowledgements, that are still run predominately by white men, that do not seek to forge a decolonial, anti-racist climate movement?

Even as these movements work to move Canada towards social justice, unequal and unjust relations continue to exist within and across movements: "In many NGOs, men are still calling the shots and women do all the work" (TT#3). We need to ask who is accountable to whom in the movement ecosystems (Int#16). There remains "power imbalance between Indigenous and non-Indigenous Peoples. That's a huge barrier. How do you go about being explicit about power imbalances and developing checks and balances that ensure that it is not going to be to the disadvantage of Indigenous Peoples when they interact with the settlers?" (Int#34).

We need to take a hard look at who has the resources and who is making the decisions. Strengthening our movements means undoing relations of domination amongst ourselves. We cannot build strong relations without mutual trust. And we cannot have trust across uneven power: "Hierarchy and domination hurt relations because they hurt trust" (TT#3). The most powerful sources of relational tension in these movements are not debates over strategies and approaches to change. The most significant barrier to widespread collaboration in these movements is power imbalance; it is the ways that racism, sexism, classism and other forms of domination continue to play out in our movements.

When the shots are being called by those with more power, the connective tissue of our ecosystem becomes weakened and battered. When white environmental activists replicate oppressive tendencies in movement spaces, the potential for building a powerful movement of movements shrinks. When environmental groups engage with Indigenous communities because Indigenous rights are useful to their narrow environmental goals, but then fail to support Indigenous sovereignty, our collective power to make change together is greatly diminished. When a coalition of large NGOs strikes a backroom deal with industry or government without the consent of the grassroots groups and directly impacted communities, relationships are destroyed and the movements' transformative capacity is weakened. When coalitions of climate organizations converge to draft up the next big strategic plan or manifesto and they invite Indigenous land defenders to the table without providing the resources necessary for those land defenders to get to that table, transformative opportunities are lost. There is a need to undo power inequity in these movements. Without this, the notion of mutually supportive relations makes no sense and the vision of a healthy movement ecosystem is off the table.

Getting better at working across difference while centring justice and equality will involve asking how power and privilege shapes where each of us is situated in the movement ecosystem. We need to be asking "when to be open and vulnerable and when to draw the lines in the sand and fight? Who to trust, and how? When are relationships worth fighting for, and when do they need to be abandoned?" (Montgomery and bergman 2017: 42). Knowing how to draw these lines, by having and respecting boundaries, is key to strong and just relationships: "Defining and developing just relationships will be a process that won't happen overnight. It must include clarity about decision-making, sharing strategies, and resource distribution" (brown 2017: 226). To get there, we need "more collective work to hold to our space with more intention and reminding each other what the overall goals are" (Int#11). "The lens of justice should be made clear from the beginning" (S#14).

In my conversations with activists and land defenders, we talked about how the ongoing inequality within and across these movements can be addressed. As one person explained: "I don't need everyone to do the exact same things I am doing. But I do need everyone to radicalize where they are at" (Int#32) — to find a way to do what they are doing but in ways that address the root causes of these crises. Another activist suggested that if we could get agreement on some shared principles that align us all towards addressing the root causes, we can at least find ways to do reduce the harm being done:

> What would NGO work be like if they always asked themselves these three things in all their strategic planning: 1) How does this impact the most vulnerable people? 2) How is this helping name the roots of the crisis? 3) How is this working towards the larger vision of changing structures and systems? It's harder to use fucked up tactics if you ask yourselves those questions. Everything we do can become radical work. It takes away the band-aid solutions or false solutions that continue to perpetuate the root causes. It challenges them pretty deeply. (Int#32)

Another activist suggested that if every group and organization in the movements agreed to adopt the Jemez Principles for Democratic Organizing, this would help align our efforts into a common force, through more just relations. The Jemez Principles were drafted in 1996 by forty people of colour and European-American representatives "with the intention of hammering out common understandings between participants from different cultures, politics, and organizations" in their work together around anti-globalization (Solis and Union 1997: n.p.). The principles include: be inclusive, emphasize bottom-up organizing, let people speak for themselves, work together in solidarity and mutuality, build just relationships among ourselves and commit to self-transformation (Solis and Union 1997).

One land defender argued that building just relations means unlearning the Western notion of power:

> Whether it's Marxism, communism, anarchism, libertarian

beliefs, whatever it is, they are fighting for the throne. This is based on a Western conception of power. To create real coalitions and healthy relationships, we must eliminate the throne. And then no one can fight for it. [Then] how do we talk about relationships? (Int#38 Mi'kmaw)

DECOLONIZING RELATIONS

Through all these conversations and all the reading I've done in these last five years, I have come to understand that *decolonizing relations* is the means and ends of the kind of change I want to see in the world. It is the path and the end goal. It is the answer to the climate crisis and it is the answer to the inequality crisis. Decolonization is a "dramatic re-imagining of relationships with land, people, and the state" (Walia 2012: 248). It is a "process whereby we intend the conditions we want to live and intend the social relations we wish to have. It is a process that forces us to reconnect with each other and the Earth" (Walia 2012: 251). The transformative relationships require not simply acknowledging the colonial power structures that govern our interactions within settler colonial states, but fundamentally changing the ways we relate to the world (Fortier 2017). To understand settler colonialism as ongoing relations of domination instead of a historical event is to allow us to see it as impermanent and to see and approach decolonization as a radical shift in relationships (Fortier 2017).

Decolonizing relations works on the personal level and it works on the levels of system and structures. Settlers seeking to develop just relationships with Indigenous Peoples must understand that solidarity in this context means "fighting against the colonization of Indigenous lands and peoples" (Walia 2012: 241). This unsettling process for settlers needs to include seeing and undoing the ways that ideas based in domination "seep into our practices, relationships, and aspirations" (Fortier 2017: 76), and it means we need to work together to disrupt "capitalist, colonial, heteropatriarchal structures, and many other institutions based on the Western notions of sovereignty and domination" (Simpson, paraphrased in Fortier 2017: 80).

This means settlers taking responsibility to transform colonial relations, which most people are still not willing to do (Int#7 Kanien'kehá:ka; Int#20 Michif Cree). Developing better relationships between settlers and Indigenous Peoples means "settlers have to do their research and then hopefully through that research they'll understand humility ... and listening" (Int#25 Dene). Settlers need to be "walking with care and real caution ... and humility. Understand settler colonialism and use your power to privilege Indigenous Nations" (Int#20 Michif Cree).

As more settler activists wake up to the reality of settler colonialism, many are looking to Indigenous Peoples to learn about different ways of doing things and different ways of relating. But this puts a lot of pressure on Indigenous communities not only to defend their lands but to also teach a bunch of activists and white folk:

> There's more and more interest in other worldviews than the settler worldview that has been dominant for so long and there's more and more interest to learn about Indigenous worldviews. However, it needs to be done correctly. It can be done wrong and hurt even more the wounds that are open. It's like "you're always taking from us, always taking everything that we have." (TT#2 Anishinaabe)

Learning needs to be done in ways that are not appropriative. Settlers should only be taking that which is offered.

Though settlers need to forge just, reciprocal and respectful relationships with land, with each other and with Indigenous Peoples, we cannot do that by taking Indigenous ontologies, relationalities or practices as our own:

> While our indigenous stories are rich in wisdom, and we need to hear them, I do not advocate for their wholesale appropriation. As the world changes, an immigrant culture must write its own new stories of relationship to place ... but tempered by the wisdom of those who were old on this land long before we came. (Kimmerer 2013: 345)

Decolonizing relations in our movements demands that settlers do not appropriate Indigenous knowledge and practices. Settlers can actively support Indigenous struggles and reflect on how our own practices of liberation and transformation can be designed so as to actively support Indigenous sovereignty.

Accountability is also critical for decolonizing relationships between settlers and Indigenous Peoples and the way to do this is through mutual struggle (Fortier 2017: 55). Settlers must fight alongside Indigenous Peoples in dismantling colonial capitalism. We do this in part by "making change in our own systems and among other settlers, taking our cue from Indigenous action and direction.... Relationship creates accountability and responsibility for sustained supportive action. This does not mean requiring Indigenous energies for creating relationship with settlers" (Irlbacher-Fox 2012: n.p.).

While working towards shared goals in intersectional organizing, we must also respect the boundaries between movements. We need to think hard about where movements can work together and where we must go at it independently, along separate paths. The task is to

> connect but not collapse ... this means that though we can and must look for points of unity and commonality across very different experiences and issues, everything cannot be blended into an indecipherable mush of lowest-common-denominator platitudes. The integrity of individual movements, the specificities of community experiences, must be reflected and protected, even as we come together in an attempt to weave a unified vision. (Klein 2017: 243)

On what bases can we forge alliances? How to we forge alliances while respecting the boundaries between movements? Kelly Aguirre helps shed some light here. She points out that though Indigenous resurgence is a turning inwards, it also inevitably involves resisting the "ongoing engines of dispossession. Confrontation with the corporate state is inevitable and necessary, and it's here that alignments with Settler and non-Indigenous movements arise" (2015: 202). Where the work of resurgence does not implicate non-Indigenous people and movements in any way, resistance is where Indigenous and non-Indigenous movements can and do converge. While Indigenous Peoples forge cultural resurgence, settler activists can "support the structural and material context of decolonization and sustain a decolonial form of relationality with Indigenous peoples" (Aguirre 2015: 202). "Settler society must ... choose to change their ways, to decolonize their relationships to the land and Indigenous Nations and join in building a sustainable future based upon mutual recognition, justice, and respect" (Simpson 2008: 14).

As I've been arguing, relational approaches to movement building that centre justice and actively work towards decolonization are deeply important. That said, we need to acknowledge the limits to this. As one activist admitted to me: "There's a lot of financial and structural incentives that are counter to those relationships having any effect" (Int#16). Indeed, during her keynote address at a conference in Toronto, pedagogical and critical race theorist Gloria Ladson-Billings was asked how to create a more unified force for change out of our fragmented movements. She told the crowd that "we're not losing because we're not unified. We're losing because the other side is playing chess. We're playing checkers." This message has stayed with me as a constant reminder that, as with all the other approaches to change, while focusing on relationships and movement cohesion is necessary, we need to be attending to other dimensions as well.

CLIMATE CHANGE AS CATALYST FOR DECOLONIZING RELATIONS

As I write the final pages of this book, Australian wildfires are wreaking unfathomable damage to wildlife, eco-systems and communities, while East Africa is dealing with record-breaking rainfall and catastrophic flooding. Another year of international climate negotiations got nowhere. Meanwhile, the most transformative force for climate change in Canada — the Indigenous communities defending their lands and waters against unwanted extractive projects while building beautiful alternatives — are continuing to be removed from their lands and arrested to make way for pipeline after pipeline. It is roughly one year since the RCMP invaded the Unist'to'ten and Gidim'ten camps with instructions to use as much violence as they wanted. Again, the RCMP has sought to enforce injunctions to allow Coastal Gaslink Pipeline to carry on with the construction of the gas pipeline. In the most recent federal election Trudeau was re-elected, promising to make sure oil and gas pipelines can be built in the country. All of this is so deeply unjust and unsustainable. And daunting.

The young folk I organize with in the climate movement and the students I teach in undergraduate environmental studies courses are wracked with anxiety for the future and anger at all this rampant injustice and inaction in the face of out-of-control crises. I feel it too, and I can't even imagine how it all feels to the people on the front lines. I struggle to know how to end this book in a way that can offer some hope without making light of how very scary and unbelievably daunting it all is — and without resorting to naïve tropes of unity and miracles of the human spirit. The hope I do hold is in the ways the intensifying crises are waking many, many people up to the existential crises that the colonial, capitalist system has wrought. We are waking up to a nightmare. We are waking up to this moment in history. Can this wake-up call spark unprecedented caring, action and transformation?

"We are in a moment of tremendous crisis and possibility" (Dixon 2014: 2). Climate change is the "furthest reaching crisis … and one that puts humanity on a firm and unyielding deadline" (Klein 2014: 459). "Time is running out fast. Climate change is going to bring so much pressure everywhere.… There is more pressure to be successful in our fight" (Int#9 Kanien'kehá:ka).

"This is a massive intersecting crisis, it relates to all the issues and there are a bunch of ways to contribute" (Int#28 Anishinaabe). "There are many solutions, and the beauty of it all is that it's such an urgent issue that no one action is enough, and all actions are necessary, and so whatever people can bring to this movement … we need everybody" (Int#23).

Climate is exposing the ugly underbelly of the economic and political system and changing people's understanding of the world. The way climate change is playing out — who is being impacted, who is taking action and who is resisting climate action — "is teaching us about power; about who has the power in society" (Int#39). Through increasing awareness of the links between climate impacts, extractivism and the ongoing violation of Indigenous rights and resistance "there is a real opportunity to rethink how our society is structured, especially colonial structures" (Int#29):

> Now there's a crack in the Western thinking of dominance. Their monopoly on truth is starting to be seen as an illusion. The climate crisis offers a pressure that forces Western society to think about self-preservation and it is one that sees Western society as the cause of the threat. When people start to understand that, they can start to shed some of this racism and might be willing to move towards an Indigenous model. How intense does the climate crisis have to get before people are ready to give up power, before

they are willing to abandon the benefits that racism has given them? What point does it have to get to? Does all of BC have to be on fire before we say, "maybe we should change the ways we live?" Climate crises might put them in the position where they no longer have the choice. (Int#38 Mi'kmaw)

Climate change is teaching settlers what Indigenous Peoples have long understood, that Western society, through colonial capitalism, is bent on destroying nature, which includes humans. "Some people won't [learn this lesson] — they'd rather die than give up these notions. But others will [begin to see] that Indigenous ways of life are how we're going to mitigate the existing destruction and reduce the rate of the ongoing extinction of life on this planet" (Int#38 Mi'kmaw).

"I believe there will come moments in which centralized systems of power will be rendered ineffective, at least temporarily, and there will be opportunities to see more decentralized democratic control, for communities and for energy systems. People living in their own communities, making decisions for their own communities" (Int#20 Michif Cree). "Communities [will] reshape the power, reshape the context of control, according to their own cultures and values, according to their own practices" (Int#21).

"The current political order is in crisis, which presents us with an enormous political opportunity" (Smucker 2017: 252). But winning will certainly take "the convergence of diverse constituencies on a scale previously unknown" (Klein 2014: 459). And indeed, climate change is creating opportunities to connect the political dots, to create links between all kind of movements, the incentive to join forces to change the systems and structures at the root of so many of the social and environmental injustices. This is where I feel the spark of hope.

But that is also why I found the racism at the Montreal climate march so demoralizing. Clearly there are people in the climate movement who are not seeing the links. There are still people in the movement who are heavily influenced by the white-dominated environmental movement of the last thirty years, which has treated the environment as something *outside*, something to protect so that we can enjoy it on the weekends and on summer vacations. It is the same kind of environmentalism that forcefully removes Indigenous Peoples from their territories so that carbon can be sequestered in the forests that these same Indigenous Peoples have been successfully living in harmony with for thousands of years. This is an environmentalism that is mired in the Western worldview that sees people as separate from nature. What we desperately need at this moment in history is the end of environmentalism. The end of seeing humans as either above and in control of nature, or as somehow inherently destructive to nature. Settlers interested in a livable planet need to understand what Indigenous Peoples have long understood: that people are nature. That violence to the Earth is suicide.

If there was one message I would like those just coming to the climate movements — including those who yelled at and shoved the Indigenous youth at that Montreal climate march — to take away from this book, it's that an anti-racist, decolonial climate movement is the only kind of climate movement that stands any chance of winning.

The conversations in this book have made clear that the exploitation of nature and the oppression of people have been, from the start, inextricable parts of the same systems. It is very hard to imagine how they could become disentangled from each other now, as some environmentalists seem to think is possible. As has happened so often in past struggles, I regularly hear climate activists and academics argue that the climate crisis must take precedence — that we can address these other social justice issues once we've secured a livable planet. While there is urgency to the climate crisis, this argument is premised on the assumption that, somehow, we could achieve environmental sustainability while our social relations of domination remain intact. But given that the people in power continue to make decisions aimed at maintaining the status quo — and their own power — it's difficult to believe they will even act to achieve environmental sustainability.

The argument is based on the very questionable assumption that people currently in positions of power are capable of securing a livable planet. The Western worldview and the white folks speaking for it have utterly failed to address the crisis and it is reasonable to assume they don't even have the conceptual tools or values systems to do so. Meanwhile there are other people with other worldviews who are equipped with ways of living and governing that are time tested and deeply rooted in respectful, reciprocal relations with each other and with the land. Indigenous Peoples, and other land-based peoples, offer significantly different and much more just and ecologically viable systems. It is (beyond) time for those white men upholding the current disastrous system and perpetuating the worldviews and relations of dominance to step the fuck aside.

But I also want those newly mobilized climate activists to understand that while we need to undo white supremacy and step back from our positions of power within movements, this doesn't mean white people have no place in building a better world. We do. To be strong enough to create a counter-force to the very powerful elites, we need everyone. But we need everyone to abandon their single-issue silos and push in a common direction, working together to target those root causes. That means climate activists must genuinely commit to anti-capitalism and decolonialism and to undoing all forms of domination.

The final reason the climate movement needs to take an active role in the fight against inequality is what Naomi Klein refers to as climate barbarism (2019). Not including inequality as a central tenant of climate action will likely mean a huge shift to the hard right; as crises mount and people are forced to migrate, borders will be closed.

Climate change "could become a galvanizing force for humanity, leaving us not just safer from extreme weather, but with societies safer and fairer in all kinds of other ways as well" (Klein 2014: 7). This vision is possible, but by no means a given: "Climate change can be a catalyst for a range of very different and far less desirable forms of social, political, and economic transformation" (Klein 2014: 8). Climate change could be a catalyst for a better world, but that really depends, in no small part, on our ability to come together and build the kind of relationalities that could generate and sustain powerful, diverse and massive movements. Many of the key lessons emerging from these conversations offer important insight into building these relationalities.

In order to build new systems, as the old ones collapse or are dismantled, we will need to be better at working together across all kinds of differences, making decisions together and choosing kindness and sharing over competition and self-interest. Right now, in our movements, we have the opportunity to practise the skills of relating, collaborating and sharing power and resources fairly. "Being really good allies, that's the only thing that matters" (Int#33). "We need to unleash the full creativity of everything. To find the things that are going to get us there, we have to support each other on a basic human level. That's how we're going to get ourselves out of the current mess" (Int#16).

As climate change is causing "us to take a look at ourselves and re-evaluate our relationship with each other, our communities, and the land" (ICA 2018: n.p.), putting heavy pressure on us to build different way of living together on Earth, "we are realizing that we must become the system we need — no government, political party, or corporation is going to care for us, so we have to remember how to care for each other" (brown 2017: 113).

To change the system, we need movements that function as a system. In other words, "we are only as strong as our connections with others" (Miller 2012: 15). To forge flourishing movement ecosystems, we need to tend to our relationships, which must be based on justice, equality and reciprocity. As Montgomery and bergman see it, "the most widespread, long-lasting, and fierce struggles are animated by strong relationships of love, care and trust" (2017: 31):

> With so much destruction in motion, this might all sound naïve to some readers; why speak of thriving and love when there are so many massive, urgent problems that need to be confronted? To write about the potential of trust and care, at this time in history, could seem like grasping optimistically at straws as the world burns. But durable bonds and new complicities are not a reprieve or an escape; they are the very means of undoing Empire. (Montgomery and bergman 2017: 24–25)

Though much of European thought has sought to subdue life through rigid dualisms and classifications, there have been some Western thinkers who theorized against the grain. Baruch Spinoza was one of these. A theorist of relationality, he "conceptualized a world in which everything is interconnected and in process" (Montgomery and bergman 2017: 28). We must take inspiration from the fact that Spinoza and other Western thinkers were able to think beyond their worldview and know that it is possible for settlers to develop relational thinking without appropriating Indigenous ontologies.

Spinoza's approach to relationality focused on processes "through which people become more alive, more capable, and more powerful together" (Montgomery and bergman 2017: 29). I hope that by reporting on these many rich conversations and raising up relational approaches to change, this book can contribute to the movements' capacity to tap into the "enduring power that arises from mutualism" (Kimmerer 2013: 275) and that, through this, we can become *more powerful together.*

That is how we're going to get from where we are … to where we need to be.

Note
* Starlight 2016.

TABLE OF CODES FOR ALL SOURCES OF DATA

Every time I included a quote from an interview, survey, think tank session or event transcription, I provided a code (e.g., Int#21) to indicate which person and which source of data the quote came from. This table provides the information about the interviewee, survey respondent, etc. associated with each code.

Codes	Date	Involvement	Gender	Type*	Capacity **	Prov.
Int#1	5/19/2017	Community/ Grassroots	M	POC	Ind	BC
Int#2	5/23/2017	Organization	M	Settler	Ind	BC
Int#3	5/26/2017	Organization	F	Settler	Rep	BC
Int#4	5/29/2017	Community/ Grassroots	M	Settler	Ind	VT
Int#5	6/1/2017	Grassroots	M	Settler	Ind	QC
Int#6	6/2/2017	Organization	M	Settler	Ind	QC
Int#7	6/5/2017	Community/ Grassroots	M	Indigenous	Ind	QC
Int#8	6/6/2017	Grassroots	M	Settler	Ind	QC, ONT
Int#9	6/7/2017	Community	M	Indigenous	Ind	QC
Int#10	6/7/2017	Grassroots	F	Settler	Ind	QC
Int#11	6/7/2017	Grassroots	F	Settler	Ind	QC
Int#12	6/9/2017	Organization	F	Indigenous	Ind	ONT
Int#13	6/11/2017	Grassroots	F	POC	Ind	QC
Int#14	6/12/2017	Grassroots	F	Settler	Ind	BC
Int#15	6/12/2017	Organization/ Grassroots	F	Settler	Ind	QC
Int#16	6/12/2017	Organization/ Grassroots	M	Settler	Ind	QC
Int#17	6/1/2017	Grassroots	F	Settler	Ind	QC
Int#18	6/15/2017	Grassroots	F	Settler	Ind	QC
Int#19	6/20/2017	Organization/ Grassroots	M	Settler	Ind	QC
Int#20	6/22/2017	Grassroots	F	Indigenous	Ind	ONT
Int#21	6/22/2017	Grassroots	M	POC	Ind	QC

Codes	Date	Involvement	Gender	Type*	Capacity **	Prov.
Int#22	6/23/2017	Grassroots/ Community	F	Indigenous	Rep	NB
Int#23	6/26/2017	Grassroots/ Student	M	Settler	Ind	QC
Int#24	6/26/2017	Grassroots/ Organization	M	POC	Ind	QC
Int#25	6/28/2017	Grassroots	F	Indigenous	Ind	QC
Int#26	6/28/2017	Organization	M	Settler	Ind	SK
Int#27	7/6/2017	Grassroots	F	Settler	Ind	QC
Int#28	7/10/2017	Organization/ Grassroots	F	Settler	Ind	ONT
Int#29	7/11/2017	Organization	M	Settler	Rep	BC
Int#30	7/13/2017	Grassroots	M	Settler	Ind	QC
Int#31	7/17/2017	Organization	F	Settler	Rep	BC
Int#32	8/7/2017	Organization/ Grassroots	F	POC	Ind	BC
Int#33	8/10/2017	Organization	F	Settler	Ind	BC
Int#34	8/11/2017	Community/ Scholar	M	Indigenous	Ind	BC
Int#35	8/18/2017	Organization	M	POC	Rep	BC
Int#36	8/19/2017	Grassroots/ Scholar	F	Settler	Ind	ONT
Int#37	8/19/2017	Organization/ Community	F	Settler	Rep	BC
Int#38	8/28/2017	Community/ Grassroots	M	Indigenous	Ind	BC
Int#39	10/3/2017	Organization/ Grassroots	F	Settler	Ind	QC
Int#40	2/20/2017	Grassroots	M	POC	Ind	QC
TT#1	10/18,2017	varied	varied	varied	Rep	QC
TT#2	9/28/2017	varied	varied	varied	Ind	QC
TT#3	6/28/2018	Organization/ Grassroots	F	Settler	Ind	QC
S#1	2/6/2017	Community/ Grassroots	M	Settler	Ind	ONT
S#3	2/6/2017	Organization	M	Settler	Rep	ONT
S#4	2/6/2017	Organization	M	Settler	Ind	MAN
S#5	2/6/2017	Grassroots	?	?		BC
S#6	2/7/2017	Organization	?	?	Rep	ONT

Codes	Date	Involvement	Gender	Type*	Capacity **	Prov.
S#7	2/7/2017	Community/ Grassroots	?	?	Rep	ONT
S#8	2/7/2017	Grassroots	F	Settler	Rep	ONT
S#9	2/7/2017	Grassroots	F	Settler	Rep	QC
S#10	2/9/2017	Union	?	?	Rep	?
S#11	2/12/2017	Community	F	Settler	Rep	?
S#12	2/16/2017	Grassroots	M	POC	Rep	ONT
S#13	3/8/2017	Organization	M	Settler	Rep	ONT
S#14	3/8/2017	Organization	?	?	Rep	ONT
S#15	3/9/2017	Organization	?	?	Rep	CAN
S#16	3/26/2017	Grassroots	M	Settler	Rep	QC
S#17	3/28/2017	Grassroots/ Scholar	F	Settler	Ind	US
S#18	3/31/2017	Organization	M	Settler	Rep	BC
S#19	4/3/2017	Community/ Organization	F	Indigenous	Rep	ONT
S#20	4/4/2017	Grassroots	M	?	Rep	?
S#21	4/10/2017	Organization	F	Settler	Rep	ONT
S#22	4/26/2017	Organization	M	POC	Rep	ALB
S#23	4/26/2017	Organization	F	Indigenous	Rep	CAN
S#24	4/28/2017	Community/ Organization	M	Settler	Rep	BC
S#25	5/3/2017	Organization	?	?	Rep	INT
S#26	5/3/2017	Funder	F	Settler	Ind	CAN
S#27	5/9/2017	Community	M	Settler	Ind	?
S#28	5/11/2017	Business	F	Settler	Rep	?
S#29	5/19/2017	Student Union	M	Settler	Rep	QC
S#30	5/23/2017	Grassroots	F	POC	Rep	ONT
S#31	5/26/2017	Student Union	M	Settler	Rep	QC
S#32	5/29/2017	Organization	F	?	Rep	ONT
S#33	5/31/2017	Political Party	M	Settler	Ind	QC
S#34	6/5/2017	Grassroots/ Arts	M	Settler	Rep	QC
S#35	6/15/2017	Community	M	Indigenous	Ind	QC
S#36	6/15/2017	Organization	F	?	Rep	CAN
S#37	6/15/2017	Organization	?	?	Ind	CAN

Codes	Date	Involvement	Gender	Type*	Capacity **	Prov.
E#2	8/16/2016	World Social Forum	M	Indigenous	Rep	Int.
E#3	8/17/2016	World Social Forum	F	Indigenous	Ind	CAN
E#9	4/17/2017	ndp/Leap Event	M	Setter	Rep	ONT
E#10	2/15/2018	Courage to Leap Event	M, F	Settler, poc	Rep	ONT
E#12	3/21/2017	Sacred Fire Network Event	M	Indigenous	Ind	BC
E#14 E#15	3/22/2017	Sacred Fire Network Event	M	POC	Ind	BC
E#16	5/25/2017	Decolonizing Divestment Webinar	M	Indigenous	Rep	Man
E#17	6/18/2017	Unsettling Canada 150 Webinar	M,F,M	Indigenous	Ind	Var.
E#18 E#19	1/03/2018	Violence Against the Land is Violence Against Women Webinar	F	Indigenous	Rep	BC, AB
E#21	11/28/2015	Corridors of Resistance Film	M	Indigenous	Ind	BC

* Settler, Indigenous or person of colour (poc)
**Ind: Speaking as individual, Rep: Representing organization

REFERENCES

Abbasi, S.A., and N. Abbasi. 2000. "The Likely Adverse Environmental Impacts of Renewable Energy Sources." *Applied Energy*, 65, 1–4: 121–144.

Abraham, Y.M. 2018. "Décroissance: How the Degrowth Movement Is Blooming in Quebec." *Briarpatch*. <https://briarpatchmagazine.com/articles/view/decroissance>.

Abson, D.J., J. Fischer, J. Leventon, et al. 2017. "Leverage Points for Sustainability Transformation." *Ambio*, 46, 1: 30–39.

Aguirre, K. 2015. "Telling Stories: Idle No More, Indigenous Resurgence and Political Theory." In E. Coburn (ed.), *More Will Sing Their Way to Freedom: Indigenous Resistance and Resurgence*. Halifax, NS: Fernwood Publishing.

Alfred, T. 1999. *Peace Power Righteousness: An Indigenous Manifesto*. Don Mills, ON: Oxford University Press.

____. 2005. *Wasase: Indigenous Pathways of Action and Freedom*. North York, ON: University of Toronto Press.

____. 2008. "Opening Words." In L. Simpson (ed.), *Lighting the Eighth Fire: The Liberation, Resurgence, and Protection of Indigenous Nations*. Winnipeg, MB: Arbeiter Ring Pub.

____. 2009. "Colonialism and State Dependency." *Journal de la santé autochtone*, 5: 42–60.

____. 2018. "It's All About the Land." In P. McFarlane and N. Schabus (eds.), *Whose Land Is It Anyways? A Manual for Decolonization*. Federation of Post-Secondary Educators of BC.

Allard, J., and C. Davidson (eds.). 2008. *Solidarity Economy: Building Alternatives for People and Planet*. Raleigh, NC: Lulu.com.

Amadahy, Zainab. 2010. "Community, 'Relationship Framework' and Implications for Activism," Rabble.ca. <http://rabble.ca/news/2010/07/community-%E2%80%98relationship framework%E2%80%99-and-implications-activism>.

Aorta Coop, 2017. "Understanding and Resisting Divide and Conquor Tactics." <https://aorta.coop/portfolio_page/understanding-and-resisting-divide-and-conquer-tactics/>.

Armstrong, E., and V. Prashad. 2005. "Exiles from a Future Land: Moving Beyond Coalitional Politics." *Antipode*, 37, 1: 181–185.

Arrighi, Giovanni, Terence K. Hopkins, and Immanuel Wallerstein. 1989. *Antisystemic Movements*. New York: Verso.

Atleo, E.R. 2011. *Principles of Tsawalk: An Indigenous Approach to Global Crisis*. Vancouver, BC: UBC Press.

Barker, A. and E.B. Lowman. n.d. "Settler Colonialism." Global Social Theory. <https://globalsocialtheory.org/concepts/settler-colonialism/>.

____. 2015. *Settler: Identity and Colonialism in 21st Century Canada*. Halifax, NS: Fernwood Publishing.

Barker, C., L. Cox, J. Krinsky, and A.G. Nilsen. 2013. *Marxism and Social*

Movements: An Introduction. Leiden, NL: Brill.

Bear, L.L. 2000. "Jagged Worldviews Colliding." *Reclaiming Indigenous Voice and Vision.* UBC Press.

Beddoe, R., R. Costanza, J. Farley, et al. 2009. "Overcoming Systemic Roadblocks to Sustainability: The Evolutionary Redesign of Worldviews, Institutions, and Technologies." *Proceedings of the National Academy of Sciences,* 106, 8: 2483–2489.

Berkes, F., J. Colding, and C. Folke (eds.). 2008. *Navigating Social-Ecological Systems: Building Resilience for Complexity and Change.* Cambridge, UK: Cambridge University Press.

Beymer-Farris, B.A., and T.J. Bassett. 2012. "The REDD Menace: Resurgent Protectionism in Tanzania's Mangrove Forests." *Global Environmental Change,* 22, 2: 332–341.

Black, T., S. D'Arcy, and T. Weis (eds.). 2014. *A Line in the Tar Sands: Struggles for Environmental Justice.* Oakland, CA: PM Press.

Bond, P. 2012. *Politics of Climate Justice: Paralysis Above, Movement Below.* Cape Town: University of Kwa Zulu Natal Press.

Bookchin, M. 1991. "Libertarian Municipalism: An Overview." *Green Perspectives,* 24: 1–6.

___. 2004. *The Third Revolution, Volume Three.* New York: Continuum.

Boothe, P., and F. Boudreault. 2016. *Sharing the Burden: Canadian GHG Emissions.* London, ON: Western University, Ivey Business School, Lawrence National Centre for Policy and Management.

Borrows, J. 2007. "Crown and Aboriginal Occupations of Land: A History and Comparison." Research paper prepared for the Ipperwash Inquiry <www.ipperwashinquiry.ca>.

Bourdieu, P. 1990. *In Other Words: Essays Towards a Reflexive Sociology* (M. Adamson, Trans.). Stanford, CA: Stanford University Press.

Bridge T., and R. Gilbert. 2017. *For Tomorrow: Canada's Building Trades and Net Zero Emissions.* Vancouver, BC: Columbia Institute.

brown, a.m. 2017. *Emergent Strategy: Shaping Change, Changing Worlds.* Chico, CA: AK Press.

Buechler, S.M. 2016. *Understanding Social Movements: Theories from the Classical Era to the Present.* Abingdon, UK: Routledge.

Bullard, R.D. (ed.). 1993. *Confronting Environmental Racism: Voices from the Grassroots.* Boston, MA: South End Press.

___. 2002. "Confronting Environmental Racism in the Twenty-First Century." *Global Dialogue,* 4, 1: 34.

Burke, M.J., and J.C. Stephens. 2017. "Energy Democracy: Goals and Policy Instruments for Sociotechnical Transitions." *Energy Research & Social Science,* 33: 35–48.

Cancian, F. 1993. "Conflicts between Activist Research and Academic Success: Participatory Research and Alternative Strategies." *The American Sociologist,* 2, 1: 92–106.

capitalism. (n.d.). In dictionary.cambridge.org. Retrieved from <https://dictionary.cambridge.org/dictionary/english/capitalism>.

Carpenter, S.R., and C. Folke. 2006. "Ecology for Transformation." *Trends in*

Ecology & Evolution, 21, 6: 309–315.

Carroll, W. K., and R.S. Ratner. 1994. "Between Leninism and Radical Pluralism: Gramscian Reflections on Counter-Hegemony and the New Social Movements." *Critical Sociology*, 20, 2: 3–26.

___. 2001. "Sustaining Oppositional Cultures in 'Post-Socialist' Times: A Comparative Study of Three Social Movement Organisations." *Sociology*, 35, 3: 605–629.

Carroll, W.K., and K. Sarker. 2016. *A World to Win: Contemporary Social Movements and Counter-Hegemony*. Winnipeg, MB: ARP Books.

Cayley-Daoust, D., and R. Girard. 2012. *Big Oil's Oily Grasp: The Making of Canada as a Petro-State and How Oil Money Is Corrupting Canadian Politics*. <https://d3n8a8pro7vhmx.cloudfront.net/polarisinstitute/pages/31/attachments/original/1411065312/BigOil%27sOilyGrasp.pdf?1411065312>.

CCPA (Canadian Center for Policy Alternatives). 2015. *The Alternative Federal Budget 2015: Delivering the Good*. <https://www.policyalternatives.ca/publications/reports/alternative-federal-budget-2015>.

Charman, K. 2008. "False Starts and False Solutions: Current Approaches in Dealing with Climate Change." Capitalism Nature Socialism, 19, 3: 29–47.

Chatterton, P., D. Featherstone, and P. Routledge. 2013. "Articulating Climate Justice in Copenhagen: Antagonism, the Commons, and Solidarity." *Antipode*, 45, 3: 602–620.

Chatterton, P., P. Routledge, and D. Fuller. 2007: "Relating Action to Activism: Theoretical and Methodological Reflections." In S. Kindon, R. Pain, and M. Kesby (eds.), *Connecting People, Participation and Place: Participatory Action Research Approaches and Methods*. London: Routledge.

Chen, C.W., and P.C. Gorski. 2015. "Burnout in Social Justice and Human Rights Activists: Symptoms, Causes and Implications." *Journal of Human Rights Practice*, 7, 3: 366–390.

Choudhury, S. 2015. *Deep Diversity: Overcoming Us vs. Them*. Toronto, ON: Between the Lines.

Choudry, A. 2010. "Global Justice? Contesting NGOization: Knowledge Politics and Containment in Antiglobalization Networks." In D. Kapoor and A. Choudry, *Learning from the Ground Up*. New York: Palgrave Macmillan.

___. 2015. *Learning Activism: The Intellectual Life of Contemporary Social Movements*. North York, ON: University of Toronto Press.

Choudry, A., and D. Kapoor. 2013. *NGOization: Complicity, Contradictions and Prospects*. London, UK: Zed Books.

Clapp, J., and P. Dauvergne. 2011. *Paths to a Green World: The Political Economy of the Global Environment*. Cambridge, MA: MIT Press.

Clark, B., and R. York. 2005. "Carbon Metabolism: Global Capitalism, Climate Change, and the Biospheric Rift." *Theory and Society*, 34, 4: 391–428.

Coburn, E. (ed.). 2015. *More Will Sing Their Way to Freedom: Indigenous Resistance and Resurgence*. Halifax, NS: Fernwood Publishing.

Coburn, E., and C.K.C. Atleo. 2016. "Not Just Another Social Movement: Indigenous Resistance and Resurgence." In W. Carroll and K. Sarker (eds.), *A World to Win: Contemporary Social Movements and Counter-Hegemony*. Winnipeg, MB: ARP Books.

Collins, P.H., and S. Bilge. 2016. *Intersectionality.* Hoboken, NJ: Wiley & Sons.

Coulthard, G.S.. 2010. "Place Against Empire: Understanding Indigenous Anti-Colonialism." *Affinities: A Journal of Radical Theory, Culture, and Action,* 4, 2: 79–83.

___. 2013. "Placing #IdleNoMore in Historical Context." *The Tyee,* Jan. 4. <https://thetyee.ca/Opinion/2013/01/04/IdleNoMore-Historical-Context/>.

___. 2014. *Red Skin, White Masks: Rejecting the Colonial Politics of Recognition.* Minneapolis, MN: University of Minnesota Press.

Cox, L. 2014. *We Make Our Own History: Marxism and Social Movements in the Twilight of Neoliberalism.* London, UK: Pluto Press.

___. 2017. "Learning to Be Loyal to Each Other." In J. Sen (ed.), *Movements of Movements: Part 1: What Makes Us Move?* Oakland, CA: PM Press.

Cox, L., and A.G. Nilsen. 2014. We Make Our Own History: Marxism and Social Movements in the Twilight of Neoliberalism. London, UK: Pluto Press.

Crawford T., and H. Mooney. 2018. "RCMP Arrest Pipeline Protesters at Kinder Morgan Site in Burnaby." *Vancouver Sun,* Mar. 17. <http://vancouversun.com/news/local-news/rcmp-arrest-anti-pipeline-protesters-at-kinder-morgan-site-in-burnaby>.

Crosby, A., and J. Monaghan. 2018. *Policing Indigenous Movements: Dissent and the Security State.* Halifax, NS: Fernwood Publishing.

Cumming, G.S., P. Olsson, F.S. Chapin, and C.S. Holling. 2013. "Resilience, Experimentation, and Scale Mismatches in Social-Ecological Landscapes." *Landscape Ecology,* 28, 6: 1139–1150.

Curtis, C. 2015. "In the Pipelines' Path: Canada's First Nations Lead Resistance." *The Gazette,* Sept. 8. <https://montrealgazette.com/news/pipeline-resistance>.

Dauvergne, P. 2016. *Environmentalism of the Rich.* Cambridge, MA: MIT Press.

Davis, J.E. (ed.). 2002. *Stories of Change: Narrative and Social Movements.* Albany, NY: SUNY Press.

Davis, L. (ed.). 2010. *Alliances: Re/Envisioning Indigenous-Non-Indigenous Relationships.* North York, ON: University of Toronto Press.

Dawson, A. 2016. *Extinction: A Radical History.* New York: Or Books.

Dawson, M.C., and L. Sinwell (eds.). 2012a. *Contesting Transformation: Popular Resistance in Twenty-First-Century South Africa.* London, UK: Pluto Press.

Day, R.J. 2005. *Gramsci Is Dead: Anarchist Currents in the Newest Social Movements.* London, UK: Pluto Press.

Deranger, E. 2018. "Violence Against the Land Is Violence Against Women Webinar." Indigenous Climate Action. <www.indigenousclimateaction.com/single-post/2018/03/19/Violence-Against-the-Land-is-Violence-Against-Women>.

___. 2019. *The Green New Deal in Canada: Challenges for Indigenous Participation.* Yellowhead Institute. <https://yellowheadinstitute.org/2019/07/15/green-new-deal-in-canada/?fbclid=IwAR2nwJtBu6-68qiOpjBUdxEdzRBSwRuBpeSzQ_K4p5ct_-v_HBNGbWuaTS4>.

Dhillon, J., and Parish, W. 2019. "Exclusive: Canada police prepared to shoot Indigenous activists, documents show." *Guardian* Dec 20 <www.theguardian.com/world/2019/dec/20/canada-indigenous-land-defenders-police-documents>.

Dixon, C. 2014. *Another Politics: Talking Across Today's Transformative Movements.* Oakland, CA: University of California Press.

Droitsch, D., and T. Simieritsch. 2010. "Canadian Aboriginal Concerns wWith Oilsands." Pembina Institute, Drayton Valley, AB. <http://www. pembina. org/ pub/2083>.

Durkheim, E. 1965. "The Elementary Forms of the Religion Life." *The Origin and Development of Religion.* Oxford, UK: Oxford Press.

Dussault, R., and G. Erasmus. 1996. *Royal Commission on Aboriginal Peoples. People to People, Nation to Nation: Highlights from the Report of the Royal Commission on Aboriginal Peoples.* Ottawa, ON: Minister of Supply and Services Canada.

Ehrenfeld, J.R. 2004. "Searching for Sustainability: No Quick Fix." *Reflections*, 5, 8: 1–13.

Environment and Climate Change Canada. 2019. *Canada's Changing Climate Report (CCCR).* Ottawa, ON: Government of Canada.

Environmental Defence. 2016. *The Elephant in the Room: Canada's Fossil Fuel Subsidies Undermine Carbon Pricing Efforts.* Toronto, ON: Environmental Defence.

Epstein, B. 1990. "Rethinking Social-Movement Theory." *Socialist Review*, 20, 1: 35–65.

Escobar, A. 2018. *Designs for the Pluriverse: Radical Interdependence, Autonomy, and the Making of Worlds.* Durham, NC: Duke University Press.

Featherstone, D.J. 2013. "The Contested Politics of Climate Change and the Crisis of Neo-Liberalism." *ACME: An International E-Journal for Critical Geographies*, 12, 1: 44–64.

Feygina, I. 2013. "Social Justice and the Human–Environment Relationship: Common Systemic, Ideological, and Psychological Roots and Processes." *Social Justice Research*, 26, 3: 363–381.

Field, C.B., V.R. Barros, M.D. Mastrandrea, et al. 2014. "Summary for Policymakers." In *Climate Change 2014: Impacts, Adaptation, and Vulnerability. Part A: Global and Sectoral Aspects. Contribution of Working Group II to the Fifth Assessment Report of the Intergovernmental Panel on Climate Change.* Cambridge, UK: Cambridge University Press.

Findlay, P. 2002. "Conscientization and Social Movements in Canada." In C. Lankshear and P. McLaren (eds.). 2002. *The Politics of Liberation: Paths from Freire.* London, UK: Routledge.

Folke, C., S. Carpenter, B. Walker, et al. 2010. "Resilience Thinking: Integrating Resilience, Adaptability and Transformability." *Ecology and Society*, 15, 4.

Folke, C., Å. Jansson, J. Rockström, et al. 2011. "Reconnecting to the Biosphere." *AMBIO: A Journal of the Human Environment*, 40, 7: 719–738.

Foran, J., and R. Widick. 2013. "Breaking Barriers to Climate Justice." *Contexts*, 12, 2: 34–39.

Ford, J.D., B. Smit, J. Wandel, et al. 2008. "Climate Change in the Arctic: Current and Future Vulnerability in Two Inuit Communities in Canada." *Geographical Journal*, 174, 1: 45–62.

Fortier, C. 2015. "Unsettling Movements: Decolonizing Non-Indigenous Radical Struggles in Settler Colonial States." Doctoral dissertation, York University,

Toronto, ON.

___. 2017. *Unsettling the Commons: Social Movements Within, Against, and Beyond Settler Colonialism*. Winnipeg, MB: ARP Books.

Foucault, M. 1971. "Orders of Discourse." *Social Science Information*, 10, 2: 7–30.

Frichner, T.G. 2010. *Impact on Indigenous Peoples of the International Legal Construct Known as the Doctrine of Discovery*. Ninth United Nations Permanent Forum on Indigenous Issues. New York: United Nations Economic and Social Council.

Fung, K.Y., I.N. Luginaah, and K.M. Gorey. 2007. "Impact of Air Pollution on Hospital Admissions in Southwestern Ontario, Canada: Generating Hypotheses in Sentinel High-Exposure Places." *Environmental Health*, 6, 1: 18.

Galtung, J. 1990. "Cultural Violence." *Journal of Peace Research*, 27, 3: 291–305.

Gauthier P. 2018. *The Limits of Renewable Energy and the Case for Degrowth*. Canadian Dimension, Sept. 25. <https://canadiandimension.com/articles/view/the-limits-of-renewable-energy-and-the-case-for-degrowth>.

Gaventa, J. 1980. *Power and Powerlessness: Quiescence and Rebellion in an Appalachian Valley*. Champaign, IL: University of Illinois Press.

Gedicks, A. 1994. *The New Resource Wars: Native and Environmental Struggles Against Multinational Corporations*. Montreal, CA: Black Rose Books Ltd.

___. 2001. *Resource Rebels: Native Challenges to Mining and Oil Corporations*. Boston, MA: South End Press.

Gibson-Graham, J.K. 2006. *A Postcapitalist Politics*. Minneapolis, MN: University of Minnesota Press.

Gioia, D.A. 1986. "Symbols, Scripts, and Sensemaking: Creating Meaning in the Organizational Experience." In H.P. Sims and D.A. Gioia (eds.), *The Thinking Organization*. San Francisco, CA: Jossey-Bass.

Glasberg, D.S., and D. Shannon. 2010. *Political Sociology: Oppression, Resistance, and the State*. Thousand Oaks, CA: Sage Publications.

Gosine, A., and C. Teelucksingh. 2008. *Environmental Justice and Racism in Canada: An Introduction*. Toronto, ON: Emond Montgomery.

Government of Canada. 2016. *The Pan-Canadian Framework on Clean Growth and Climate Change*. <http://publications.gc.ca/collections/collection_2017/eccc/En4-294-2016-eng.pdf>.

___. 2019. "Greenhouse Gas Emissions from the Trans Mountain Project." <https://www.canada.ca/en/environment-climate-change/news/2019/06/greenhouse-gas-emissions-from-the-trans-mountain-project.html>.

Graham, N., S. Daub, and B. Carroll. 2017. *Mapping Political Influence: Political Donations and Lobbying by the Fossil Fuel Industry in BC*. <https://www.policyalternatives.ca/sites/default/files/uploads/publications/BC%20Office/2017/03/ccpa-bc_mapping_influence_final.pdf>.

Gramsci, A. 1971. *Selections from the Prison Notebooks of Antonio Gramsci* (Q. Hoare, and G. Nowell-Smith, trans.). London, UK: ElecBook.

___. 2000. *The Gramsci Reader: Selected Writings, 1916–1935*. New York: NYU Press.

Green, D. 2016. *How Change Happens*. Oxford, UK: Oxford University Press.

Greene, J. 2014. *Moral Tribes: Emotion, Reason, and the Gap Between Us and Them*. London. UK: Penguin.

Griffin, A., and S. Vukelich. n.d. "Taking Back the Grid: Struggles for Energy Democracy in Canada and Beyond." The Leap. <https://theleap.org/portfolio-items/taking-back-the-grid-struggles-for-energy-democracy-in-canada-and-beyond/>.

Guha, R. 2014. *Environmentalism: A Global History*. London, UK: Penguin UK.

Guy, S., and P. Suess. 2017. *No Oil Pipelines on Stolen Land* [Video File]. May 31. <https://www.youtube.com/watch?v=M-hOiDJg-GQ>.

Habermas, J. 1987. *The Philosophical Discourse of Modernity* (trans. F. Lawrence). Cambridge, MA: MIT Press.

Hansen, J. 2012. "Game Over for the Climate." *New York Times*, May, 12. <https://www.nytimes.com/2012/05/10/opinion/game-over-for-the-climate.html?ref=global>.

Harvey, D.2014. *Seventeen Contradictions and the End of Capitalism*. Oxford, UK: Oxford University Press.

Head, L. 2016. *Hope and Grief in the Anthropocene: Re-Conceptualising Human–Nature Relations*. Abingdon, UK: Routledge.

Hill, G. 2010. *500 Years of Indigenous Resistance*. Oakland CA: PM Press.

Holling, C.S., and L.H. Gunderson. 2002. *Panarchy: Understanding Transformations in Human and Natural Systems*. Washington, DC: Island Press.

Howarth, R.W. 2015. "Methane Emissions and Climatic Warming Risk from Hydraulic Fracturing and Shale Gas Development: Implications for Policy." *Energy and Emission Control Technologies*, 3: 45–54.

Hughes, J.D. 2018. *Canada's Energy Outlook: Current Realities and Implications for a Carbon-Constrained Future*. Vancouver, BC: Canadian Centre for Policy Alternatives.

Human Rights Watch. 2018. *World Report 2018*. <https://www.hrw.org/world-report/2018/country-chapters/canada>.

ICA (Indigenous Climate Action). 2018. "Violence Against the Land Is Violence Against Women." March 18. <https://www.indigenousclimateaction.com/single-post/2018/03/19/Violence-Against-the-Land-is-Violence-Against-Women>.

IPBES, E., E.S. Brondizio, J. Settele, S. Díaz, and H.T. Ngo. 2019. *Global Assessment Report on Biodiversity and Ecosystem Services*. Bonn: Intergovernmental Science-Policy Platform on Biodiversity and Ecosystem Services (IPBES).

IPCC. 2018. "Summary for Policymakers." In V. Masson-Delmotte, P. Zhai, H.-O. Pörtner, et al. (eds.), *Global Warming of 1.5°C. An IPCC Special Report on the impacts of global warming of 1.5°C above pre-industrial levels and related global greenhouse gas emission pathways, in the context of strengthening the global response to the threat of climate change, sustainable development, and efforts to eradicate poverty*. Geneva, Switzerland: World Meteorological Organization.

Irlbacher-Fox, S. 2012. "#IdleNoMore: Settler Responsibility for Relationship. Decolonization." December 12. <https://decolonization.wordpress.com/2012/12/27/idlenomore-settler-responsibility-for-relationship/>.

Jacobson, M.Z., M.A. Delucchi, Z.A. Bauer, et al. 2017. "100% Clean and Renewable Wind, Water, and Sunlight All-Sector Energy Roadmaps for 139 Countries of the World." *Joule*, 1, 1: 108–121.

Jay, Dru Oja. 2014. "NGOization: Depoliticizing Activism in Canada." *New Socialist*.

<https://newsocialist.org/ngoization-depoliticizing-activism-in-canada/>.

K.N.N. Collective. 2014. *The Winter We Danced: Voices from the Past, the Future, and the Idle No More Movement.* Winnipeg, MB: ARP Books.

Kaijser, A., and A. Kronsell. 2014. "Climate Change Through the Lens of Intersectionality." *Environmental Politics,* 23, 3: 417–433.

Kallis, G., and H. March. 2015. "Imaginaries of Hope: The Utopianism of Degrowth." *Annals of the Association of American Geographers,* 105, 2: 360–368.

Kamat, S. 2004. "The Privatization of Public Interest: Theorizing NGO Discourse in a Neoliberal Era." *Review of International Political Economy,* 11, 1: 155–176.

Kerr, J. 2014. "Western Epistemic Dominance and Colonial Structures: Considerations for Thought and Practice in Programs of Teacher Education." *Decolonization: Indigeneity, Education & Society,* 3, 2.

Kimmerer, R.W. 2013. *Braiding Sweetgrass: Indigenous Wisdom, Scientific Knowledge and the Teachings of Plants.* Minneapolis, MN: Milkweed Editions.

King, H. 2015. "The Problem with 'Indigenous Peoples': Re-Considering International Indigenous Rights Activism." In E. Coburn (ed.). *More Will Sing Their Way to Freedom: Indigenous Resistance and Resurgence.* Winnipeg, MB: Fernwood Publishing.

Kinsman, G. 2006. "Mapping Social Relations of Struggle: Activism, Ethnography, Social Organization." In C. Frampton, G. Kinsman, and A. Thompson (eds.), *Sociology for Changing the World: Social Movements/Social Research.* Winnipeg, MB: Fernwood Publishing.

Klein, N. 2007. *The Shock Doctrine: The Rise of Disaster Capitalism.* London, UK: Macmillan.

___. 2014. *This Changes Everything: Capitalism vs. the Climate.* New York, NY: Simon and Schuster.

___. 2017. *No Is Not Enough: Resisting the New Shock Politics and Winning the World We Need.* New York: Knopf Canada.

___. 2019. *On Fire: The (Burning) Case for a Green New Deal.* New York: Simon & Schuster.

Kohn, M., and K. Reddy. 2017. "Colonialism and Imperialism." *Stanford Encyclopedia of Philosophy.* <http://hiskingdom.us/wp-content/uploads/2019/10/Colonialism-and-Imperialism.pdf>.

Kothari, A. 2014. "Radical Ecological Democracy: A Path Forward for India and Beyond." *Development,* 57, 1: 36–45.

Kovach, M. 2010. *Indigenous Methodologies: Characteristics, Conversations, and Contexts.* University of Toronto Press.

Krznaric, R. 2007. *How Change Happens: Interdisciplinary Perspectives for Human Development.* Oxfam, GB.

Laboucan-Massimo, M. 2018. "Violence Against the Land Is Violence Against Women Webinar." Indigenous Climate Action. <www.indigenousclimateaction.com/single-post/2018/03/19/Violence-Against-the-Land-is-Violence-Against-Women>.

Ladner, K. 2008. "Aysaka'paykinit: Contesting the Rope Around the Nations' Neck." *Group Politics and Social Movements in Canada.* Peterborough, ON: Broadview.

Laville, S., and J. Watts. 2019. "Across the Globe, Millions Join Biggest Climate Protest Ever." *Guardian,* Sept. 21. <www.theguardian.com/environment/2019/sep/21/across-the-globe-millions-join-biggest-climate-protest-ever>.

The Leap. 2019. "What Is a Green New Deal?" The Leap Website. <https://theleap.org/portfolio-items/green-new-deal/>.

Lee, D. 2011. "Windigo Faces: Environmental Non-Governmental Organizations Serving Canadian Colonialism." *Canadian Journal of Native Studies,* 31, 2: 133.

Lipset, S.M., M.A. Trow, and J.S. Coleman. 1956. *Union Democracy: The Internal Politics of the International Typographical Union,* Vol. 14. New York: Free Press.

Long, N., and J.D. Van Der Ploeg. 1989. "Demythologizing Planned Intervention: An Actor Perspective." *Sociol Ruralis,* 29, 3/4: 226–249.

Loorbach, D. 2014. "To Transition! Governance Panarchy in the New Transformation." *Inaugural Address.* Rotterdam, NL: Erasmus University.

Lukes, S. 1974. *Power: A Radical View.* London, New York: Macmillan.

MacKay, K. 2017. *Radical Transformation: Oligarchy, Collapse, and the Crisis of Civilization.* Toronto, ON: Between the Lines.

Mackenzie, C.A., A. Lockridge, and M. Keith. 2005. "Declining Sex Ratio in a First Nation Community." *Environmental Health Perspectives,* 113, 10: 1295–1298.

Macy, J., and C. Johnstone. 2012. *Active Hope: How to Face the Mess We're in Without Going Crazy.* Movato, CA: New World Library.

Manuel, A. 2017. *Until Canada Gives Indigenous People Their Land Back, There Can Never Be Reconciliation.* Rabble.ca, Jan. 18. <http://rabble.ca/blogs/bloggers/views-expressed/2017/01/until-canada-gives-indigenous-people-their-land-back-there-ca>.

Manuel, A., and Grand Chief Derrickson. 2017. *Reconciliation Manifesto: Recovering the Land, Rebuilding the Economy.* Toronto, ON: James Lorimer.

Manuel, K. 2018. "Violence Against the Land Is Violence Against Women Webinar." Indigenous Climate Action. <www.indigenousclimateaction.com/single-post/2018/03/19/Violence-Against-the-Land-is-Violence-Against-Women>.

Martinez-Alier, J., L. Temper, D. Del Bene, and A. Scheidel. 2016. "Is There a Global Environmental Justice Movement?" *Journal of Peasant Studies,* 43, 3: 731–755.

Marx, K. 1976. *Capital, Volume 1.* Toronto, ON: Pelican Books.

Mascarenhas, M. 2007. "Where the Waters Divide: First Nations, Tainted Water and Environmental Justice in Canada." *Local Environment,* 12, 6: 565–577.

Maynard, R. 2017. *Policing Black Lives: State Violence in Canada from Slavery to the Present.* Halifax, NS: Fernwood Publishing.

McAdam, D., J.D. McCarthy, M.N. Zald, and N.Z. Mayer (eds.). 1996. *Comparative Perspectives on Social Movements: Political Opportunities, Mobilizing Structures, and Cultural Framings.* Cambridge, UK: Cambridge University Press.

McFarlane, P., and N. Schabus (eds.). 2017. *Whose Land Is It Anyway? A Manual for Decolonization.* Vancouver, BC: Federation of Post-Secondary Educators of BC. <https://fpse.ca/sites/default/files/news_files/Decolonization%20Handbook.pdf>.

McGlade, C., and P. Ekins. 2015. "The Geographical Distribution of Fossil Fuels Unused When Limiting Global Warming to 2 C." *Nature,* 517, 7533: 187.

Meadows, D. 1997. "Places to Intervene in a System." *Whole Earth,* 91, 1: 78–84.
___. 2008. *Thinking in Systems: A Primer.* Hartford, VT: Chelsea Green Publishing.
Merchant, C. 2006 "The Scientific Revolution and the Death of Nature." <https://nature.berkeley.edu/departments/espm/env-hist/articles/84.pdf>.
Miller, E. 2010. "Solidarity Economy: Key Concepts and Issues." In Emily Kawano, and Tom Masterson and Jonathan Teller-Ellsberg (eds.), *Solidarity Economy I: Building Alternatives for People and Planet.* Amherst, MA: Center for Popular Economics.
___. 2012. "Occupy! Connect! Create! Imagining Life Beyond 'The Economy.'" In Amber Hickey (ed.), *A Guidebook of Alternative Nows.* Los Angeles: Journal of Aesthetics and Protest Press.
Monaghan, J., and K. Walby. 2017. "Surveillance of Environmental Movements in Canada: Critical Infrastructure Protection and the Petro-Security Apparatus." *Contemporary Justice Review*, 20, 1: 51–70
Montgomery, N., and c. bergman. 2017. *Joyful Militancy: Building Thriving Resistance in Toxic Times.* Chico, CA: AK Press.
Moore, J. 2016. *Anthropocene or Capitalocene? On the Origins of Our Crisis.* Oakland, CA: PM Press.
Moore, M.L., O. Tjornbo, E. Enfors, et al. 2014. "Studying the Complexity of Change: Toward an Analytical Framework for Understanding Deliberate Social-Ecological Transformations." *Ecology and Society*, 19, 4.
Morin, B. 2015. "Trudeau Says Indigenous People Can Teach the World How to Care for the Planet. APTN, Nov. 30. <http://aptn.ca/news/2015/11/30/trudeau-says-indigenous-people-can-teach-how-to-care-for-the-planet/>.
Natural Resources Canada. 2018. "Crude Oil Facts." NRC website. <https://www.nrcan.gc.ca/science-and-data/data-and-analysis/energy-data-and-analysis/energy-facts/crude-oil-facts/20064>.
Nikiforuk, A. 2019. "When Indigenous Assert Rights, Canada Sends Militarized Police." The Tyee, January. <https://thetyee.ca/Analysis/2019/01/17/Indigenous-Rights-Canada-Militarized-Police/>.
Nimana, B., C. Canter, and A. Kumar. 2015. "Energy Consumption and Greenhouse Gas Emissions in the Recovery and Extraction of Crude Bitumen from Canada's Oil Sands." *Applied Energy*, 143: 189–199.
Olsson, P., V. Galaz and W.J. Boonstra. 2014. "Sustainability Transformations: A Resilience Perspective." *Ecology and Society,* 19, 4: 1.
Owusu-Bempah, A., and S. Wortley. 2014. "Race, Crime, and Criminal Justice in Canada." *The Oxford Handbook of Ethnicity, Crime, and Immigration*, 321–359.
Parks, B.C., and J.T. Roberts. 2006. "Globalization, Vulnerability to Climate Change, and Perceived Injustice." *Society and Natural Resources*, 19, 4: 337–355.
Paulson, S. 2017. "Degrowth: Culture, Power and Change." *Journal of Political Ecology,* 24, 1: 425–448.
Pepermans, Y., and P. Maeseele. 2016. "The Politicization of Climate Change: Problem or Solution?" *Wiley Interdisciplinary Reviews: Climate Change*, 7, 4: 478–485.
Perkins, P.E. 2009. "Feminist Ecological Economics." In J.M. Gowdy (ed.), *Economics Interactions with Other Disciplines*, Vol. II: 192–205. <https://www.eolss.net/Sample-Chapters/C13/E6-29-04-05.pdf>.
Pimentel, D., I. Aymar, M. Lawson, et al. 2000. "Reward Work, Not Wealth."

Oxfam. Oxford, UK. <https://d1tn3vj7xz9fdh.cloudfront.net/s3fs-public/file_attachments/bp-reward-work-not-wealth-220118-en.pdf>.

Pines, A.M. 1994. "Burnout in Political Activism: An Existential Perspective." *Journal of Health and Human Resources Administration,* 16, 4: 381–394.

Piven, F.F., and R.A. Cloward. 1979. "Electoral Instability, Civil Disorder, and Relief Rises: A Reply to Albritton." *American Political Science Review,* 73, 4: 1012–1019.

Plumwood, V. 2002. *Feminism and the Mastery of Nature.* Abingdon, UK: Routledge.

Powell, J.A. 2016. "Resistance and the Rebirth of Inclusion." *Berkeley Blog,* Nov. 28. <https://blogs.berkeley.edu/2016/11/28/resistance-and-the-rebirth-of-inclusion/>.

Ramos, H., and K. Rodgers. 2015. *Protest and Politics: The Promise of Social Movement Societies.* Vancouver, BC: UBC Press.

Raworth, K. 2017. *Doughnut Economics: Seven Ways to Think Like a 21st-Century Economist.* Hartford, VT: Chelsea Green Publishing.

Reid, J. 2010. "The Doctrine of Discovery and Canadian Law." *The Canadian Journal of Native Studies,* 30, 2: 335–359.

Reinsborough, P., and D. Canning. 2010. *Re:Imagining Change: How to Use Story-Based Strategy to Win Campaigns, Build Movements, and Change the World.* Oakland, CA: PM Press.

Research and Degrowth. 2020. Definition. <https://degrowth.org/definition-2/>.

Riddell, J.K., A. Salamanca, J.D. Pepler, et al. 2017. "Laying the Groundwork: A Practical Guide for Ethical Research with Indigenous Communities." *The International Indigenous Policy Journal,* 8, 2: 6.

RIPESS (Intercontinental Network for the Promotion of Social Solidarity Economy). 2015. *Global Vision for a Social Solidarity Economy.* <http://www.ripess.org/wp-content/uploads/2017/08/RIPESS_Vision-Global_EN.pdf>.

Ripple, W.J., C. Wolf, T.M. Newsome, et al. 2017. "World Scientists' Warning to Humanity: A Second Notice." *BioScience,* 67, 12: 1026–1028.

Robbins, P. 2011. *Political Ecology: A Critical Introduction,* Vol. 16. Wiley & Sons.

Rockström, J., W. Steffen, K. Noone, et al. 2009. "Planetary Boundaries: Exploring the Safe Operating Space for Humanity." *Ecology and Society,* 14, 2.

Rowlands, J. 1997. *Questioning Empowerment.* Oxford, UK: Oxfam.

Russell, E.D. 2018. "Resisting Divide and Conquer: Worker/Environmental Alliances and the Problem of Economic Growth." *Capitalism Nature Socialism,* 29, 4: 109–128.

Russell, P. 2010. "Oka to Ipperwash: The Necessity of Flashpoint Events." In L. Simpson and K. Ladner (eds.), *This Is an Honour Song: Twenty Years Since the Blockades.* Winnipeg, Manitoba, Arbeiter Ring Publishers.

Salick, J., and A. Byg. 2007. *Indigenous Peoples and Climate Change.* Norwich, UK: Tyndall Centre Publication.

Santos, L. 2008. "Genetic Research in Native Communities." *Progress in Community Health Partnerships: Research, Education, and Action,* 2, 4: 321–327.

Schaufeli, W.B., and P. Buunk. 2002. "Burnout: An Overview of 25 Years of Research and Theorizing." In M.J. Schabracq, J.A.M. Winnubst, and C.L.

Cooper (eds.), *The Handbook of Work and Health Psychology*. Wiley & Sons.

Scheidel, A., L. Temper, F. Demaria, and J. Martínez-Alier. 2017. "Ecological Distribution Conflicts as Forces for Sustainability: An Overview and Conceptual Framework." *Sustainability Science*, 1–14.

Schweickart, D. 2009. "Is Sustainable Capitalism an Oxymoron?" In J. Harris (ed.), *The Nation in the Global Era*. Leiden, NL: Brill.

Serebrin, J. 2018. "Montreal Vigil Channels Outrage Over Acquittal in Colten Boushie's Killing." *Montreal Gazette*, Feb. 13. <http://montrealgazette.com/news/local-news/montreal-vigil-channels-outrage-over-acquittal-in-colten-boushies-killing>.

Sharife, K., and P. Bond. 2009. "False Solutions to Climate Crisis Amplify Eco-Injustices." *Women in Action*, 2.

Shingler, B. 2019. "'We Are Changing the World': Greta Thunberg Addresses Hundreds of Thousands at Montreal Climate March." CBC, Sept. 27. <https://www.cbc.ca/news/canada/montreal/montreal-climate-march-greta-thunberg-1.5298549>.

Shoemaker, N. 2015. "A Typology of Colonialism." *Perspectives on History*, 53, 7: 29–30.

Simpson, L.B. (ed.). 2008. *Lighting the Eighth Fire: The Liberation, Resurgence, and Protection of Indigenous Nations*. Winnipeg, MB: Arbeiter Ring Pub.

___. 2011. *Dancing on Our Turtle's Back: Stories of Nishnaabeg Re-Creation, Resurgence and a New Emergence*. Winnipeg, MB: Arbeiter Ring Pub.

___. 2017. *As We Have Always Done: Indigenous Freedom Through Radical Resistance*. Minneapolis, MN: University of Minnesota Press.

Simpson, L., and K.L. Ladner. 2010. *This Is an Honour Song: Twenty Years Since the Blockades*. Winnipeg, MB: Arbeiter Ring Pub.

Smith, A. 2016. "Heteropatriarchy and the Three Pillars of White Supremacy: Rethinking Women of Color Organizing." *Women in Culture: An Intersectional Anthology for Gender and Women's Studies*, 404.

___. 2017. "Indigenous Feminism and the Heteropatriarchal State." In J. Sen (ed.), *Movements of Movements: Part 1: What Makes Us Move?* Oakland, CA: PM Press.

Smith, L.T. 1999. *Decolonizing Methodologies: Research and Indigenous Peoples*. London, UK: Zed Books.

Smith, S. 2017. "A Marxist Case for Intersectionality." *Socialist Worker*, August 1. <https://socialistworker.org/2017/08/01/a-marxist-case-for-intersectionality>.

Smucker, J. 2017. *Hegemony How-To: A Roadmap for Radicals*. Chico, CA: AK Press.

Snow, D.A., and R.D. Benford. 1992. "Master Frames and Cycles of Protest." *Frontiers in Social Movement Theory*, 133: 155.

Snow, D.A., E.B. Rochford Jr., S.K. Worden, and R.D. Benford. 1986. "Frame Alignment Processes, Micromobilization, and Movement Participation." *American Sociological Review*, 464–481.

Snow, D.A., S.A. Soule, and H. Kriesi (eds.). 2008. *The Blackwell Companion to Social Movements*. Hoboken, NJ: John Wiley & Sons.

Solis, M. 2018. "When Dismantling Power Dismantles You Instead." *Vice*, Dec. 7. <https://www.vice.com/en_us/article/3k95kk/>.

when-dismantling-power-dismantles-you-instead-v25n4>.

Solis, R., and S.P.W. Union. 1997. *Jemez Principles for Democratic Organizing*. Chicago, IL: SouthWest Organizing Project.

Solnit, R. 2016. *Hope in the Dark: Untold Histories, Wild Possibilities*. Chicago, IL: Haymarket Books.

Solomon, S., D. Qin, M. Manning, et al. 2007. *Climate Change 2007 — The Physical Science Basis Contribution of Working Group I to the Fourth Assessment Report of the IPCC*. Cambridge, UK: Cambridge University Press.

Stainsby, M., and D.O. Jay. 2009. "Offsetting Resistance: The Effects of Foundation Funding from the Great Bear Rainforest to the Athabasca River." <http://www.offsettingresistance.ca/>.

Starblanket, T. 2018. *Suffer the Little Children: Genocide, Indigenous Children, and the Canadian State*. Gardena, CA: SCB Distributors.

Starlight, T. 2016. "Experiencing Colonization and Decolonization Efforts." *The Dominion*. Montreal: The Dominion News Co-operative.

Stewart, G. 2015. "First Nations Bear the Risks of Oilsands Development." *The Star*, Aug. 28. <https://www.thestar.com/news/atkinsonseries/2015/08/28/first-nations-bear-the-risks-of-oilsands-development.html>.

Symbiosis. 2019. "Vision and Strategy." < https://www.symbiosis-revolution.org/vision-and-strategy/>.

Tarrow, S.G. 2011. *Power in Movement: Social Movements and Contentious Politics*. Cambridge, UK: Cambridge University Press.

Taylor, D. 2014. *Toxic Communities: Environmental Racism, Industrial Pollution, and Residential Mobility*. New York: NYU Press.

Taylor, K.Y. 2016. *From# BlackLivesMatter to Black Liberation*. Chicago, IL: Haymarket Books.

Temper, L., and S. Bliss. 2015. *Decolonising and Decarbonising: How the Unist'ot'en Are Arresting Pipelines and Asserting Autonomy*. Barcelona, ES: EJOLT.

Temper, L., and D. Del Bene. 2016. "Transforming Knowledge Creation for Environmental and Epistemic Justice." *Current Opinion in Environmental Sustainability*, 20: 41–49.

Temper, L., M. Walter, I. Rodriguez, et al. 2018. "A Perspective on Radical Transformations to Sustainability: Resistances, Movements, and Alternatives." *Sustainability Science*. <https://www.academia.edu/36182171/A_perspective_on_radical_transformations_to_sustainability_resistances_movements_and_alternatives>.

There are no others. 2011. Othering 101: What Is "Othering"? Dec. <therearenoothers.wordpress.com/2011/12/28/othering-101-what-is-othering/>.

Tokar, B. 2018. "On Social Ecology and the Movement for Climate Justice." In S. Jacobsen (ed.), *Climate Justice and the Economy*. Routledge.

TRC (Truth and Reconciliation Commission of Canada). 2015. *Final Report of the Truth and Reconciliation Commission of Canada: Honouring the Truth, Reconciling for the Future*.

Tuck, E., and K.W. Yang. 2012. "Decolonization Is Not a Metaphor." *Decolonization: Indigeneity, Education & Society*, 1, 1.

___. (eds.). 2013. *Youth Resistance Research and Theories of Change*. Routledge.

Tucker, B. 2017. "Social Movements Played a Huge Part in Derailing Energy East." CBC, Oct. 12. <http://www.cbc.ca/news/opinion/ social-movements-energy-east-1.4344080>.

Tupaz, V. 2015. "Indigenous Peoples to World Leaders: We Carry Burden of Climate Change." *Rappler*. <https://www.rappler.com/world/ global-affairs/114613-cop21-world-leaders-indigenous-peoples-pay-highest-price-climate-change>.

Unist'ot'en Camp. 2017. "Heal the People, Heal the Land." Website. <http:// unistoten.camp/>.

United Nations. 2007. UN General Assembly, United Nations Declaration on the Rights of Indigenous Peoples: Resolution / adopted by the General Assembly. <A/RES/61/295. https://www.refworld.org/docid/471355a82.html>.

___. 2008. *Climate Change*. New York: Department of Economic and Social Affairs — Indigenous Peoples.

Vowel, C. 2016. *Indigenous Writes: A Guide to First Nations, Métis, and Inuit Issues in Canada*. Winnipeg, MB: Portage & Main Press.

Waldron, I. 2018. *There's Something in the Water: Environmental Racism in Indigenous and Black Communities*. Halifax, NS: Fernwood Publishing.

Walia, H. 2011. "Reflecting on Social Movement Successes in Canada." *Canadian Dimension*, Oct. 30. <https://canadiandimension.com/articles/ view/2011-reflecting-on-social-movement-successes-in-canada>.

___. 2012. "Decolonizing Together: Moving Beyond a Politics of Solidarity toward a Practice of Decolonization." In E. Shragge, A. Choudry, and J. Hanley (eds.), *Organize! Building from the Local for Global Justice*. Oakland, CA: PM Press.

___. 2019. "My Timeline Is Full." April 19. <https://www.facebook.com/harsha. walia> [Facebook update]. <https://www.facebook.com/harsha.walia/ posts/10157101443974337>.

Waring, M., and G. Steinem. 1988. *If Women Counted: A New Feminist Economics*. San Francisco, CA: Harper & Row.

Weber, M. 1905. *The Protestant Ethic and the "Spirit" of Capitalism and Other Writings*. London, UK: Penguin Classics.

___. 1978. *Economy and Society: An Outline of Interpretive Sociology*, Vol. 1. Berkeley, CA: University of California Press.

Westley, F., P. Olsson, C. Folke, et al. 2011. "Tipping Toward Sustainability: Emerging Pathways of Transformation." *Ambio*, 40, 7: 762.

Whyte, K. 2017. "Indigenous Climate Change Studies: Indigenizing Futures, Decolonizing the Anthropocene." *English Language Notes*, 55, 1: 153–162.

Wilson, A. 2015. "A Steadily Beating Heart." In E. Coburn (ed.), *More Will Sing Their Way to Freedom: Indigenous Resistance and Resurgence*. Halifax: Fernwood Publishing.

Wolfe, P. 2006. "Settler Colonialism and the Elimination of the Native." *Journal of Genocide Research*, 8, 4: 387–409.

Wynes, S., and K.A. Nicholas. 2017. "The Climate Mitigation Gap: Education and Government Recommendations Miss the Most Effective Individual Actions." *Environmental Research Letters*, 12, 7: 074024.

Yellowhead Institute. 2019. *Land Back. A Yellowhead Institute Red Paper*. Toronto, ON: Yellowhead Institute.

INDEX

Page numbers in *italics* denote illustrations.

Aamjiwnaang First Nation, 11, 37, 193
actions for systemic change, 95–111
  collective actions, 96–97
  confronting power, 100–104
  creating solutions, 104–111
  engaging with the electoral system, 98–100
activist burnout, 106, 124, *140,* 140–142, 165, 175, 187
activist culture, 54–55, *140,* 142–143
Africa, East, 207
agroecology, 105
Aguirre, Kelly, 87, 206
Alberta tar sands, 19, 28, 33, 37, 120
Alfred, Taiaiake, 64, 65, 94, 115, 116
alternatives, 54–72
  decarbonization, 55–58
  decentralization, 58–61
  decolonization, 61–69
  energy systems, 105, 119
Alton Gas, Nova Scotia, 130, 189
anarchism, 59–60, 71, 120
Another Politics (Dixon), 183
anti-globalization, 203
anti-pipeline resistance, 9–12, 15–16, 22, 29–31, 126, 150, 194
  See also environmental/climate justice movements; land defenders; mainstream environmental movement; oil and gas pipelines
Athabasca Chipewyan First Nation (ACFN), 3–4, 36
Atleo, E. Richard, 180
Australia, 207

Bacon, Francis, 51
barriers to change, external, *126,* 126–140
  capitalism, 132–134
  corporate influence on the political system, 134–136
  false solutions and false understanding, 129–131
  lack of alternatives and fear of job loss, 128–129
  lack of public will, 127–128
  the legal system and criminalization of dissent, 136–139
  the state, 139–140
  See also possible solutions
barriers to change, internal, *140,* 140–160
  activist culture, 142–143
  bias, self-interest, privilege, 158–160
  centralized, hierarchical and top-down structures, 157–158
  fractured movements/us *vs.* them, 143–146
  lack of financial resources and activist burnout, 141–142
  NGOization, 152–157
  relational tensions, 146–152
  See also possible solutions
Barrow, Kai, 183
Batchewana First Nation, 2–3
Benford, R.D., 85–86
bergman, c., 196, 212
bias, *140,* 158–160, 198
Bilge, S., 90, 183, 185
biodiversity, 7–8
bio-environmentalists, 26–27
bitumen, 30, 33
  See also tar sands
Black Panthers, 108
Bolduc, Jessica, 2–3
Bookchin, Murray, 49, 60
Borrows, John, 23
Bourdieu, Pierre, 81
Braiding Sweetgrass (Kimmerer), 182
brown, adrienne marie, 184–186, 196
burnout (activist), 106, 124, *140,* 140–142, 165, 175, 187
Burnt Church, 23

Cahill, Caitlin, 182–183
Caledonia, 23
Calls to Action (TRC), 3

Canada's Energy Outlook, 57
Canadian Boreal Forest Agreement, 28,
    156
Canadian Centre for Policy Alternatives,
    135
Canadians
    energy consumption of, 56–57
    media influence on, 131
    self-perception of, 16, 38
Canning, D., 86
capitalism
    alternatives to, 106–107
    as barrier to change, *126*
    and Christianity, 48
    and community, 175
    damage from, 177
    and decision making, 157–158
    and dualisms, 179, 197
    and economic growth, 128,
        130–131, 132–134
    and lack of public will, 127
    as root cause of environmental and
        inequality issues, 5, 43–46
    solutions to, 190
    symptoms of, 33–34
    as a way of life, 100
    See also colonialism; possible solu-
        tions; systems change
Capitalism, A Ghost Story (Roy), 154
carbon trading/capture/taxation,
    129–130, 209–210
Caroll, W.K., 188
Carson, Rachel, 25
Cerecer, David Alberto Quijada, 182–183
Chevron's Pacific Trail pipeline, 30
Choudry, Aziz, 10, 152–153, 155
Christianity, 48, 50–51
civil disobedience, 103–104, 119, 165,
    194
civil rights movement, 27, 103
Clapp, J., 26
clear-cut logging, 25
climate barbarism, 211
climate change, 207–213
    and capitalism and colonialism, 53
    failure of government to act on, 5
    and gender justice, 36
    and power, 34–35
climate crises, 32–53
    causes, 38–47
    impacts, 34–38
    justifications for, 47–52
    and oil and gas development in
        Canada, 18–20
Climate Justice Edmonton, 29
Climate Justice Montreal, 29
climate justice movement, 27–29
climate march, *see* Global Climate Strike,
    2019
Cloward, R.A., 97, 155
Coastal GasLink pipeline, 43, 130, 207
Coast Salish Nation, 37
collective action frames, 85–86, 119
collective power, 202
Collins, P.H., 90, 183, 185
colonial-capitalism, 53, 54, 117
    See also capitalism; colonialism
colonialism
    and capitalism, 46, 53, 177
    and gender justice, 36
    and power relations, 39
    as root cause of environmental and
        inequality issues, 5, 38, 42
    settler understanding of, 152
    symptoms of, 33–34
    See also colonization
colonization
    and Canadian culture, 38
    and Christianity, 40, 49–51
    and climate issues, 38
    and land, 45–46, 64–65
    resistance to, 23, 68
    and resource extraction, 20
    See also decolonization; settler
        colonialism
communities, self-determining/autono-
    mous, 60–61, 70, 71, 107, 195,
    209
cooperation and coordination, 58, 119,
    123, 169–172, 211
    See also movement ecosystems
Corntassel, Jeff, 181
Corporate Mapping Project (CCPA), 135
Corridor Resources (resource extraction
    company), 130
Coulthard, Glen, 24, 39, 46, 50, 61, 94,
    102, 115–116
counter-hegemonic force

building of, 84, 107, 114, 144, 157, 161
coalitions of, 95
legitimacy of, 108
requirements of, 188
story work as crucial, 88
Cox, L., 89
Cree Nation, 66
criminalization of dissent, *126,* 136–139, 141
critical holism, 200–201
cultural genocide, 21

Dauvergne, Peter, 26
Dawson, Ashley, 43
decarbonization, 9–10, 55–58, 72, 130, 133, 150, 195
   See also barriers to change, external; barriers to change, internal
decentralization, 54–55, 58–61, 70, 71, 157–158, 166, 192
decolonization, 61–69, 125–160
   and decarbonization, 4
   description, 204
   dual strategies, 95
   and government, 98
   non-reform reforms, 195
   and other social movements, 25, 115
   of relationships, 204–207
   See also barriers to change, external; barriers to change, internal
"Decolonization Is Not a Metaphor" (Tuck and Yang), 64
Decolonizing Methodologies (Smith), 13
Deranger, Eriel Tchekwie, 1, 3–4, 32, 36, 65
Derrickson, Grand Chief, 68
Descartes, 51
direct action
   controversy with, 148, 154, 184
   criminalization of, 10, 137, 140–141
   flash point events, 23, 119
   funding of, 167
   including solutions, 189
   kinds of, 190–191
   in leadership position, 77–78
   in mainstream environmental movement, 25
   necessity of, 102–104

personal transformation through, 83
success as strategy, 24, 123
training of, 162–163
diversity, 120–121, 123, 145, 171–173, 184, 191, 200–201
divestment campaigns, 123
Dixon, Chris, 10, 183
Dixon, E., 196
Doctrine of Discovery, 40, 63
dualisms, 49–51, 178–179, 197, 200

eco-imperialism, 28
ecology, 185
economics, 35, 106–107, *126,* 132–134
education, 85, 165
electoral system, engaging with, 98–100, 184
Elsipogtog Nation, 23, 130
Enbridge pipeline, BC, 28
Energy East pipeline, 30
Enfors, E., 86
environmental and equality issues, 18–31
   connection of, 164
   hope for, 208–210
   interconnection of, 8–9
   root causes of, 5, 32, 46–47, 52–53
environmental/climate justice movements, 27–29
Environmentalism of the Rich (Dauvergne), 26
environmental racism, 35–36
Environment and Climate Change Canada, 18
extractivism, 41–42, 53

Farmer, Paul, 72
Feygina, Irina, 49
Financial Reports and Political Contributions (FRPC) System, BC, 135–136
First Nations, *see* individual nations
500 years of Resistance (Hill), 94
Fortier, Craig, 159
Foucault, Michel, 113–114
4Rs Youth Movement, 2
fractured movements/us *vs.* them, *140,* 143–146

Gabriel, Ellen, 22

gender justice, 36, 41, 45, 49, 52
Gibson-Graham, J.K., 106, 187–188
Gidimt'en chekpoint, BC, 42–43, 207
Global Assessment Report on Biodiversity and Ecosystem Services (United Nations), 7–8
Global Climate Strike, 2019, 1–3, 53, 71, 160, 201, 209–210
globalization, 27, 100, 132, 182, 203
Global North, 29
Global South, 29, 32, 34
Gobby, Jen (research), 9–14
Gorski, Paul, 142, 160n1
governments
    as barrier, 139–140
    corporate influence on, *126,* 134–136
    electoral system, 98–100, 119–120, 184
    new forms of, 105
    varied approaches to, 77
Gramsci, Antonio, 82
Grande, Sandy, 10
grassroots funding, 167–169
Gray, Vanessa and Beze, 11
Great Bear Rainforest deal, 156
Green, Duncan, 74, 194
Green, Joshua, 196–197
green building, 105
greenhouse gases (GHGS), 6, 18–19, 22, 56, 129
Green New Deal (GND), 56–57
Greenpeace, 26
grounded normativity, 116
Gustafsen Lake, BC, 23

Habermas, Jürgen, 81, 188
Haida Nation, 66
Hansen, James, 19
Harley, Anne, 10
Harper government, 24
heteropatriarchy, 15, 61, 72, 91, 177, 207
    See also patriarchy
Hill, Gord, 94
How Change Happens (Green), 74, 194
human-Earth relationships, 8, 127
human-human relationships, 8
Human Rights Watch, 21

Idle No More, 24, 68, 138
imperialism, 46
INCITE!, 154
Indigenous Climate Action (ICA), 2, 3, 29, 36
Indigenous Peoples
    activist strategies (compared to settler's), 148–149
    climate impact on, 3, 7–8, 20, 33, 35, 36–37
    incarceration of, 138
    and land, 46, 64–65, 67, 71, 115–116, 192–193
    land defence movement, 16–17, 19, 22–25, 31, 102, 139
    land title, 20, 23, 63
    leadership of, 92–95, 119, 123
    loss of rights, 21, 33, 38, 42
    personal transformation, 84
    and relationships, 180–181
    self-determination, 62–63, 65–67, 109, 151, 192
    Traditional Knowledge, 67–68, 116, 189, 205
    youth delegation, 2–3, 47, 71, 201, 210
    See also land defenders; racism; Royal Commission on Aboriginal People (1996); Truth and Reconciliation Commission (TRC)
industrialization, 48
inequality, economic/social, 5, 6–7, 35
institutionalists, 26–27
interdependence, 179–181
Intergovernmental Panel on Climate Change (IPCC), 6
International Covenant on Civil and Political Rights, 63
International Covenant on Economic, Social and Cultural Rights, 63
intersectionality, 91, 113–115, 123, 147, 179–180, 193, 206
Inuit, 37
Ipperwash, ON, 23

Jay, Dru Oja, 156
Jemez Principles for Democratic Organizing, 203
Jones, Robert, Jr., 72

Joyful Militancy: Building Thriving Resistance in Toxic Times (Montgomery and Berman), 196

Kamat, S., 155
Kanien'kehá:ka (Mohawk) Nation, 51, 66, 150
Kapoor, Dip, 10, 152–153
Khasnabish, Alex, 10
Kimmerer, Robin Wall, 182
Kinder Morgan pipeline, 30, 51, 94, 109, 123, 189
King, Hayden, 72n1
Klein, Naomi, 5, 31, 44, 68, 79–80, 177, 211
Klima Forum, 29
Kothari, Ashish, 7

Laboucan-Massimo, Melina, 52
Ladson-Billings, Gloria, 207
Lakey, George, 173
land
    colonization of, 45–46, 64–65
    connection/disconnection, 33–34, 52–53, 69–70, 115–116
    See also land defence movements; land defenders
Land Back (Yellowhead Institute), 67
land claims, *see under* Indigenous Peoples
land defence movements, 16–17, 19, 22–25, 31, 102, 139
    See also environmental/climate justice movements; mainstream environmental movement
land defenders
    criminalization of, 137–140
    future for, 54–55, 94
    and police, 42–43, 51, 81, 130
    See also voices
#LANDBACK, 71
Langdon, Jonathan, 10
Leap, *see* The Leap
Lee, D., 156
legal system, *126*, 136–139
    See also governments
2slgbtqqia people, 36
Liberal Party of Canada, 18, 33, 148
liquified natural gas (lng) industry, 113, 130, 133

lobby groups, 134–135, 136, 190–191
logging, 25
Loorbach, D., 188
Lubicon Cree First Nation, 52
Lukes, Steven, 101

MacKay, Kevin, 83, 107, 188
Macy, Joanna, 105, 186–187
mainstream environmental movement, 25–27
    See also environmental/climate justice movements; land defence movements
Mannheim, Karl, 81
Manuel, Arthur, 20, 22, 30, 64, 65, 68
Manuel, Kanahus, 36
market liberals, 26–27
Martinez-Alier, J., 26
Marx, 78
Mascarenhas, M., 36
Meadows, Donella, 91
media influence, 131
mental health, 127
Merchant, Carolyn, 51
Mi'kmaq Nation, 66, 130, 189
Miller, Ethan, 106–107, 184–185, 187
missing and murdered Indigenous women, 21, 36, 64
Mohawk Nation, *see* Kanien'kehá:ka (Mohawk) Nation
Monaghan, J., 138
Montgomery, N., 196, 212
Montreal climate march, 2019, *see* Global Climate Strike, 2019
Moore, M.L., 86
Moral Tribes: Emotion, Reason, and the Gap between Us and Them (Joshau Green), 196–197
movement ecosystems, 171–176, 200, 212
Movement for Black Lives, 112
movements, *see* environmental/climate justice movements; land defence movements; mainstream environmental movement
movements, taking stock, 122–160
    successes and challenges, 122–125
    See also barriers to change, external; barriers to change, internal

natural gas, 113, 130, 133
neoliberalism, 44–45, 100, 134–135
The New Green Deal in Canada (Deranger), 1, 32
NGOization: Complicity, Contradictions and Prospects (Choudry and Kapoor), 152–153
"NGOization: Depoliticizing Activism in Canada" (Jay), 156
NGOS, 26, *140*, 152–157, 166–167, 173, 201
Nilsen, A.G., 89
non-governmental organizations (NGOS), 26, *140*, 152–157, 166–167, 173, 201
North American Tar Sands Coalition, 156
Norway, 133
Nova Scotia, 130, 189
NYC Climate Convergence, 4

Offsetting Resistance (Stainsby and Jay), 156
oil and gas pipelines
    building of, 19, 22
    and climate change, 18–20, 34
    resistance to, 11, 22, 23, 29–30
    siting of, 35–36
    See also individual pipelines
Oka, QC, 23
Ontario Far North Act, 28
oppressions, 71, 91
othering, 146, 197
"Our Relationships Keep Us Alive: Let's Prioritize Them in 2018" (Dixon, E.), 196

Pacific Trail pipeline (Chevron), 30
Pan-Canadian Framework on Clean Growth and Climate Change, 32–33
Paris Agreement, 133
Parks, B.C., 35
patriarchy, 36, 49, 54, 114–115
    See also heteropatriarchy
Paulson, S., 58
Peace, Power and Righteousness: An Indigenous Manifesto (Alfred), 65
Pembina Institute, 136

People's Climate March, 2014, 4
pipelines, *see* Chevron's Pacific Trail pipeline; Coastal GasLink Pipeline; Enbridge Pipeline, BC; TransCanada's Energy East pipeline; Trans Mountain Kinder Morgan pipeline
Piven, F.F, 97, 155
police brutality, 21
Policing Indigenous Movements (Monaghan and Walby), 139
political system
    corporate influence, *126*, 134–136
    engaging with, 98–100, 184
Potawatomi Nation, 182
power
    about, 81–82
    analysis of, 90
    building from below, 96–97, 119
    confronting and dismantling, 100–104, 119
    inequities, 116, 201–202
    and land, 39–40, 158–159
    relational, 113–115, 119, 147, 171, 179, 183, 198
    Rowlands's forms of, 114
Powershift, 29
Principles of Tsawalk (Atleo), 180
prior informed consent (PIC), 63
privatization, 44
Project Sitka, 138

Québec, 149–150

racism, 3, 4, 39, 40, 45, 53
Rainforest Action Network, 26
Ramos, H., 26
Raworth, Kate, 6, 8
Raymond, Tayka, 4
Reconciliation Manifesto (Manuel and Derrickson), 68
Red Skins, White Masks (Coulthard), 61
Reinsborough, P., 86
relational tensions, *140*, 146–152, 177, 202
relational theories and approaches to systems change, 177–199
    thinking and working across difference, 183–196

working across the us/them divide, 196–199
relationships, 111–117, 119, 163, 175–176, 200–204, 212
repatriation, 64–67, 151–152, 192–193
residential school system, 41, 62
    See also Truth and Reconciliation Commission (TRC)
resistance movements, 19, 22, 23, 94
Resistance Research and Theories of Change (Tuck and Yang), 73
The Revolution Will Not Be Funded (INCITE!), 154
Robbins, Paul, 188
Roberts, J.T., 35
Rodgers, K., 26
Rodriguez, I., 81–82
Rowlands, J., 114
Roy, Arundhati, 154
Royal Canadian Mounted Police (RCMP), 42–43, 51, 81, 138, 207
Royal Commission on Aboriginal People (1996), 21, 62, 63–64

Sarker, K., 188
Saudi Arabia, 19
Schweickart, D., 59
Secwepemc Nation, 20, 36, 37, 94, 109, 189
Secwepemc Women Warriors, 36
settler colonialism
    and capitalism, 46
    description, 39, 50, 204
    and Doctrine of Discovery, 41–42
    impacts of, 20–22
    solutions to, 61–62
    See also colonialism; decolonization
settlers
    activist strategies (compared to Indigenous Peoples), 148–149
    education of, 124
    and Indigenous Peoples leadership, 93–95, 119
    personal transformation, 84
Shelbourne, Nova Scotia, 193
The Shock Doctrine: The Rise of Disaster Capitalism (Klein), 79–80
Shragge, Eric, 10
Silent Spring (Carson), 25

Simpson, Leanne Betasamosake, 22, 39–40, 67, 87, 94, 115, 181
Smith, Andrea, 116
Smith, Linda Tuhiwai, 13
Smith, S., 92
Snow, D.A, 85–86
social-ecological systems, 76–77
social greens, 26–27
social movements, 9, 22–31
    environmental/climate justice movements, 27–29
    Indigenous land defence movements, 22–25
    mainstream environmental movement, 25–27
possible solutions
    to capitalism, 190
    creation and promotion of, 104–111
    current systems, 200–213
    with direct action, 189
    overcoming barriers, external, 162–163
    overcoming barriers, internal, 165–176
    to settler colonialism, 161–162
Spinoza, Baruch, 212–213
Standing Rock, 168
storytelling, 85–88, 119, 187, 205
strategic planning, 166
sustainability, 32
Symbiosis network, 60
systems analysis, 88–92, 114, 119
systems change, 73–121
    context, 76–80
    justification for current system, 47–52
    Macy's approaches to, 186–187
    possible solutions, 200–213
    relationships, 111–117, 212
    theory of, 75
    thinking together, 1–17
    See also actions for systemic change; barriers to change, external; barriers to change, internal; relational theories; values

Tarrow, S.G, 76–77
tar sands, 19, 28, 33, 37, 156
Taylor, Keeanga-Yamahtta, 45

Temper, L., 81–82, 114, 188
The Leap, 11, 29
This Changes Everything: Capitalism vs. the Climate (Klein), 5, 44
Tiny House Warriors, 36, 109, 189
Tjornbo, O., 86
Traditional Knowledge, 25, 67–68, 116, 189, 205
TransCanada's Energy East pipeline, 30
Trans Mountain Kinder Morgan Pipeline, 30, 51, 94, 109, 123, 189
treaties, 40–41, 63, 84–85
Treaty Truck House, 189
Trudeau (Justin)/Trudeau government, 16, 18, 33, 51, 56, 207
Truth and Reconciliation Commission (TRC), 3, 20, 62, 64
Tuck, E, 64, 73, 177, 182–183
2SLGBTQQIA people, 36

Unist'ot'en camp, BC, 11, 23–24, 83, 104, 109, 189, 207
United Nations
    Committee on the Elimination of Racial Discrimination, 21
    Declaration on the Rights of Indigenous Peoples (UNDRIP), 41, 63, 72n1
    Framework Convention on Climate Change (UNFCCC), 18, 28
    Global Assessment Report on Biodiversity and Ecosystem Services, 7–8
United States, 27

values, 80–95
    Indigenous Leadership, 92–95
    narratives, changing of, 85–88
    personal transformation, 83–85
    systemic analysis, 88–92
    See also voices
Venezuela, 19
voices
    amplified, 12–17, 64, 92, 95, 117, 119, 123
    importance of, 6, 87, 157–158
    sidelined, 3, 25, 28, 38, 143

Walby, K., 138

Walia, Harsha, 10, 27–28, 65
Walker, Alice, 69
Walter, M., 81–82
Ward, Sakej, 14
Warning to Humanity, 6
Watch House, Burnaby Mountain, BC, 189
Weber, M., 96–97
West, Cornel, 69
Wet'suwet'en Nation, 37, 42–43, 130
Whyte, Kyle, 46
Wilson, Alex, 180–181
Wilson-Raybould, Jody, 139
Women of Colour against Violence, 154
World Social Forum in Montreal, 2016, 81

Yang, K.W., 64, 73, 177, 182–183
Youth Resistance Research and Theories of Change (Tuck and Yang), 177

Zapatistas, 185